STATE, PEOPLE AND LAW OF BHUTAN

STATE, PEOPLE AND LAW OF BHUTAN:
A Study in Historical Perspective

Madhu Rajput

ISBN : 978-93-5128-076-7

Price : 860

First Published, 2015

Published by

Kalpaz Publications
C-30, Satyawati Nagar,
Delhi-110052, Ph. : 9212142040
E-mail: kalpaz@hotmail.com

Laser Typesetting : Future Computer, Delhi
Printed at : G. Print Process, Delhi

Cataloging in Publication Data—DK
Courtesy: D.K. Agencies (P) Ltd. <docinfo@dkagencies.com>

Rajput, Madhu, author.
State, people and law of Bhutan : a study in historical perspective / Prof. Dr. Madhu Rajput.
pages. cm.
Includes bibliographical references (pages).
ISBN 9789351280767

1. Bhutan—History. 2. Bhutan—Politics and government. 3. Bhutan—Social life and customs. 4. Law—Bhutan. I. Title.

DDC 954.98 23

Contents

Preface

Bhutan is a country which despite small size has always attracted the attention of international community. As a nation which remained steeped in medieval conditions and extreme backwardness at a time when other South-Asian countries were striving to develop, Bhutan opened up to modernisation late with the help of India. The Wangchuck dynasty caringly served the nation and was instrumental in transformation from a monarchy to a constitutional monarchy, making the concept of Gross National Happiness a parameter for development.

To understand this multi-lingual and multi-ethnic nation, it was imperative to visit personally to get an insight into its uniqueness. I had an opportunity to visit 11 out of 20 dzongkhags (districts) of Bhutan during the time of transition – politically and economically. The State has gracefully absorbed the process of transformation and has carved a place in the community of nations for itself.

It has carefully earned the image of a nation which cares for its people. In the development projects, emphasis has been on disseminating the fruits of modernisation to each and every corner of the country. It is evident in the field of infrastructure as well as education. Roads are being built, remote places are being connected to mainstream, Basic Health Care Units have been established in most of the dzongkhags, electricity and telephone facilities are spreading far and wide. A thoughtful effort is being put towards changing the attitude of people, to convince them to embrace a progressive life-style. The measure of success can be gauged by the way education has caught the attention of people, even in the villages where only a few years back government officials had to convince the parents to get their children enrolled in schools. Now, with the government sponsoring education till 10th standard, students have to compete for enrolment. In higher education, the enrolments are now merit based.

Bhutan can boast of vividness in culture and language which has seen off late the outside creeping influences. Till now, the efforts to keep traditions and development in balance have been successful but with exposure and opportunities what will happen in future is eagerly awaited. Will Bhutan retain ethnic charm in the era of sweeping cosmopolitanism is a big question?

In this book, an effort has been made to trace the transition of the State, People and Laws of Bhutan since the coming of Wangchuck dynasty in 1907 till now. Its close ties with India have been the main focus. Bhutan has recently seen momentous changes in every sphere and is striding into future with confident but cautious approach. It would be interesting to observe this Buddhist nation's tryst with modernisation.

Madhu Rajput

Acknowledgement

This book owes to the valuable time and co-operation extended by many Bhutanese who are playing vital role in the process of modernisation. I had an opportunity of meeting and interacting with many of them which gave an authentic character and depth to my study. At the outset, I would like to express my gratitude to the Ministry of Education for granting permission to visit the educational institutions in the country and openly interacting with the people concerned. Despite his busy schedule, the Honourable Minister of Education, Lyonpo Thakur Singh Powdyel spared his valuable time and gave me an insight into the development of education in the form of various 'waves' in Bhutan. His concern and involvement in the ongoing process was inspiring and overwhelming.

I am extremely indebted to the Chief Justice of Bhutan Lyonpo Sonam Tobgye, who expounded the legal system of Bhutan and formulation of the constitution. The clarity with which he spoke has helped me to understand the judiciary more closely.

The readiness with which the Chief Election Commissioner Dasho Kunzang Wangdi and the two Election Commissioners Aum Deki Pema and Dasho Chogyal Dago Rigdzin provided me with material and detailed information about the election process and the role of women in it was heartwarming.

The Anti-Corruption Commission chief Aum Neten Zangmo who is a role model for most of the young Bhutanese women exuded authority, grace and remarkable agility. She was forthcoming in her opinions and gave an insight into the grey areas of Bhutanese society.

I am extremely indebted to the following people who extended their sincere co-operation during my visits to Bhutan:

Aum Sangay Zam, Education Secretary of Bhutan, Dr. Pema Thinley, Vice-Chancellor, Royal University of Bhutan, Thimphu, Tshewang Lhamo, Member of Parliament, Chhukha Constituency, Jigmi Rinzin, Member of Parliament, Pema Gatsel Constituency, Aum Kunzang Choden, the first woman English writer of Bhutan, Dorji Penjore, Senior Researcher, Centre for Bhutan Studies, Gyonpo Tshering, Director, National Library and Archives of Bhutan, Singye Namgyel, Director, Sherubtse College, Kanglung, Dorji Wangchuck, Director, College of Natural Sciences, Lobesa, Karma Tshering, Director, Royal Institute of Management, Simtokha, Thimphu, Thubten Gyatsho, Director, Paro College of Education, Paro, Lhato Jamba, Director, Geddu College of Business Studies, Geddu, Chhukha, Nim Dorji, Chief Administrative Officer, Dagachhu Hydro-Power Corporation Ltd., Dagapela, Dagana, Dr. C. T. Dorji, Former Director, National Museum of Bhutan, Paro, Dr. Sonam Wangmo, Dean of Academy Affairs and Lecturer of Botany, Sherubtse College, Kanglung, Phuntsho Dolma, Dean, Student Affairs, College of Education, Paro, Kunzhang Lhamu, Chief Planning Officer, GNH Commission, Dasho Karma Debu, the then Secretary, Women Association of Bhutan, Chimi Wangmo, Secretary, RENEW, Yangdey Penjor, Secretary, Youth Development Fund, Yangchen Pelden, Program Officer, National Women's Association of Bhutan, Norbu Gyaltshen, Head, Programs/ Secretariat Services, National Commission for Women and Children, Phuntshok Chhoden, Consultant and Secretary-General of BAOWE (Bhutan Association of Women Entrepreneurs), Tshering Pem, Programme Specialist, United Nations Development Programme, Thimphu, Karma Tshering, Director, MPC Bhutan Entertainment, Pema Choden Tenzin, Chief Editor, Yeewong magazine, Phuntsho Choden, Producer, Bhutan Broadcast Service (BBS), Namkhai Norbu, Managing Director, Bhutan Times, Kinley Wangmo, Reporter, Kuensel News paper, Indra Maya Timsin, General Manager, Kisa Hotel, Thimphu, Rekha Chhetri, Lecturer, CNR (Centre for Natural Resources), Lobesa, Tulsi Gurung, Lecturer, CNR (Centre for Natural Resources), Lobesa, Pema Chhodeup, Principal, Bumthang Higher Secondary School, Kinley Pem, Principal, Lungtenzampa Middle Secondary School, Thimphu, Cheku Dorji, Principal, Trongsa

Lower Secondary School, Gomchen Tenzing, Principal, Kanglung Primary School, Sonam Wangmo, Teacher, Computer and IT, Sherubtse College, Kanglung and Moloy Kumar Bose, Executive Vice-President, Druk PNB Bank Ltd., Thimphu.

I also appreciate the encouragement extended by Prof. B. C. Upreti, Director, South Asian Studies, University of Rajasthan, Jaipur, Dr. Gretchen Legler, Associate Professor, Department of Humanities, University of Maine, Farmington, Dr. Salam Irene, Associate Professor, Department of History, University of Manipur, Prof. Niru Hazarika, Department of Political Science, Guwahati University, Guwahati, Prof. Asha Shukla, Head, Department of Women Studies, Barkatulla University, Bhopal, Prof. Bashir Dabla, Head, Department of Social work, Kashmir University, Dr. Asifa Jan, Associate Professor, Department of Political Science, Kashmir University, Dr. Ranaja Mishra, Associate Professor, University of Mumbai, Prof. P. K. Shrivastava, Department of Western History, University of Lucknow, Dr. Amita Sonker, Department of Western History, University of Lucknow, Dr. Shalini Gupta, Associate Professor, Department of Commerce, M.P.G. College, Mussoorie, Dr. B. B. Kumar, Editor, 'Dialogue', Dr. Kashinath Zena, Department of Political Science, Tripura University, Tripura, Dr. Manjil Hazarika, Assistant Professor, Institute of Paleo-Environment and Heritage Conservation, Mekelle University, Ethiopia, Dr. Shubhra Rajput, Department of English, D. N. College, Kanpur.

I would also like to acknowledge the support provided by the staff of various libraries during my research work such as Library, J. N. U., New Delhi, Nehru Memorial Library, New Delhi, National Library, Thimphu, Bhutan, Library, Sherubtse College, Kanglung, Trashigang, Library, Paro College of Education, Bhutan and Tagore Library, University of Lucknow.

I am also grateful to the Indian Embassy in Thimphu, Bhutan for their optimum fecilitation during my frequent visits in 2010 and 2011. I am also thankful to Mr. Afzal Ahmed (Advocate) for his support and encouragement.

1

Founding of Monarchy

In South Asia, Bhutan is a country which is synonymous with monarchy, a country which emerged from civil war like situation fragmented into small factions under *Desis*. It was only in 1907 that with the establishment of the Wangchuck dynasty, the modern political system started taking shape with the coronation of Ugyen Wangchuck as the king. Under the sheltered patronage of this dynasty, Bhutan was embarking on the road which would take it through the turns of development and its recognition in international society. The mountainous kingdom which can be termed as a living place in its own time zone was shaken by the decisions taken by first king in order to bring medieval Bhutan in touch with the developed societies of other parts of the world.

Bhutan is situated along the southern slopes of great Himalayan range. It is bounded by Tibet on the north, the plain of Jalpaiguri district of Assam on the south, the Chumbi valley (Tibet), Sikkim and Darjeeling district of West Bengal on the west, and the Kameng district of the North East frontier Agency Assam on the east.[1]

Bhutan is situated 88°45’ to 92°7’ longitude East and 26°5’ to 28°5’ latitude North, in the Lower Himalayas in the south.[2]

The country extends 350 km. from west to east and about 130 km from north to south, covering an area of 46,500 sq. km. The area is well comparable in size to Switzerland (41,000 sq. km.).[3] It is bordered on the north by Republic of China (Tibet) and on the south-west and east by Republic of India. Both the west and east are hugged by mountains, which form the natural boundary. In the south, however the network of mountain spurs disappears abruptly into Duars. Interaction between Bhutan and India was through these Duars.

The present Bhutan, which is divided into 20 Dzongkhags (districts) was ruled by 57 *Desis* at the time when the first king who was a strategist and by faith a Buddhist thought of uniting them and established relations with British India. Bhutan, situated between the two giant countries China and India was always seen as a state which, if Chinese had their way, would have been a possible danger to the Indian interests. The secret exchange of letter between the political officer John Claude White and the Secretary of State in October 1908 revealed the true intent of policy towards Bhutan. The letter mentions; "Indeed, the establishment of Chinese influence in Bhutan could raise complications of grave kind on Northeast Frontier and eventually might necessitate the location of considerable force on our side of the border." John Claude White advised his government to propose new treaty with Bhutan.

His successor Charles Bell began to enforce active policy towards Bhutan. He suggested, "We should have the right to intervene only in case of disputes. If Bhutan at any time in future agrees to Chinese intervention in her affairs, e.g., by receiving Chinese Agent in Bhutan, we should endeavour to persuade Bhutan to place her foreign relations under the British government while the latter should abstain from interference in the internal administration of the country." His recommendations largely determined the subject matter of treaty, signed in Punakha on August 8, 1910.

When Sir Charles Bell came to Punakha to negotiate the treaty, His Majesty personally attended and took delight in introducing each of his senior officials. The ten-clause treaty contained an article that 'British India would recognise Bhutan's independence, while Bhutan would remain guided by the latter in her external relations'. Bhutan gained many benefits from this treaty like the formal settlement of border issues with British India, opening of trade link and the raise in British annual subsidy from Rupees 50,000 to Rupees 100,000. The treaty placed Bhutan now in a secure zone as an independent buffer state.

The exchanges of delegates between Bhutan and British India became almost regular. In 1911, His Majesty visited Delhi to attend the Coronation Durbar of King George V with thirteen officials. His Majesty was keen to know all about the change, advertent to even the new rifles that the troops displayed, which were shorter than the ones he saw earlier. Sir Charles Bell attended to him as the interpreter. In response to question on how far His Majesty had come, he said, "Owing to the excellent administration of the British government, there is a railway up to the borders of Bhutan, which brought me to Delhi in two days. I had also a journey of seventeen days in my own country." The most impressive of His Majesty's comment was, "When coming to present myself to His Majesty [the King of England], no distance seems far".

His Majesty faithfully adhered to the treaty of 1910 and tried to keep British India at ease. During the Great World War (1914), His Majesty donated Rupees 200,000 to the Imperial Indian War Relief Fund. He encouraged recruiting Gurkhas and Bhutanese warriors from his territory and offered them remission of rent and taxes for three years. His Majesty closed down Bhutanese bars in the border areas as requested by the British Government and controlled the Bhutanese rioting in the Indian territories.

British India maintained close ties with His Majesty, and stood by his side even during his personal crisis. For example, the British Government awarded him the Grand Cross of the Indian Empire (GCIE) when His Majesty was deeply overwhelmed by the loss of Her Majesty Ashi Tsundru Lhamo.[4]

Speaking on the status of culture and religion during the reign of Ugyen Wangchuck, Karma Ura says, "His relations were not only good with British officials, as a man of great faith he had affectionate relations with many Tibetan lamas. He venerated holy artefacts in Lhasa like the Jowo, on whose altar he sponsored 1,000 butter lamps every month from Bhutan. One can imagine a regular supply of butter cargo being carried over the mountains to Lhasa.

The fact is, King Ugyen Wangchuck was a deeply spiritual man. He received empowerment and initiations from very high lamas, like Lama Serkong Dorji Chang. Serkong was invited to Bhutan soon after the 1878 battle with Paro Penlop Tshewang Norbu. King Ugyen Wangchuck was also very close to Karmapa Khachab Dorji and drew strength from Buddhism. We know from the colophon of the terms text of the Chimed

Sogthig that King Ugyen Wangchuck extended patronage to Terton Zilnon Namkhai Dorji while the terton was writing religious texts in Bumthang.

The middle Lhakhang in Kujey, with towering Guru statue, was built in 1894 by King Ugyen Wangchuck at considerable cost. One must bear in mind that there was no technology and machinery in those days; everything had to be done manually, and therefore it was a major undertaking.

His Majesty was great benefactor to the Dratsangs (monastic bodies) throughout the country. As part of his vision for scholarship and education of young Bhutanese, he sent two Bhutanese groups to study up to geshey level in Tibet. In 1915 and 1917, he sent young monks like Tenpa Rinchen, Acho Pasang, Rinchen Dorji, Pema Tshering, Kelzang, Rigzang, Ugyen Penjor, Mindru and Nim Dorji to Tibet. Some went to Zhenphen Choki Nangwa in Dokham and later returned and became influential *geshes* and lamas, serving as radiant sources spreading Buddhist teachings.

His Majesty's commitment was not limited to religious education. Following his visits to Calcutta and Delhi, he began to establish schools. The schools were opened in Lame Goenpa and Wangdicholing, with 14 Bhutanese boys from eastern and western Bhutan. Later, the number increased to 46. By then, students were being sent to Kalimpong. The first school was opened under the Sikkimese teacher Phento and Pasa Kutshab Norbu. The first batch of students became important officials in the 1930s and 1940s. The king took the initiative to sow seeds of western education, as well as strengthen the roots of dharma in Bhutan.

I mentioned the construction of Kurjay as a leading example of his artistic and architectural heritage. But his contributions were not only within the country, one of the iconic pilgrimage centres of Buddhism is the Boudanath Temple in Kathmandu, which was renovated almost entirely with King Ugyen Wangchuck's personal funds. The renovation was supervised by Kagyu Lama Togden Sacha Shri, with whom Ugyen Wangchuck corresponded a great deal. King Ugyen Wangchuck sent *geshey* Sherub Jorden to assist Togden Sacha Shri in this task. In total, Ugyen Wangchuck spent some Rs. 70,000, a great deal of money in today's terms. But these sponsorships, education, construction and so forth, are somewhat external to the individual. Buddhism should be internalised.

His Majesty spent considerable amount of time practising meditation. When he got older, he built small meditation centre for himself- Tshamkhang Kunzangcholing above Lame Goenpa. He was inaccessible every day until one in afternoon, kept an attendant and 12 dogs to guard him. Later on, he moved to a holier place near Kujay and Jampa Lhakhang, and then built Phodrang Thinley Rabten, where he continued his prayerful and contemplative life.[5]

A closed and isolated country like Bhutan with physical barriers to protect, the economy was thoroughly based on whatever grown and importing was not easy, as it could only be carried on horseback and on the backs of people. Trade fairs were held on the border of Tibet and Bhutan and it was mostly the southern borders from where the trade was carried with Kalimpong, Gaudama and Siliguri.

These were times when the state used to receive income from society unlike today where money is pumped into economy and the state is considered responsible for reforms, generating new avenues. During that time, there were many taxes imposed such as grain tax, textile tax, handicraft tax, gunpowder tax, metal tax, dairy produce tax, bamboo and timber tax. In short, whatever was needed was taxed. The story was not different as it was the medieval times in Europe, where the rich were not taxed and the poor had to bear the burden. To evade tax burden, many people fled to places like Pasakha, Darjeeling, Kalimpong and Arunachal Pradesh.

His Majesty abolished certain taxes, reduced others, and encouraged the return of those who left the country to elude taxes. In his *Kasho*, His Majesty encouraged the return of Bhutanese exiles: "Under the charge of the king, you may return and those who come back will be allowed to settle wherever there are empty lands. Except for the official *woola*, no royal minister, big or small, shall command any other pottering and *woola* on any troublesome pretext." Furthermore, the *Kasho* mentions, "Those *who* are coming back should submit their names in writing to Haa Drungpa through Chichab Sahib, with the indication of where they would like to settle."[6]

Even the regions had disparity in paying taxes. Labour tax was heavy for Dzongs. Irrigation channels, mule track highways and bridges to carry official cargos, were built by them. According to Karma Ura, "There was one tax called *Sarim Woola*. Sarim stood for express delivery. As soon as a piece of cargo was dropped in a village, that village had to continue carrying it onwards whether it was night or day, rain or shine, and if necessary, negotiating footpaths at night with wooden torches. With *sarim woola*, a back load would reach Thimphu from Tashigang within four nights and four days.

However, deaths due to famine and starvation on a wide scale seemed not to have occurred in our history-even though it was a subsistence economy. The dzongs had granaries, which held extra food stocks, to cover localised famine or crop failures. The local dzongs also issued loans of grain. The farming system was designed to avert huge risks. A household grew many kinds of crops on plots, which were scattered in a valley, so that the crops would not fail at the same time. The same principle applied to livestock holding. A household had a few of every livestock such as chickens, sheep, cattle horses, and pigs.

Nevertheless, both the people and government were helpless when epidemics like smallpox struck. There was no remedy and no immunisation in those days. In general, the economy was geared towards being self-sufficient primarily at the village level. People had to grow many types of crops to diversify risks. It was in this kind of economic environment that Ugyen Wangchuck became the first king of Bhutan."[7]

He was open in his relations with British and helped them in 1904 when Tibet Mission under Col. Sir Francis Edward Younghusband was moving towards Lhasa. In 1905, he earned the title 'Knight Commander of the Indian Empire', KCIE, for assistance rendered through the British expedition to Tibet. In 1907, Ugyen Wangchuck was formally elected King of Bhutan by an assembly comprising representatives of monastic community, officials and the common people.

The British Government was represented by Claude White who spoke on the occasion thus- "I am convinced that you have taken a wise step in thus consolidating the administration of the State. Sir Ugyen has been my friend for many years and you could not have made a better choice. His integrity, uprightness and firmness of character commend him to everyone and his accession to the Maharaja status is not only a gain to Bhutan, but of great advantage to the British Government, who will henceforth have settled government with man of strong character as its head, to negotiate with."[8]

This brought an end to the dual system of government prevalent in Bhutan and marked the beginning of hereditary monarchy in Bhutan. National day is celebrated on December 17 each year commemorating the day in 1907 when Ugyen Wangchuck became the king. He died in 1926 having established peace and foundation for the future prosperity of Bhutan. He was cremated at the temple of "Kuje".[9]

During his time, the biggest constraint was from where to get the money so that basic infrastructure for development could be laid. The people were already overtaxed and so was the need to explore other avenues. One could get aid from British India, as the first king has turned out to be a solid ally for the British, but after the retirement of Claude White in 1908, it was not possible. Even J. C. White wrote, "I wish it has been possible to remain in India till at least he had commenced some of the schemes of reforms." The other was to offer license for capturing elephants in the forests adjoining Bhutan, Assam and Bengal. The forest ranges covering Assam, Bengal and southern Bhutan were divided into three elephant capturing zones: Goalpara, Kamrup and Daang, which we call Dirang. Bhutan had to be involved in this enterprise because the best traps could be set up on the Bhutanese side. Elephants were valuable for logging, transport and pageantry all over India. It appears that a decent amount of money was generated, but not enough for any significant development in the Kingdom. His Majesty taking an unusual step reduced interest rate from 25 per cent to 20 per cent through a *Kasho* (Royal decree) in 1908.[10]

With King Ugyen Wangchuck, sovereign dynastic monarchy was established. Religious leaders who earlier had a say no longer found themselves in the realm of political activities. The country was centralised and the power flew from the king, who was to be apprised of any development or law and order situation. The important positions of the kingdom were now shared by the people close to the Royal family, which is a trend till present date. Isolation was still preferred which meant that backwardness and underdevelopment become partners. The kings enjoyed the support of the feudal as well as the British India.

When the second king Jigme Wangchuck ascended throne in 1926, Bhutan was a picture of underdevelopment and several risks, although the reign was peaceful one. The king managed to ensure security and streamline administration in some sections. He was not only proficient in the local dialects, but knew Hindi as well, which made it easy for him to discuss matters with British officials as well as Indian. The renewal of Treaty of Friendship with India in 1949 with appropriate changes was fruitful when India got independence. One area which needed his attention was to streamline the tax system, which was too heavy for ordinary people to bear with. Getting financial aid from Government of India was something which could not be postponed any more. But at the backdrop of Second World War, it was not easy to seek. Left with the only option, the king had to change the labour and commodity tax system.

At the first instance, he wanted to study the entire tax system along with his Royal secretaries. The findings were complicated due to many layers in administration, which could be eliminated without affecting the service, law and order and regulations of the kingdom. He realised that there were far too many dungkhags. We know from records that in 1747, Bhutan had 126 dungkhags. The problem was that dungkhags subsisted on taxes from constituent's households. Households had to provide goods and services to the dungpa's office and the dungpa.

The burden of taxation was compounded when it came to dzongkhag level, with many officials like dzongpon, droenyer, zimpon, tapon, gorab, at the expense of the people. As a result, His Majesty boldly dismantled large number of dungkhags to reduce tax burden on the people. In the mid 18th century, Bhutan had 126 dungkhags according to the list given in Desi Sherab Wangchuck's biography. And, this must have been roughly the number of dzongkhags (districts) that existed when His Majesty contemplated abolishing most of them. Contemporary generations do not realise what major reform it was at that time. Since the founding of Bhutan, taxes had gone up periodically without proportionate benefit accruing to people. The second king reduced taxes and made them uniform throughout the country. It was a sweeping decision.[11]

During his time, farming system and medical services were given concentrated attention for development. Allopathic health services were spread in the entire country. Karma Ura in his book 'Leadership of the Wise' says that another way of promoting an agrarian society was to propagate high-yielding varieties of fruits and cash crops and this became the mainstay of Bhutan's First and Second Five-Year Plans. His Majesty

Jigme Wangchuck anticipated the introduction of cash crops and established a medicinal plant centre in Dachenling- a place I have yet to identify. He visited Dechenling to supervise the planting on his way to Gelephug via Surey, according to a Kasho. Although, he was not a plant breeder by any training, using his powerful intuition he attempted to grow rice in the temperate region. During the 1940s, His Majesty's efforts to grow rice in Garpang in Chekhor were successful, but he could not diffuse this technology due to the lack of administrative and extension agents. As a result, his success was confined to the planting experiment at Garpang where he did get a rice harvest. As a man of religion, His Majesty sent a symbolic amount of three dre (one dre= 1.37 kg) from the first harvest as an offering to the Jowo in Lhasa.[12] He particularly promoted the Kargyue sect.

In terms of the conduct of societal relations, the traditional norms persisted whether the relations were between the government and citizens, Royalty and commoners, or officials and villagers. Within that context, His Majesty the king was considered a Buddhist monarch and a patron of Dharma and *Dratshang*. He promoted Bhutanese culture and religion, though this was not obvious to everyone due to poor documentation of his reign.

His Majesty renovated Tashigang Dzong in 1936, and that dzong we see today is largely what was reconstructed that year. It was a major renovation. Kuenga Rapten Palace and Domkhar Tashichholing Palace were constructed in 1929 and 1937 respectively. His Majesty also constructed the Samchiling Palace for Ashi Pema Dechen in early 1930s. Kuenga Rapten Palace is fairly well preserved but the Samchiling Palace has fallen into a derelict condition. Major renovation was carried out in Tongsa Dzong in 1930 and in Wangdiphodrang Dzong in 1948.

The building projects were completed without any technological or mechanical devices, and thus, these were major undertakings during two decades of his reign. In addition, he established many other Buddhist institutions, such as Chitokha Lhakhang in Wangiphodrang in 1948, and the Nimalung and Tharpaling Shedras during the 1930s. He rebuilt Gogona Lhakhang in Wangdi and Jigjay Lhakhang in Tondsa in 1933. He enriched the monastic accoutrements for mask dances in many dzongs, most notably in Punakha Dzong. In 1928, he completely refurnished the mask dance costumes in Punakha with the most expensive silk brocade. [13]

In 1935, a dispute arose between Bhutan and Tawang over pastural rights on the Tawang-Tashigang border in which an officer of the Tashigang Dzong injured a gelong of Gauden Namgyal Lhatse Monastery of Twang. Bhutan had to settle the matter by paying monetary compensation to the Gauden Namgyal Monastery for the injury.

The policy of isolation was given up by the king and Mr. Ludlow and Mr. Sheriff, two botanists of the British Museum in 1933 were allowed to collect plants in eastern Bhutan. In 1947, the Asian relations conference was held in New Delhi in which Bhutan also participated. Before the signing of the treaty of 1949 at Darjeeling with independent India, Bhutanese delegation visited New Delhi for preliminary talks.

The king's policies both internally and externally were directed towards integrating Bhutan and slowly opening it to the world.

References

1. Surveyor General of India, Government of India, New Delhi, 1969, pp. 8-9.
2. Dasho Rigzin, Dorji 'A brief Religious, Cultural and Secular History of Bhutan', the Asia Society Galleries, New York, 1989, p. 9.
3. Main Plan Document, Seventh Five-Year Plan, 1992-1997, Vol. I, Planning Commission, Royal Government. of Bhutan, Thimphu, December 1991, p. 5.
4. Dorji Lham, 'The Wangchuck Dynasty, 100 Years of Enlightened Monarchy', 2008, The Centre of Bhutan Studies, p. 14.
5. Ura Karma, 'Leadership of the Wise: Kings of Bhutan', 2010, pp. 39-42.
6. *Op. Cit.*, p. 16.
7. Ura Karma, 'Leadership of the Wise: Kings of Bhutan', 2010, pp. 34-35.
8. Das Nirmala, 'The Dragon Country, A History of Bhutan', p. 39.
9. Gupta B.S., 'Bhutan', 1999, pp. 26-27.
10. Ura Karma, 'Leadership of the Wise: Kings of Bhutan', 2010, pp. 37-38.
11. *Ibid*, pp. 49-50.
12. *Ibid*, p. 52.
13. *Ibid*, pp. 55-56.

2

Consolidation

Through his farsightedness, the third king perceived if Bhutan was to have place in the modern world, it had to leave isolation and adopt an approach which was not copied but was indigenous yet modern. He rose to the challenge by clearly making strategic shift towards development. His time from 1952 to 1972 saw some major shifts in policy making. He was convinced that modernisation cannot be given a second thought. The kingdom had to be opened to the world and steadfast relations had to be established with neighbouring India. The country could not maintain its medieval existence where travelling was still based on mules. In 1966, *The Times'* special correspondent described, "Bhutan is a land of valleys, full of a rushing silence that used to be broken only by the far-carrying hails of the muleteers, the melodious tonking of their caravans' bells, and steady snapping of a prayer flags at a windy bend on the track. Now, the blare of horns heralds a convoy of lorries winding up a new road....the snorting of tractors."[1]

With Indian support Bhutan entered two international organisations Universal Postal Union and United Nations Organisation. The beginning of the extensive road network which was to be built by Dantak (Indian Border Road Organisation) later on, was made with the Phuentsholing- Paro road. This was the time when all the Himalayan entities Ladakh, Sikkim and other Asian kingdoms had lost their glory. Bhutan was the only one which was still standing tall with its Buddhist culture. So, the question was to preserve the ancient heritage along with environment but at this part of time, one could not neglect western science and technology. The decision was in favour of opening Bhutan, but with cautious approach.

Foreign aid had to be sought to embark on planned development and India could be one option which could offer assistance and play a crucial role in Bhutan's development. With the visit of the Indian Prime Minister Jawaharlal Nehru in 1958 accompanied by Indira Gandhi, the help was not only promised it was given in abundance to see that development in Bhutan started. 1959 was the year when the first road was built. In 1961, the-first Five Year Plan came into being. It marked the beginning of the motorable road to reach Thimphu and Bhutan government transport service was started. By 1966, Samtse, Thimphu, Paro and several other places in Bhutan were connected by motor road. Indian planners started to work on developing infrastructure in Bhutan.

First Five-Year Plan [1961-62 to 1965-66]

The total outlay of the first Five-Year plan was 107.2 million Ngultrum (Nu., which is equivalent to Rs.) was fully financed by the government of India.

Table 1

Provision	*Nu in million*
Public Works Department	62.9
Road Transport/ Aviation	7.5
Health	3.1
Education	9.4
Power	1.5
Trade and Industries	1.1
Agriculture	2.0
Miscellaneous	9.10[2]

The plan was seriously handicapped by shortage of manpower and technical skills.

Road Transport

The 66 per cent of the outlay was utilised for major network connecting India. More than 900 km of roads were constructed during the First-five year plan, which completely changed the life pattern in Bhutan. The 208 km road linking Bhutan with Shillong on the West Bengal border with Paro and Thimphu, crossing altitudes as high as 10,000 feet opened western Bhutan in remarkable manner. The road leading to Paro was extended to Ha, a smaller town further west. At the eastern end, Trashigang is linked with Darranga roads from southern hill towns of Sarbhang and Gelephu north of Chirang and Tongsa in southern and central Bhutan.[3]

With the construction of roads, ancient methods of transport came to an end and vehicular traffic started on regular schedule to some important places of Bhutan with outside world. The Bhutan government transport service organised within the last three years runs passengers and freight services on all roads.

Communication Facilities: 36 post offices have been set up in Bhutan and the mail is now carried by jeeps as far as possible. Bhutan has its own philatelic bureau where beautiful stamps are designed. Most of the district headquarters have wireless connections with Thimphu. There is also a telephone and telegraph connection between Paro, Thimphu and Phuentsholing. The former two places have got automatic telephone exchange.

Education: Before planning commenced, there were only 36 lower primary schools and 23 upper primary schools in various parts of Bhutan. The total enrolment was about 2,500 children. During the first five-year plan, over 108 schools including two public schools catering to 15,000 students, one teacher training institute and one technical schools were established.[4]

Health: In the valleys and plains, there was menace of malaria. Considerable advance has been made in eradicating malaria. A public health department under a chief medical officer was set up in Thimphu. The old hospitals were renovated and qualified doctors appointed. Besides, three new hospitals were constructed and over 40 new dispensaries have been established.

Agriculture: During the first plan period, programmes were started for development of agriculture. A regular department of agriculture was established which has extended a large number of model agricultural farms, seed multiplication farms, agricultural research station and development of extension work. Since horticultural crops yield considerable income to the Bhutanese, efforts were made to increase the area under fruit and vegetable cultivation.

Animals and Animal-husbandry: There is ample wealth of livestock in Bhutan. Poultry and dairy animals hold an important place in social economy. A department of animal husbandry was set up during the first plan period. Half a dozen livestock farms in different parts of the country were established.

The establishment of sheep breeding farm, a mithun breeding centre in eastern Bhutan and availability of veterinary services throughout the country represent solid achievements made after the inception of planning.

Forests: The Forest department of the government of Bhutan initiated wide range of measures for conserving forest wealth and exploration of forest products. The sale of timber has been well organised. A wildlife sanctuary was developed at Manas.

Minerals: Extensive deposits of minerals like coal, dolomite, graphite, gypsum and lime stone have been discovered in Bhutan in substantial quantities. Mica is found everywhere and there are immense potentialities for its exploitation. A unit of the Geological Survey of India has worked in Bhutan for some years to assist the Government of Bhutan in every way to locate minerals deposits.[5]

Industry: A fruit preserving plant, processes oranges and pineapple, and a distillery yields sizeable revenue to the Bhutan government. It is located at Samchi. Orange juice and other fruit products of the government food preservation factory find good market in India. Ginger is also processed in a factory near Samchi. Handicraft products are diverse including many textiles, metal ware, leather goods and wooden articles. An important craft is the production of handmade paper from the bark of local bushes and the ancient art of weaving woollen and cotton fabrics. The making of blankets supports a large number of people chiefly women. Possibilities for setting up of rayon and paper pulp factory and match factory were explored.

Trade: Trade routes exist between north and west Bhutan and Tibet for many centuries, on the north and on the south between Bhutan and the neighbouring states of Assam and Bengal in India. With the Chinese occupation of Tibet in 1959-60, trade with Tibet and China virtually came to an end. Now, Bhutan has to export her products consisting of woollen hand-woven material carpets, fruits, etc., to India, which also supplies the items required for it.

Power: Torrential rivers and streams in Bhutan have hydroelectric potential. In most areas, the mountains surface and high precipitation favours the development of waterpower. The system of the Torsa, Raidak and

Sankosh in the west and its large tributaries in the east, offers several promising sites for power development. The engineers of the Indian Central Water Power Commission have helped Bhutan government in setting up a Hydel Directorate by loaning the services of technical personnel to Bhutan. The Hydel Directorate had constructed a 400 kw Hydel project to serve the capital Thimphu and another hydel project (400 kw) to serve the needs of western Bhutanese town of Paro.[6]

In 1961, India and Bhutan signed a pact to harness Jaldhaka River for hydro electric power; the plant generates 18,500 kw of power of which Bhutan receives without charge 250 kw daily and India pays a royalty of Rs. eight per unit annually for the rest.[7]

Second Five-Year Plan (1966-77)

The second Five-Year Plan commenced in 1966 with total outlay of NU 202.2 million. The whole amount was provided by India. The barter economy gave way to money economy affecting larger segment of economic activity and interaction between the inaccessible regions. Development led to the emergence of middle class, which began to have a say in country's governance.

Bhutan started revenue raising schemes in the small-scale industries in the second plan. The breakup of expenditure in various fields under the Second plan are shown in the Table 2 below[8].

Table 2

Item	*Provision in millions (Nu.)*
Developing Wing Headquarter and office–of F.A. and C.A.O.	6.5
Agriculture	21.6
Animal Husbandry	5.8
Cottage Industries	0.8
Education	35.7
Forest	6.9
Health Services	35.7
Postal	5.7
Publicity	1.7
Transport	15.3
Mechanical Workshops	5.9
Power (Hydel)	7.3
BES (Roads, Water supply, Electrification,	68.0
Industries and exploitation of natural Resources	0.9
Preservation of ancient monuments	0.4

The Second Plan concentrated mainly on the improvement of agricultural and horticultural output, the level of education and creating cadre of qualified technical personnel, improvement in animal husbandry scheme, establishment of network of communication for surplus production to the plains of India, restoration of depleted forest reserves in southern Bhutan and proper forestation in northern Bhutan.

The main aim was further development of infrastructure, which was achieved by expenditure of Rs. 200 million.

In 1961, Department of Agriculture was established for the modernisation of agriculture. The main emphasis was on increasing food production by regional specialization of crops, provision of improved seeds, implements and fertilizers, introducing new and improved varieties, popularising fruit and vegetable cultivation and research in new plantation such as apple, snero fruit etc.

By 1971, there were nine regional agricultural research stations and extension farms, three agricultural research and extension stations, four orchards and sericulture research stations in Bhutan.[9]

For improvement of cattle, six livestock farms were established. A cheese making plant was set up at Sa-Ganga and a mithun breeding farm at Thromeng along with small pisciculture units. A special unit of mule and horse breeding was opened at livestock farm at Bidung. Steps were taken to control the grid disease of yaks and common disease like rinderpest etc.[10]

Roads: About 70 million were spent on roads and electrification. The 480 km east-west lateral road between Paro and Tashigang through the heart of the country was opened to facilitate and integrate the eastern and western regions of Bhutan for future development. The Bhutan government started a transport service in 1964 with a fleet of passenger buses and trucks.

The work on new hydel projects was started to electrify Wangdue and Tashigang. The foothill towns of Sarbhang, Bhur, Gelephu and Samdrup Jongkhar and Deothang were linked with Assam grid to get supply power.

In the first two plans, investment was mainly on roads, because without roads, the cost of everything was high It took a longer period to get the work done. Without communication, the country could not have been integrated.

In 1971, entry of Bhutan at the United Nations created an opening for economic aid from other sources than India that had till now financed entire five-year plans. However, the political and economic stance was changed and serious efforts were made to diversify to have a dependable economic or political system. It was a turning point in the traditional pattern of relationship between Bhutan and India.

The king through the resolution of the first National Assembly granted manumission to the serfs in 1953. The resolution reads as follows:

"It was resolved that henceforth all the serfs under any landlord should be allowed to cultivate the land on contract basis as per the following arrangement. If the total produce from the land is 20 pathis, the serf should pay 12 pathis and retain eight pathis. However, the landlord should not provide the early livery as done earlier. If the serfs do not desire to undertake cultivation on contract basis but still desire to continue to stay with their landlords, the landlords must keep them as servants and not as serfs. Serfs who are neither willing to undertake cultivation on contract basis nor to stay with their landlords should be taken over by the government."[11]

Karma Ura says, "His Majesty was inherently interested in emancipation: the idea of giving greater freedom to all individuals so that human development and potential could become possible. In the context of Bhutan, there were small groups in our society who were bonded labourers. They were not slaves. Slavery has a different connotation; these groups were indentured labourers. These consisted of textile labourers. These consisted of textile weavers (thagma), garto, zaabs, drabs for aristocratic households. Indentured labourers for prominent families consisted of zaabs and drabs. In return, they would receive food, lodging and clothes, but the systems of what the indentured labourers received varied greatly. As soon as His Majesty became the king, the labourers who worked on the royal lands were turned into tenants and sharecroppers instead of indented labourers. Later, similar indentured labourers were set free in other parts of the country,especially in some parts of eastern Bhutan where they were concentrated.

Knowledge of the actual social and economic situation of Bhutanese peasants was crucial to His Majesty's planning reforms. As there were no social scientist except wise elders who gave him information by way of conversation, this knowledge had to be a personal quest. As a result, His Majesty went to observe the realities and identify the problems himself. In 1957, a year after he became the king, he travelled to eastern Bhutan with 150 officials. It was an area unknown, but as the bulk of Bhutanese population was living there, the region had to be studied from the point of view of development potential.

In 1953, His Majesty was preoccupied with another matter. He realised the decision of the king and that of high officials need to be shared so that the outcome's acceptable to everybody. As a result, His Majesty opened the National Assembly of Bhutan in 1953, in Punakha. For the first time elders from different gewogs were invited to voice their concerns, ideas and solutions for the future of this country. At the same time, it was a forum for His Majesty to share his larger vision for Bhutan in the years to come.

In 1955, he intensified the conversion of commodity taxes to cash taxes, by assessing land for cash taxation. Land holdings were measured by cadastral surveys using simple chain links. The inaccuracies involved were to cause considerable anxieties to the people later in 1970s, 1980s, and 1990s during remeasurements. Cash taxes were nominal, but moving from commodity taxes to cash taxes was a radical step.[12]

The king separated his personal expenses from that of the State's. Earlier the taxes and revenues were collected and paid directly to the king. In his proposal for the separation in National Assembly 1959, he proposed:

Until now government accounts were not separated from His Majesty's personal accounts. As both revenue and expenditure were handled by His Majesty, there was considerable confusion among the public as to whether the revenue was treated as public money or formed of His Majesty's privy purse. Therefore, in the earlier sessions it was resolved to distinguish between the two. It was decided that henceforth, all expenditure and maintenance costs pertaining to developmental activities would be accounted separately and verified by the National Assembly each year. The revenue and expenditure related to His Majesty's privy purse would be marked 'private'.[13]

After the National Assembly was established in 1953, His Majesty drafted and devised a series of progressive laws for the Kingdom.

Previously it was customary practise for disputes and litigations that could not be solved by elders and mediators in the village to be directed to the king. The Royal Secretaries arbitrated the litigations and the final verdicts were given by His Majesty or in the name of His Majesty by the Royal Secretaries. This process was considered insufficient and the king brought out a holistic set of laws covering fundamental aspects of Bhutanese life such as marriage, inheritance, properties and so forth. The Thrimzhung Chenmo (Supreme Law) was approved in 1959. His Majesty was the author of almost all the provisions contained in it. The influence of His Majesty's intelligence is evident: the laws are very organic and coherent among its provisions and to the reality, which was traditional. This is not so with the new legislations, which have obvious extraneous origins, as is apparent from their convoluted attempts at translations into Dzongkha, and jar on a traditional audience. The comment that the Bhutanese legislators and bureaucrats cannot understand new draft of laws, if there is no English translation is not completely satirical.

The reduction of taxes was continuous aim from the second king onwards and His Majesty continued to make significant reduction. Apart from better laws and tax reforms, The Royal Bhutan Army was formally established. Furthermore, the entitlement of officials were converted from commodities to cash and new designations were given. Until then there were penlops, dzongpons, dzongtshabs, dronyers, zimpons, and so forth, but no ministers or deputy ministers; they were to become new inventions of His Majesty with the establishment of ministries in 1968.

Along with the promulgation of Thrimzhung Chenmo, a mechanism to implement and enforce laws became necessary. His Majesty decided to initiate the establishment of judiciary, first with the appointment of Thrimpons (now called Drangpons) in districts, and finally with the High Court in 1968. These administrative and social reforms were prior to any economic modernisation programmes. From certain perspective, they were preconditions for modernisation."[14]

About culture and education system during his reign, Karma Ura continues, "The third king established Simtokha Rigzhung Lobdra in 1967, where a new breed of traditional scholars could graduate, with Dilgo Kyentse Rinpoche (1910-1991) as the founding principal. His Majesty increased the number of monks in many dratshangs. He understood that as a nation, we collectively stood to benefit more if we preserved and promoted our culture and traditions, whether it be the preservation of textiles, architecture, language or values.

His Majesty is the father of Dzongkha as national language. The phonology and grammar of Dzongkha were adapted and devised under the command of the third king. The brilliant brain engaged in this challenging task was Lopen Gyembo Tenzin. For the first time, a unity of tongues emerged, although continued to preserve the diversity of languages. As kingdom that was moving, merging and integrating together, Bhutan needed a common tongue.

To propagate culture and tradition in schools, to study scientific disciplines and humanities, the king established modern education. He established two centres of educational excellence, inaugurating one public school, Yangchenphug, in western Bhutan in 1969, and the other, Kanglung, in eastern Bhutan in 1968. An agriculture department was opened to improve nutritional qualities and generate income. The kingdom's free health service was founded.[15] In his time; Hindi was replaced by English as the medium of instruction in schools. His Majesty firmly believed that only English can act as a means of connecting and communicating with the world.

His Majesty's first priority was to deepen the excellent relation with India. That he did successfully, visiting India many times. The second priority was to diversify the relation with other countries. Bangladesh figured quite high in his scheme of things. Bhutan was the first nation after India to recognise the independence of Bangladesh. In 1971, His Majesty raised Nu. six million for the victims of flood in Bangladesh.[16]

His Majesty's period coincided with that in the world when de-colonialisation process was on in Africa and Asian countries. Having had education outside Bhutan in Kalimpong and London, his exposure definitely gave him broader vision in which he understood that legislature, executive and judiciary had to be separated. Medieval bureaucracy had to be replaced by modern bureaucracy and the democratic de-centralisation had to be thought about. His may be only a beginning but his intention was surely to establish a state where civil administration, law and justice could be followed. He laid the foundation of representative institutions in Bhutan.

With the consolidation of country, it was time to see that the chaotic conditions of the past could not be repeated in present. "Since that had been accomplished, the third Wangchuck ruler concluded his principal task was to reform and restructure the existing system to allow power and functions shared on pragmatic terms with other institutions. This was considered essential if the monarchy was to survive in a changing world."[17]

The third king's half brother, Prince Namgyal Wangchuck in his speech at the United Nations' General Assembly in September 1971 summed up the reign of the third king in the most appropriate way, "Our government and people are fully committed to a policy of modernisation, although we are at the same time aware of the importance of preserving our national identity by retaining the best in our ancient culture and tradition. None of us imagine that this will be an easy thing to do- to achieve this fine balance and synthesis but with all our mind and effort directed towards this goal, we are confident of our success.

As we present before this Assembly a short outline of present developments in our country, it is important to emphasise the fact that all the radical changes in the country have been initiated by the king himself. In the field of government and administration, it has been our aim to reform our traditional institutions to meet the needs of the present age. Representative institutions like the National Assembly, Council of Ministers and the Royal Advisory Council have been established. The sovereign powers of the monarch have been voluntarily handed over to the National Assembly. The judiciary is separated from the executive and a uniform legal court based on custom and present necessity has been introduced."[18]

The king's intentions matched his vision. As a result, a country which did not even have motorable roads could boast of firm infrastructure on which development and modernisation were inevitable. The king's contribution justified the title which is used for him 'The Founder of Modern Bhutan'.

The year 1972 saw the demise of the third King and ascending of his son Jigme Singye Wangchuck on the scene of Bhutan as the youngest monarch of the world at 17 years of age. He suggested that a Council of Regents could be appointed by the National Assembly until he reaches the age of 21. This was in accordance of the provision Clause 7 of the agreement drawn up in the National Assembly in 32nd session held in 1970. The agreement was not recorded in the resolutions of the session but was a separate document. But, this request was not considered by the National Assembly. On the other hand, the National Assembly resolution said:

His Majesty had commanded the National Assembly to form a resolution as to the appointment of the member of the council. An unanimous decision, however, was reached by this assembly, without any need of debate, that since the aforesaid Agreement was originally drawn up with the case in mind of a Crown Prince too young in age to reign in a proper manner, and in view of the fact that the Crown Prince was now eighteen years old and fully capable of reigning as King, and taking into consideration the fact that he himself had given a clear declaration to this Assembly that he intended to follow the policies laid down by his Late Father, the entire public overjoyed, and with full faith submitted that it would be most grateful if His Majesty would take upon himself the right to rule.[19]

The formal coronation of the king took place on 2nd June 1974. That was the beginning of series of decisions, which were to change the complexion of the State of Bhutan. The nation embarked on its journey of modernisation in true spirit. The agrarian society had to co-exist with industrial development. During his time, an effort was made to maintain the balance between the tradition and the change, between liberalising various political institutions and bringing contentment to the nation. Even the idea of Gross National Happiness which was to be born in 1980s had its germination in initial years. Self-reliance was the key word, which he was to emphasise again. And, it required that he forge a friendship with India which was based on deep understanding and trust with other nations of the world, isolation could no longer be followed.

His economic policies reflected his desire to make optimum use of resources which were available with maximum support from India, which could see this land-locked country develop to its full potential. The constraints which Bhutan felt as a mountainous country were very clearly stated in Chapter-I of the Fifth Five-Year plan of 1992-97 of the Royal Government of Bhutan, which read as follows:

(a) Bhutan is geographically isolated from other countries in the region being a land-locked country, and is distant from the nearest sea port in Calcutta, India. This isolation makes the transport of goods into and from Bhutan costly.
(b) Because of the extremely mountainous terrain, the area of land, which is suitable for agricultural production is relatively small. This limits the potential for increasing the output from agricultural sector and increases the risk of environmental degradation.
(c) The population is distributed in remote scattered settlements, to take advantage of the limited land suitable for agricultural production.
(d) The above factors have made the provisions of roads and communication networks difficult, and the delivery of health and education services costly.
(e) Unlike most other developing countries, Bhutan has relatively small population and the supply of manpower is a major constraint.
(f) As most of the population has been subsistence farmers until recently, the level of monetisation has remained low. [Royal Government of Bhutan, 1991:92].

In his *Casho* (order) issued on 15th Day of the 7th Month of the Fire Tiger Year (September 27, 1986), he outlined his vision for development of Bhutan in the coming years. It read as follows:

> *"In the year 1960, my late father, His Majesty Jigme Dorji Wangchuck broke the isolationist policy of our country and introduced planned development activities in the country. He initiated a new era of community and economic development, strengthened our sovereignty, and made it possible for Bhutan to get all the entitlements of independence, which other countries get as a right. Therefore, looking at the improvement in the living standard of our communities, which were never heard before, we are reassured without any doubt that our goals be achieved well in future just as in the past. We now understand more about our incomplete works, our inabilities and the problems that arise with development activities.*

Besides, we all know that the number of people who think they should not be too greedy but should strive to lead life just without problems and hardship, is increasing. Further, because of the existence of good religion and discipline from the times of our parents in our country, we enjoy perennial peace and happiness. Today, during my reign, firstly with the blessings of our Kencho sum, secondly by the grace of our committed government and thirdly because of our luck, there is adequate improvement in the living standard and public welfare. However, we should endeavour more in future for the betterment of the country and people. If there is any one contravening the objectives of our country by going against the interests of our country or if anyone disobeys the orders of leaders, they will be given whatever punishment they are liable for, without any exception.

Since it is time to begin the work for our Sixth plan, I am commanding the Planning Commission to form policies, and plan our programmes in such way that we can achieve our goals. The policy should be compiled to include all the systems of community and economic development, and our political system. Moreover, our policies should be made according to the need of time and we should think deeply about the future activities that are important for our country. Moreover, it was decreed that we should frame such policies, the execution of which will not affect our political system, our traditional etiquette, culture and religion.

Having thought of our country's objectives and interests, it is hereby decreed that our policies and plans should be made according to the following orders:

Our policies should altogether support the economic development, culture, religion and political system in order to achieve the objectives of our country and to strengthen and safeguard our identity.

We should find ways of improving the per capita income from the internal resources to achieve the objective of self-reliance.

We should endeavour to work harder for the public welfare and the development activities should be distributed according to the needs of all the villages.

The objectives should be to increase the revenue according to the percentage of revenue received as expenditure for the development works within the planned period by the Planning Commission.

We should protect intact our environment in order to enjoy a better health.

Every individual must understand the need and importance of the objectives of the government and bear equal responsibility to promote the system of co-operation between our people and government.

Our government should be able to bear the responsibility of executing functions for the benefit of the people and the country, and our people should support in creating a strong and trustworthy government.

Further, it has been decided that the basis for the evaluation of the achievements of the objectives of the Sixth plan is to see whether the people are happy and live comfortable life.

This policy decree clearly shows our government's endeavour for economic development and the peace of our country. It indicates what our government should do, what development path our country should take and how impartial laws and security of our country should be maintained."[20]

In his Coronation Address on June 2, 1974, His Majesty stressed the need "to attain self-reliance and preserve Bhutan's sovereignty and independence." HM also stressed that development undertakings should be a genuine collaboration between the people and the government. He conceived of grand, long-term goals in the industrial, hydro-power and communications sectors. These came to fruition in the 1980s. But during the 1970s, His Majesty's immediate aims for rural households unfolded in terms of intensive valley projects, cash crops-especially potatoes-irrigation, and resettlement.[21]

In 1972, in Trashigang and Tsirang, projects were undertaken to achieve self-sufficiency in food and to generate more income. These projects called upon people to contribute labour to build the infrastructure such as roads, irrigation channels and dispensaries. This was the beginning of a positive co-operation between people and the government. Similar projects were initiated in Monger and Pemagatshel. This led to the idea where any development programme will have the full participation of the local officials as well as central officials to prepare the developmental plans. It led to the formation of Dzongkhags Yargay Thogchungs (DYTs/ District Development Committees). Careful planning ensured that potatoes were harvested in Bhutan, when they were sown in Bengal and Assam. The emphasis was on high altitude farming and by 2006, as a result of large scale production of potatoes in Khaling and Chapcha, the export reached 60,000 metric tonnes. In the district of Dagana, cardamom and orange plantation was started. These cash crops are now major source of rural income as 3,400 metric tons of cardamom, 55,558 metric tons of oranges and 7,400 metric of apples were produced in 2006 due to initiatives in 1970s.[22]

Canal system through which the water is supplied throughout the country was revised. The old ones were revived and new canals were initiated so that fresh drinking water and water for irrigation can be supplied to the densely populated areas. Bhutan was divided into eight major irrigation zones.

Fourth Five-Year Plan (1976-77 to 1980-81)

The total outlay of the plan was Nu 1,106.2 million. Many new hydro-electric projects and industrial projects were taken up. Even tourism was given attention. Farming was not totally neglected; forest and education were seen in new light and were levied.

Foreign aid was Nu 193 million for the fourth plan. There was six-fold increase in overseas finance, mainly from the UN system, from three per cent to 18 per cent. Serious problem lies in mobilisation of internal resources, which went down from seven per cent to five per cent of the total financing. Major contribution was made by India (90 per cent).

At the end of the Fourth Five-Year Plan, serious review of the success and challenges were undertaken. The result was an entirely new shift in the system of economic development form the Fifth Five-Year Plan (1981-86) onwards. Bhutan was now set for decentralisation in which all the Dzongdas were to play a pivotal role dispersing the responsibility of managing public financing and co-ordinating district development lands. They were the chairman of DYTs. The king had firmly believed that until the decisions are taken at the local level, the development would not be practical and suited to local needs.

Fifth Five-Year Plan (1981-82 to 1986-87)

Decentralisation and people's participation at grass-root level was the hallmark. Each district had its own plan which projected its resources and priorities which were to be discussed in the National Assembly (Tshogdu). Now the projects were undertaken according to the necessity of the region and the Centre fully assisted them.

Chukha hydro-electric power plant was inaugurated by President of India Shri R. Venkatraman, on October 21st 1988. This completely changed the revenue situation and the financial capacity of the country. It paved the way for many projects with Indo-Bhutanese co-operation in coming years.

Since 1981, the kingdom entered a new phase of economic development. Trade agreements for financial assistance from Kuwait Development Fund, membership of World and Asian Development Fund, membership of World and Asian Development Bank, setting up consulate in Singapore and South Korea were prominent. The UNDP, the FAO, the WHO and the UNESCO had increased role in Bhutan.

Druk Airlines began in 1983 between Paro and Calcutta.

Highest priority was given to general government as necessity of streamlining the administrative structure of the country had increased. Public Works Department claimed huge resource form health and agriculture.

Sixth Five-Year Plan (1987-88 to 1991-92)

The main aim of this plan was to achieve socio-economic development in the country and improving the lives of Bhutanese people considerably through the objectives of:

1. Strengthening of the government administration.
2. Preservation and promotion of the national identity.

3. Mobilization of internal resources.
4. Enhancement of rural income.
5. Improvement of rural housing and resettlement.
6. Consolidation and improvement of development services.
7. Human resource development
8. Promotion of people's participation
9. Promotion of national self-reliance.[23]

The process of decentralisation was further enhanced with several major steps taken during the Sixth plan.

The king who was the chairman of the Planning Commission relinquished his post and appointed Dasho C. Dorji, the Deputy Minister, Planning Commission Secretariat as the new Chairman of the Planning Commission.

The Policy and Planning Division (PPD) and technical committee comprising of secretaries of the government and heads of the departments were created to ensure a wider representation in decision making process within the government.

Development services were carried out effectively despite severe financial constraints and disruptive activities by the anti-national elements in southern Bhutan.

Seventh Five-Year Plan (1992-93 to 1996-97)

The Seventh Five-Year Plan saw the Bhutanese government trying to achieve internal mobilisation of sources, decentralisation and people's participation with private sector also being added to the existing structure. Protection of environment and national security were also prime concerns.

His Majesty the fourth king personally visited each dzongkhag and held extensive discussion with the people on the subjects and objective of the Seventh Five-Year Plan.

An Indian delegation visited Thimphu in October 1991 to discuss Indo-Bhutan cooperation projects of the seventh plan. The Royal Government also held talks with other donors at the round table meeting in Paris in March 1992. This was an opportunity for the donors to discuss Bhutan's development strategy and request for assistance as outlined in the Seventh Plan.

In the words of His Majesty, "Decentralisation should go from the centre to the dzongkhag. It should not stop there. It should go past the dzongkhag, the Dzongkhag Yargay Tshochungs and finally to the Gewog Yargay Tshochungs." More effective assignments were made to promote genuine people's participation in the implementation of shared decision.[24]

In the Seventh plan, the Royal Government continued to pay particular attention to ensure that there was balanced development throughout the kingdom with same services and facilities in all parts of the kingdom. Self-reliance with emphasis on internal resource mobilisation, sustainable development with emphasis on environmental protection, development of the private sector, human resource participation and decentralization, promotion of balanced development in all the districts and above all, strengthening and ensuring the security of the country were the main objectives.

Eighth Five-Year Plan (1997-2002)

In the Eighth Five Year Plan, the emphasis was on human resource development and proper application of technology for development and community participation. All development was to be environmental-friendly keeping in consideration with the culture of the country. Bhutan's national security is envisaged to benefit from continued collaboration with friendly neighbours and donors. As far as possible, equal access to basic services and facilities of comparable equality to all Bhutanese, were to be provided, wherever they reside. Improving access of the people to basic services like education, health and facilities such as clean drinking water, sanitation and communications was stressed. Government's objective is to mobilise continued community participation for essential services to further decentralised functions on a selective basis. The privatisation efforts made during the Seventh Five-Year plan continue in the Eighth plan.

At present, Bhutan receives external assistance from as many as fifteen multilateral organisations, nineteen individual donor countries (bilateral assistance), four financial institutions (ADB, World Bank, IFAD and KFAED) and some non-governmental organisations.[25]

Ninth Five-Year Plan (2002-2008)

Ninth Five-Year Plan began at the backdrop of historic move made by the fourth king, when he commanded the drafting of written constitution for the country. As a result, the local officials were to get more powers and people more representation. The Ninth plan was made of 201 Gewog plans formulated by the communities and their elected representatives. After intensive consultation, the micro-economic situation of the country was taken into consideration and the priorities and objectives of the development were framed.

There was an increase of about 75 per cent over the Eight plan expenditure and the guiding philosophy of this plan was the Gross National Happiness, which reflected a balance between material progress and spiritual well being. High priority was given to infrastructural development, improvement in quality of social services, preservation and promotion of culture and environment and development of private sector was also considered necessary for progress.

Social indicators saw improvements in terms of poverty reduction, expanded educational enrolment, impressive decline in child and maternal mortality and securing high access level in provisions of water and sanitation facility.

Ninth plan also witnessed Bhutan's first general elections (March 2008) and the country change into a democratic constitutional monarchy.

The table below shows a comparative study of various developmental aspects projecting the growth between 1985 and 2006:[26]

Table-3

Year	*Infant Mortality Rate*	*Maternal Mortality Rate*	*Water Supply Scheme*	*Households having Electricity*	*National Income (billions)*
1985	142	7.7%	150	10,000	Nu. 2.4
2006	60	2.6%	3,852	65,000	Nu. 36.9

The development programme during the fourth king's time were carried out in the length and breadth of the country, transforming it in a positive way and changing the lives of the Bhutanese people which was beyond imagination. When he took over, he had said, "The most important task before us at present is to achieve economic self-reliance to ensure the continued progress of our country in the future. Bhutan has a small population, abundant land and rich natural resources and sound planning on our part will enable us to realise our aim of economic self-reliance in the near future."

His vision was to come true in the coming years with careful planning and hard work. The goals set by him were as follows:

(a) Social and Economic Prosperity
(b) Efficient Administrative System
(c) Preservation of Culture and Religion
(d) Preservation of Natural Environment
(e) Planned Population Growth
(f) One Nation, One People
(g) Decentralisation
(h) Gross National Happiness

Hydro-Electric Power Projects

The prestigious Indo-Bhutanese joint venture Chukha Hydel Project estimating Rs. 244 crore was formally commissioned by the then President of India R. Venkataraman on October 21, 1988 with an assurance that India would continue to provide assistance to various projects in the Himalayan Kingdom. Since Bhutan is at the dawn of industrial growth, she uses this power in kingdom's domestic lighting and few mills. Over 95 per cent of power is supplied to India. West Bengal has the highest share of 35 per cent and Sikkim the lowest i.e. 1.5 per cent.

Kurichu Hydel Project (45 MW) was implemented from 1993 to 1997 at Gujelpo shing near kurizanpa. It formed the node for high voltage eastern grid, a key project in industrial and rural development of eastern Bhutan.

Tangsibji or Central Hydel Project (45 MW) was completed between 1995 and 1998 and the project feeds power into the central grid. It connects Tongsa, Shemgang, Damphu and Gelephu. At Gelephu it is connected with the Indian grid system. Another hydel project named Yonglachu hydel project (1 Megawatt) was implemented between 1994 and 1996. Rangjung hydel project (1 Megawatt) was started in 1992 and completed in 1993 mainly to supplement power generated by Chhenary and Khaling power stations.

On January 4th 1993 a Memorandum of Understanding with India for Sankosh multipurpose project was signed. The cost of this project was Nu 25,000 million and it was to generate power of 1,525 megawatts.

Following the bilateral agreement signed on March 5, 1996, Tala Hydroelectric Project (1,020 Megawatt) on Wangchu river (downstream of Chukha Project) was launched. This is a Run-of-the-river (RoR) project with six units of 170 mw each. The initial estimate of Rs 1,408 crore (at 1993 price levels) now have been revised to Rs 2,816 crore (at 1998 price levels). The project is funded under the "PLAN" funds of GOI, with 60 per cent grant and 40 per cent loan repayable at nine per cent interest per annum. The surplus power would be sold to India at mutually agreed rates. To oversee the implementation of the project, an eight member Tala Hydro Electric Project Authority (THPA) has been constituted.

Two other big power projects Punatshangchu I and II are under construction at Wangduephodrang. These two projects built with Indian support will change the topography of the region remarkably as well as earn huge revenue.

Education

The firm belief that it was educating the people which would see all round improvement in Bhutanese growth, government took upon itself the task of the expansion and improvement of education facilities. Education was to be free at all levels. Free boarding facilities and stationary were given to students. Primary schools were established all over the country. The emphasis was on increasing the enrolment by considerable numbers. A non-formal education network was established to benefit school drop outs or those who could not go to school. Technical and vocational colleges were opened and even monastic schools were encouraged, so that the preservation of culture could also be maintained. In a *Kasho* which he issued to Special Commission established in 1986, the king commanded, "I am saddened that our people copy the culture of other countries despite the existence of our distinct culture and etiquette. If we do not think now, we cannot show our religion and culture to the world in the future. This, as you know will affect our sovereignty."[27]

In a *Kasho* issued to the Minister of Health and Education on the 13th Day of the 9th Month of the Earth-Tiger Year (2 November 1998), he directed:

Bhutan is a very small and landlocked country. Our government should not create a situation where any educated Bhutanese can not get an opportunity of joining a service of his choice according to the policy of making every Bhutanese a productive citizen. Nevertheless, the citizens should also serve our country with full dedication.

The sole responsibility of our people is to safeguard the sovereignty of our country and endeavour to attain fruition for all time to come by serving our country with solemn oath and allegiance. And, since the stability of our country lies in the hands of our youth, it is very important to enable them to bear the responsibilities efficiently and effectively.

So, in order to develop our youth, our government has been coordinating the programmes of counselling and guidance of our youth. The Youth Guidance and Counselling Centre established by the Ministry of Health and Education in Thimphu with different programmes should be made accessible to about one hundred thousand of students in the schools ranging from primary schools to colleges. Further, for the continuity and sustainable promotion of such programmes, there is a need to ensure self-sufficiency.

Although our government is to spend Nu three million for the advancement of education in the eighth five year plan, youth guidance and counselling, and development programmes can not be implemented with this amount. Moreover, according to our policy of achieving self-reliance, we have to spend our revenue on regular administration.

Therefore, it is decreed that a permanent trust fund be established, for which the government will invest US $ One million to make the Centre self-reliant. Further, you should seek for maximum of foreign aid.[28]

His Majesty's vision has bore fruits and he has been able to guide his nation onto the path of formal education. The table below provides an insight into the development of education which has taken place through the dedicated efforts over the years. Proper educational infrastructure has been laid out across the country and people have become aware of its significance.

Table 4: Number of Enrolment and Teaching Staff in Schools, Institutes, Non Formal Education Centres and Day Care Centres, 2008[29]

Type of Schools, Centres and Institutes	*Enrolment Male*	*Female*	*Total*	*Teachers Bhutanese*	*N/Bhutanese*	*Total*
School Education						
Community Primary Schools	15,174	14,528	29,702	998	2	1,000
Primary Schools	11,516	11,297	22,813	792	7	799
Pvt. Primary School	917	843	1,760	108	15	123
Lower Secondary Schools	24,113	24,593	48,706	1,537	90	1,627
Pvt. Lower Secondary Schools	486	428	914	51	13	64
Middle Secondary Schools	16,481	15,811	32,292	982	195	1,177
Higher Secondary Schools	8,491	7,664	16,155	510	244	754
Pvt. Higher Secondary Schools	2,349	2,421	4,770	120	81	201
Sub-Total Institutes	79,527	77,585	157,112	5,098	647	5,745
Sherubtse College	741	350	1,091	88	42	130
Institute for Language and Cultural Studies	213	125	338	56	1	57
Samtse College of Education, Samtse	425	234	659	78	9	87
Paro College of Education, Paro	537		839	77	3	80
Jigme Namgyal Polytechnic, Desathang	244	63	307	57	2	59
College of Science and Technology, Rinchending	189	58	247	62	14	76
Royal Institute of Health Science	131	126	257	41	2	43
National Institute of Traditional Medicine College of	32	3	35	15	-	15
Natural Resources, Lobesa	117	23	140	69	2	71
Royal Institute of Management	177	100	277	75	2	77
National Institute for the Disabled	30	20	50	13	-	13
Jigmecholling Sanskrit Patshala	18	-	18	1	-	1
Vocational Training Institute, Khuruthang	118	50	168	15	-	15
Vocational Training Institute, Samthang	88	9	97	12	-	12
Vocational Training Institute, Chumey	136	91	227	13	-	13
Vocational Training Institute, Rangjung	121	53	174	16	-	16
Vocational Training Institute, Shershong	79	56	135	9	-	9
National Institutes for Zorig Chusum	61	42				
Trashiyangtse Institute for Zorig Chusum	245	135	380	26	-	26
Sub- Total	3,702	1,840	5,542	737	77	814
Early Childhood Care (Day Care Centres)	143	151	294	26	-	26
Non Formal Education Programme	4,183	9,647	13,830	736	-	736
Total	87,555	89,223	176,778	6,597	724	7,321

(*Source:* General Statistics 2008.

Health Services

Health was a priority and it was focused for development by establishing Basic Health Units within easy distance from every village. Regional Referral Hospitals where serious cases can be treated were established in various Dzongkhags. Health services were provided free of cost in the country along with government sponsored treatments outside the country for those who could not be cured locally. Thimphu and Mongar have well equipped hospitals each with qualified doctors but the country still has to come up with a Medical College to provide training to its doctors. Most of the doctors go to Bangladesh or India for Medical degree. Though efforts are to expand the existing facilities to optimum where the most advanced medical facilities could be made available to people. Still Bhutan has achieved success in its health programmes such as leprosy control, expanded programmes of immunisation, iodine deficiency disease. essential drugs programme. The Information, Education and Communication for Health (IECH) was established to educate the public on the need for better health, hygiene and nutrition practices.

Under His Majesty the fourth king, the education and health sectors jointly launched a project for planned population growth in September 1990 through the schools and the Royal Institute of Health Science in Thimphu. The project aimed at educating people on the interrelationships between population and development, environment and natural resources and the quality of life. His Majesty believed that a planned population growth was an essential component of sustainable development.

His *Kasho,* issued to the Deputy Minister for the Health and Education on third Day of the second Month of the Fire Ox Year (11 March 1997) commanded:

> *In Bhutan, whether it is the external fence or the internal wealth, it is our people. One of the most important and planned development objectives of Bhutan is to bring up a productive community by promoting the physical health of the children and the citizens of Bhutan.*
>
> *In order to achieve the above objective of making cent per cent health services available everywhere, 655 basic health units have been established in all. Further, with our government spending a lot of money every year, there are people who have passed out as doctors and dungtshos. However, the mosi important thing is to ensure that we provide health services to our people continuously and make ourselves self-sufficient. Although the development results of our health services*

are very encouraging currently, if we can not produce medicines necessary for treatment now, there may arise inconvenient times where our government can not take care of people's health. As a result, there is a risk that whatever has been invested in the basic health facilities till today will not benefit the community. So, it is extremely important to become self-sufficient. In order to enable the regular production of medicines on our own without any obstacle in future, steps should be taken to set up a trust fund for production of medicines with the beginning of the 8th Five Year Plan. For this matter, it is decreed that the Finance Ministry should grant US $ one million for creating a trust fund. The department of health should take steps to find additional capital, and the interest of the trust fund should enable us to produce medicines yearly on a regular basis.[30]

Even the remote areas in Bhutan today have access to health facilities. Superstition which was prevalent due to lack of knowledge and the cure for the diseases earlier has given way to acceptance of modern medicine. The table below shows the type and number of health facilities in various dzongkhags.

Table 5: Type of Health Facilities in Dzongkhags, Bhutan, 2008[31]

Dzongkhag	*Hospitals*	*Basic Health Unit*	*Outreach Clinic*
Bumthang	1	4	14
Chhukha	3	8	47
Dagana	1	8	16
Gasa	0	4	13
Ha	1	4	15
Lhuentse	1	11	33
Mongar	1	24	57
Paro	1	3	27
Pemagatshel	1	12	33
Punakha	1	6	9
Samdrupjongkhar	2	8	36
Samtse	3	9	18
Sarpang	2	10	11
Thimphu*	5	7	19
Trashigang	3	19	57
Trashiyangtse	1	7	23
Trongsa	1	6	19
Tsirang	1	4	13
Wangdue	1	10	23
Zhemgang	1	14	38
Bhutan	31	178	519

[***Source***: Annual Health Bulletin (AHB) 2009, MOH].

[**Note**: BHU's figure excludes those which are not functioning.

*Indigenous hospital included under hospital].

Preservation of Forests and Promotion of Tourism

The king emphasised on preservation of natural resources and to maintain a balance between economic development and industrialisation. The National Forest Policy of 1974 stated that Bhutan must maintain 60 per cent of forest cover for all times to come.

The forest sector was allocated a budget of Nu. 160 lakh in the Third Five-Year Plan, which has kept on increasing since then. Forests are considered as a living entity in Bhutan and conservation is a strategy followed religiously. The largest logging organisation Geddu Wood Manufacturing Corporation was closed down in 1995 due to its adverse environmental consequences. The slash and burn agriculture known as *tseri* cultivation was also abolished. Some new laws were also passed. The Forest and Nature Conservation Act was passed in 1995. National Forestry Master Plan was made for the 1996-2010 period, National Environment Commission was set up, National Biodiversity Action Plan was made operational, National Environment Strategy was consolidated in 1998 and Environment Assessment Act was passed in 2000.[32] In Bhutan people primarily depended on wood for the daily work but with the hydro-electric power projects coming up and electricity being available, now the pressure on forests is eased out.

Tourism became a promising industry but was very carefully laid out as high value and low volume, according to which only selective tourists could enter the country after getting permission from the government. This was to control the problems related to uncontrolled tourism which was happening in neighbouring Nepal. Tourists can only travel to Bhutan in groups and through tour operators. But, this policy is relaxed in case of SAARC countries. The limited entry permit to tourists in Bhutan has ensured a charm of Bhutan as a paradise to be visited even if it requires a high cost payment, i.e., 250 dollars per day.

Decentralisation of Power

Reign of the fourth king stands out politically for his unprecedented move to decentralise the state power, empower the local communities to govern themselves and devolution of his personal powers to the various political institutions in the country. His careful planning was first to establish democratic institutions and practices in village communities. Once, the villages were democratised, the process could move upwards in the districts and then to the centre. District and Block Development Committees were set up. The Fifth Five Year Plan carried decentralisation as the main agenda. The coming years witnessed the making of a constitution, holding of the first general elections and his retirement at a very young age in 2006. He fully believed in the ability of his own people who had grown to live under his secure guidance but his vision was different from that of his own people. As he said,

> *"As far as you, my people, are concerned, you should not adopt the attitude that whatever is required to be done for your welfare will be done entirely by the government. On the contrary, a little effort on your part will be much more effective than a great deal of effort on the part of the government."*[33]

Judicial System

The justice system received His Majesty's increasing attention to make it fair, simple, and accessible (at low cost). This required as HM wrote in a Casho in 1989, a selection of capable and upright people with impeccable values as judges. He foresaw that integrity of judges was more important than qualifications. In 1974, there were nine district courts and four sub-district courts. In some places, dzongdags arbitrated minor cases at that time. The Annual National Judicial Conference was introduced to broaden legal education and standards in 1976. Courts were established in dungkhags. The National Legal Course was introduced in 1995. A Penal Code to aid the judges in the proper interpretation of laws and effective adjudication came in 1995, followed by an Anglo-Saxon oriented Civil and Criminal Procedure Code in 2001. If the rule of law were to be attested by the number of laws enacted during His Majesty's 34-year reign, some 87 laws were enacted.[34]

International Relations

Till 1970, Bhutan did not have a full fledged Foreign Ministry to take care of its external relations. They had no communication links with other countries and the tourists had to come to India to obtain inner line permits from Indian government to visit Bhutan. Since 1958, when the then Indian Prime Minister Jawahar Lal Nehru had visited Bhutan, the relationship has grown and matured over time. After 1974, relations were established with other nations and the period between 1980 and 1990 was fruitful in terms of diplomacy when Bhutan established diplomatic relations with 17 countries and became associated with 12 organisations of United Nations.

During his reign, His Majesty received many high level foreign visitors to Bhutan. In chronological order, they included the following:

- The Prime Minister of India, Mr. Rajiv Gandhi, and PLO Chairman Yasser Arafat in 1985;
- HRH Prince Naruhito of Japan in 1987;
- HRH Princess Galyani Vadhana of Thailand, the King and Queen of Nepal, and President Muhammad Ershad of Bangladesh in 1988;
- Un Secretary General, Perez de Cuellar in 1989;
- SAARC Chairman, President Maumoon Abdul Gayoon of Maldives, and HRH Prince Vajiralongkorn in 1991;
- SAARC Chairman, President Ranasinghe Premadasa of Sri Lanka in 1992;
- Indian Prime Minister Narasimha Rao in 1995;
- SAARC Chairperson, Prime Minister Begum Khaleda Zia of Bangladesh, and King Carl XVI Gustaf and Queen Silvia of Sweden in 1994;
- Indian Foreign Minister, Mr. I. K. Gujrat in 1996;
- Australian Deputy Prime Minister, Mr. Tim Fischer and Their Imperial Highnesses the Prince and Princess Akishino of Japan in 1997;
- HRH Prince Charles, the Prince of Wales; former Prime Minister of Japan Toshiki Kaifu; and SAARC Chairman, President Maumoon Abdul Gayoom of Maldives came to Bhutan in 1998.[35]

Bhutan, in 1962 was admitted in Colombo Plan which marked its entry into the international community. Then in 1969, came the membership of Universal Postal Union and in 1970 Bhutan attended the United Nation's assembly as an observer and with India's support in became the member of UNO on 21 September 1971. In 1973, Bhutan joined the non-aligned movement. It was one of the Founder Member of SAARC in 1984.

Bhutan was selective while deciding to have diplomatic relations with other countries. According to Bhabani Sen Gupta (Bhutan, Towards a Grass-root Participatory Policy, p.133), Bhutan established diplomatic relations keeping in mind the following:

(a) Relations based on the principle of selective, utilitarian engagement.

(b) Universalism of the UN system.

(c) Very large space allowed by the Non-Aligned movement.
(d) Extensive constructive engagement with India.
(e) A Special kind of friendship forged with a number of countries with whom Bhutan has no resident diplomatic relations, and
(f) Conflict control and preventive diplomacy with its second great neighbour, China.

Special care was taken by the fourth king to nourish the good relations with India. Although there were testing times because of India's size and power and the Nepalese problem which Bhutan faced, the relations continued and flourished as India went out of its way to support Bhutan by giving it economic aid, by helping it to get into international forums and chose not to comment on the government there. While India is one of the largest democracies in the world, Bhutan chose to remain a monarchy till 2008. The Indian Embassy in Bhutan can boast of the most picturesque and spacious area for itself in Thimphu. Bilateral talks are held regularly to upgrade the existing relations. The 1949 Treaty was revised by signing of Friendship Treaty of 2007, and the cordial spirit still remains as was envisaged by the third king Jigme Dorji Wangchuck in New Delhi in 1968:

"The ties that bind our two countries are a matter of history. Our spiritual heritage which we consider our greatest treasure stems from the teachings of the great son of India, Lord Gautam Buddha. The bonds of understanding and friendship have been further consolidated as a result of growing economic and technical co-operation between our two countries, and I am fully convinced that nothing can ever shake or destroy our friendship."[36]

The fourth king led by example and has proved his calibre for statesmanship and concern for his people. When he chose to retire at the age of fifty-one, he set a rare paradigm in history. At the height of his reforms, he chose to give his successor and people the responsibility to carry on from where he left. This was reflected in the last *Kasho* given at Tashichho Dzong on the 20th Day of the 10th Month of the Fire-Dog Year,corresponding to the nineth Day of December 2006:

As I had announced during the National Day Celebrations last year about my abdication, and also briefed the Lhengye Zhungtshog on this decision, the time has now come for me to hand-over my responsibilities to Trongsa Penlop Jigme Khesar Namgyal Wangchuck.

While we prepare ourselves for parliamentary democracy in 2008, we must all pledge with our body, speech and mind to be unwavering and steadfast in our efforts to strengthen the sovereignty and security of Bhutan, to secure the blessings of liberty, ensure justice and peace in our country, and enhance the unity, happiness and well-being of our people for all time to come.

In taking note of the progress that our country has made over the past 34 years, I would like to state that whatever we have achieved so far is due to the merit of the people of Bhutan. I therefore, wish to express my gratitude to the Clergy, the officials of the Royal Government, the members of the business community and our security forces, and to all the people of the 20 dzongkhags for their unfailing support and loyalty to me and our country.

I am confident that a very bright and great future lies ahead for Bhutan with the leadership of a new king and a democratic system of government that is best suited for our country, as enshrined under the Constitution. I have every confidence that there will be unprecedented progress and prosperity for our nation in the reign of our fifth King.

As I hand over my responsibilities to my son, I repose my full faith and belief in the people of Bhutan to look after the future of our nation, for it is the Bhutanese people who are the true custodians of our tradition and culture and the ultimate guardians of the security, sovereignty and continued well-being of our country.

May the blessings of Ugyen Guru Rimpoche, the father of our nation Zhabdrung Ngawang Namgyal and our Guardian Deities continue to guide the destiny of our country and protect the future of the glorious Palden Drukpa![37]

November 2008 saw the coronation of the fifth Druk Gyalpo His Majesty Jigme Khesar Namgyal Wangchuck. Like his father, welfare and development of Bhutan is his prime concern as is evident in his address to 87th National Assembly. He said "We must always stand united in spirit and purpose. We must always be one nation with one shared goal- one nation one goal."

His Majesty Jigme Singye Wangchuck has also sown the seeds of democratization. He asserted, "It is now my solemn duty to work with the people and ensure that the roots of democracy take strong and unshakeable hold in our nation."[38]

In his address to the graduates in 2007, he outlined the areas he wanted to strengthen. He emphasized on a strong education system, an effective and strong bureaucracy, a strong private sector, an uncompromised respect for law, strong infrastructure, good leadership at all levels, spirit of innovation, creativity and enterprise and a culture of hard work, dynamism and excellence in whatever we do.

He further added "the three things that influence all the decisions that I take, are peace, security and prosperity for Bhutan now and in the future, second is the achievement of the goals of the Gross National Happiness and third is building a vibrant democracy for the country."[39]

While most of the work on the "Friendship Treaty" revision was done during the time of the fourth king, the actual signing of the revised treaty was carried out under the signature of the fifth king who at that time was the crown prince in 2007. This treaty was signed in New Delhi which reaffirms the close relationship between India and Bhutan. Apart from it, it lays the firm foundation of bilateral relationships. The fifth king also has the honour of being the first "Constitutional Monarch" of Bhutan.

The Tenth Five-Year Plan for development has been implemented in his time which focuses on fulfilling the fundamental objectives of achieving broad based and sustainable growth improving the quality of life, ensuring the conservation of natural environment, preserving the country's rich culture and strengthening good governance. These have been the themes and spirit of all the Five-Year Plans undertaken by the country since the inception of development activities in the country.

The total development outlay for the Tenth Plan is presently estimated at Nu 148.074 billion out of which Nu 72.64 billion have been allocated for current expenditure and Nu 73.61 billion for capital investments. The major investment projects for hydropower development such as Punatsangchu and Dagachu are not included in the current plan. Domestic revenue of Nu 75.39 billion is expected to be sufficient to fund only 52 per cent of the total planned outlay. External resources of Nu 57.49 billion is to be mobilised through grants and loans.[40]

In October 2011, the Royal wedding gave Bhutan an occasion to rejoice and relax as the fifth king His Majesty Jigme Khesar Namgyal Wangchuck married Her Majesty the Queen Jetsun Pema Wangchuck. The wedding was scheduled on October 13, 2011. The preparations were carried out throughout the country weeks before to receive the Royal couple after the wedding in various dzongkhags. The magnitude of the happiness which was evident everywhere saw the Bhutanese celebrating it in the capacities they could manage. The markets, the houses and the offices were flooded by the snaps of the Royal couple. Schools prepared cultural functions, many indigenous parks were built by children, songs were prepared in their honour, children ran marathon and cycle races. Receptions were held in their honour in Thimphu, Punakha, Paro and various other dzongkhags. It was a celebration unprecedented which drew attraction of one and all. A collection of poems, greetings, essays, prayers and drawings of the king and the Royal bride-to be was launched on October 5, 2011 by the Education Ministry for the Royal wedding. It was titled, 'This Moment, This Mood, Our Prayers Forever'. The book carries 116 glossary pages of dedication, both in English and Dzongkha from the education family across the country. The Bhutan Media Foundation in collaboration with the Nehru Wangchuck Cultural Centre organised a week long exhibition of the felicitation messages from the people of Bhutan to the people's King and Queen which started on October 14, 2011.

In response to its call for messages, over 3,000 messages were received from people across the country, including children, youth, monks, nuns, rural and urban population. It included messages from outside. The Assembly Speaker Tshogpon Jigme Tshultim inaugurated the exhibition and launched the Royal wedding book of congratulations.

The tourism industry boomed with the Royal wedding with hotels in Thimphu, Punakha and Paro cramped to capacity. According to Tourism Council of Bhutan, about 4,296 tourists exclusive of Indians visited Bhutan. This was a Royal wedding which was watched by thousands of people across the country and outside on their television sets. People walked from all parts of the country for hours to reach the wedding venue in Punakha as well as the reception ground of Changlingtham Stadium in Thimphu later. The stadium was overflowing with people who had already secured their place in it by early morning and those who were late, had to be contented with standing outside and striving for a glimpse of the couple. I was a witness to these unbelievable moments of joy which was shared between the Royal family and the people of Bhutan. Indeed the bond today still remains the same.

The Royal wedding took place at the Dewachhenpoi Phodrang (The Palace of Great Happiness) in Punakha. Adorned in an intricately patterned national dress dominated by gold threads, the Royal bride arrived at the Mochu Zam and was received by the reception party. The Royal bride, accompanied by the members of her family, was led in a Chhipdrel procession across Bazam. Their Royal Highnesses the Princesses from His Majesty the fourth Druk Gyalpo received the Royal bride at the Kabuna (entrance hall) before the courtyard of the Dzong and escorted the Royal bride to the ceremonial reception in the main court yard. The Royal bride offered a Tashi Jel-dar to His Majesty the King and His Majesty the King granted a Tashi Jel-dar in return to the Royal Bride. Once inside, the Royal Couple took part in the purification ceremony. After the blessings, His Holiness the Je Khenpo began the sutras for the crowning of the Queen with the accompaniment of the monastic orchestra. His Majesty the King graced the adornment of the Royal Bride with the Royal Crown, bestowing the crown of Druk Gyal-Tsuen upon the royal bride proclaiming her the Queen of the Kingdom of Bhutan. Her Majesty the Queen Jestun Pema Wangchuck ascended the throne of the Queen of the Kingdom of Bhutan. The ceremony was attended by the Royal family, foreign guests, diplomats, and the Royal Couple's chosen personal guests.

After the ceremony, the newly married Royal Couple visited the general public, over 1,500 who had gathered at the celebration ground. Along with entertainment, refreshments and lunch was also served to all the people who had gathered there.

The journey of monarchy in Bhutan has been closely associated with king's involvement with its people. The development process in spirit remains the same, only today it is more pronounced. The king introduced changes in Bhutan, not in response to violent upheavals but at a time of peace, stability and progress. It is not surprising that for Bhutanese the king is like a father and they have firm faith that a father will always remain a father and will never neglect his children. They have full faith in royal decisions. They see royal decisions as wisdom unfolded. According to traditional wisdom, a royal command has always been heavier than the mountains, more precious than gold.

The trust is mutual. For His Majesty thinks the transformation of kingdom can only be achieved with people's active participation. His Majesty says "I have been saying for thirty years, that the destiny of the nation lies in the hands of people," he further adds, "I have always made it clear that the people are more important than the king. We can not leave the future of the country in hands of one person. The constitution will be the fulfilment of our country's destiny being placed in the hands of our people."[41]

King's firm belief in people of Bhutan is a unique example of a ruler whose every move is for its people as he is confident that Bhutan will bravely face the challenges of future as the Bhutanese people have the integrity, perception and capability to carry out the important responsibility of shaping the destiny of the nation.

References

1. Dorji Lham, 'The Wangchuck Dynasty, 100 Years of Enlightened Monarchy', The Centre for Bhutan Studies, p. 47.
2. Singh Nagendra, 'Bhutan: A kingdom in Himalayas' New Delhi, 1988, p. 164.
3. Trumbull Robart, 'Bhutan Planning Four Roads to India' The New York Times, p. 4.
4. Sigh Nagendra, 'Bhutan: A kingdom in Himalayas', New Delhi, 1988, p. 165.
5. Pilgrim e.g. Note on the Geology of a Portion of Bhutan Records Geological Survey of India, xxxiv (1906) pp. 22-30.
6. Colombo Plan Bureau, Progress of the Colombo Plan, 1963, (Colombo), p. 6.
7. *Ibid,* pp. 7-8.
8. Central Statistical Office, Planning Commission Royal Government of Bhutan, Thimphu, Statistical Year Book of Bhutan, 1989, p. 78.
9. Singh Nagendra, 'Bhutan: A kingdom in Himalayas', New Delhi, 1988, p. 1569.

10. *Ibid,* p. 160.
11. National Assembly, Vol. 1, pp. 10-11.
12. Ura Karma, 'Leadership of the Wise: Kings of Bhutan", 2010, pp. 63-64.
13. National Assembly, Vol. 1, p. 32.
14. *Op.cit,* pp. 65-66.
15. *Ibid,* pp. 69-70.
16. *Ibid,* p. 71.
17. Rose E. L., 'The Politics of Bhutan', p. 151.
18. Maj. Gen. (Retd.) Sood Shubhi, 'Bhutan: Hundred Years of Wangchuck Vision', 2008, pp. 119-120.
19. National Assembly, Vol. 2, p. 110.
20. Nishimizu Mieko, 'Portrait of a Leader', The Centre for Bhutan Studies, 2008, pp. 10-12.
21. Ura Karma, 'Leadership of the Wise: Kings of Bhutan", 2010, p. 85.
22. *Ibid,* p. 87.
23. Achievements in Planned Development (Review of Sixth Plan) 1987-1992, Thimphu, September 1991, p. 7.
24. Achievement in Planned Development, Review Sixth Five Year plan, Planning Commission, Royal Govt. of Bhutan, Thimphu, September 1992, p. 22.
25. Eighth Five Year Plan (1997-2002) Main Document, Vol.1, Ministry of Planning, Royal Government of Bhutan, Thimphu, September 1996, pp. 73-76.
26. Ura Karma, 'Leadership of the Wise: Kings of Bhutan", 2010, pp. 98-100.
27. Quoted in Kinga Sonam's, 'Polity, Kingdom and Democracy', p. 264.
28. Nishimizu Meiko, 'Portrait of a Leader', The Centre for Bhutan Studies, 2008, pp. 95-96.
29. Statistical Yearbook of Bhutan 2009, National Statistics Bureau, Royal Government of Bhutan, p. 39.
30. Nishimizu Meiko, 'Portrait of a Leader', The Centre for Bhutan Studies, 2008, p.91.

31. *Op. cit,* p. 19.
32. Statistical Yearbook of Bhutan 2009, National Statistics Bureau, Royal Government of Bhutan, p. 267.
33. Ibid, p. 273.
34. Ura Karma, 'Leadership of the Wise: Kings of Bhutan", 2010, pp. 108-109.
35. *Ibid,* pp. 95-96.
36. Upreti B.C., 'Bhutan, Dilemma of Change in a Himalayan Kingdom', p. 110.
37. Nishimizu Mieko, 'Portrait of a Leader' 2008, The Centre for Bhutan Studies, pp. 128-129.
38. Translated from Dzongkha Source, Source Kuensel, Windows on Bhutan 2007-08, Welcoming the Winds of Change, p. 11.
39. *Ibid,* p. 29.
40. Tenth Five Year Plan (2008-2013) Main Document.
41. Speech Record of King Jigme Singye Wangchuck when first draft of constitution was drafted in 2002.

3

Demographic Study

Bhutan may be predominantly a Buddhist country, but it consists of several sects. They have their own ancient ethno-lingual characteristics, which makes study of Bhutan interesting. Culturally rich and ethnically diverse, it symbolises an amalgamation of groups over the years. Therefore, the knowledge of its society is very essential. A study of Bhutanese society reveals the contrast with other South Asian societies. It is a society, which has developed in isolation with few influences. Therefore, its study will reveal some interesting aspects. It was only after 1980s that specific figures began to emerge in different fields after the National Statistical Bureau and Centre for Bhutan Studies were established for research purposes.

Key Facts about Bhutan[1]

Land Area	38,394 sq. km.
Forest Cover	72.5per cent
Population, 2008	671,083
Average Household Size, (BLSS, 2007)	5.0
National Language	Dzongkha
National Currency	Ngultrum (Nu.)
Hospitals, 2008	30
Doctors, 2008	171
Civil Servants, 2008	19,848
Schools, Institutes and Non Formal Education Centres, 2008	1,299
Teachers (including in institutes and NFE), 2008	7,231
Students ((including in institutes and NFE), 2008	176,778
Labour Force Participation Rate, (BLSS, 2007)	67.3per cent
Unemployment Rate, (BLSS, 2007)	3.7per cent

Cellular Mobile subscriber, 2008	149,439
Postal Infrastructure, 2008	127
Total Road Length, 2008	5,363 km
Registered Vehicles, 2008	40,659
Electricity Generation, 2008	6,564.2 MU
Electricity exports, 2007/2008	5,429.12 MU
Tourist arrivals, 2008	27,636
Revenue earned from tourism, 2008	38.8 Mn US $
Total establishments, 2008	28,073
Balance of trade, 2008	2,921.6 Mn. Nu
Exchange rate, Nu. Per US $, 2008	43.5
Gross international money reserves, 2008/09	694.5 Mn US $
Total Ninth plan budgetary outlay (2002-07)	70,000 Mn Nu.
GDP, 2008 (current price)	54,149.9 Mn. Nu.
Average Inflation rate, 2008	8.31%
Purchasing Power of Nu. 2008 (base year =2003)	0.76 Nu.

The Inhabitants

The Bhutanese are strongly built, usually of medium height, and are agile and athletic. They are cheerful and tend to take life as it comes, an attitude due largely to their Buddhist tradition. Polite and courteous, they do not appreciate brashness and expect a courteous though frank attitude from others.[2] They are not very open and forthcoming at the beginning of an acquaintance but slowly they do open up and become good friends. Ignorance is long bygone now; a visit to the country now reveals that education has taken deep roots. The modern Bhutanese youth are conscious of their health, education, career, law, culture and media, family and community. Even the older generation which presently spearheads the development of Bhutanese— be in government offices or in farms, the emphasis is on educating their children. In most of the educational institutions, children are from all spheres. In short, they are embracing the developments of change.

With regard to the general character of the people, George Bogle wrote:

"The simplicity of their manners, their slight intercourse with strangers and strong sense of religion preserve the Bhutanese from many vices to which more polished nations are addicted. They are strangers to false-hood and ingratitude. Theft and every other species of dishonesty to which the lust of money gives birth are little known. Murder is uncommon and in general is the effect of anger and not covetousness. The celibacy of a large part of the people however is naturally productive of many irregularities. The coldness of the climate inclines them to an excessive use of spirituous liquor. The more I see of the Bhutanese, the more I am pleased with them. The common people are good- humoured, downright and, I think thoroughly trusty. The statesmen have some of the art which belongs to their profession. They are the best built race of men I ever saw. Many of them very handsome with complexions as fair as the French."[3]

The distribution of population in Bhutan is determined by its topography. The high mountains, climatic variations and the major factor of productivity of land. Some areas are virtually empty, others are crowded but quite clearly the kingdom as whole is by Asian standards one of low density. The areas densely populated are the Inner Himalayan valleys of the Central region. There are eight main valleys, where population in Central and Eastern Bhutan is concentrated. They are:

(a) Ha
(b) Paro
(c) Punakha
(d) Thimphu
(e) Tenchu
(f) Trange
(g) Bumthang and
(h) Eastern Bhutan[4]

The Population and Housing Census of Bhutan 2005 revealed that urban population (30.9) was 2.2 times less than the rural areas (69.1 per cent). Spatial distribution of the population differed significantly across the dzongkhags. The most populated dzonghkhag was Thimphu with 98,676 persons accounting for 15.5 per cent of the total population followed by Chukha with 74,387 persons (11.7 per cent) and Samtse with 60,100 persons (9.5 per cent). These three most populated dzongkhags together account for 36.7 per cent of the total population. The least populated dzongkhag was Gasa with 3,116 persons (0.5 per cent) followed by Haa with 11,648 persons (1.8 per cent) and Pemagatshel with 13,864 persons (2.2 per cent).[5]

The population of Bhutan can be divided into four broad, but not necessarily mutually exclusive categories. The first is composed of several groups of people of Tibetan origin. Some of whom may have migrated to Bhutan as early as the ninth century and others as recently as 1959-60. Second, there

Table 1: Total Surveyed Population by Age, Gender and Area of Residence, Bhutan, 2010[6]

Age	Bhutan			Rural			Urban		
Group	Male	Female	Total	Male	Female	Total	Male	Female	Total
0-4	29,800	29,200	59,000	18,900	18,300	37,200	10,900	10,900	21,800
5-9	36,300	36,600	72,900	24,900	24,800	49,600	11,400	11,800	23,200
10-14	40,800	39,900	80,600	29,200	26,800	55,900	11,600	13,100	24,700
15-19	32,900	39,000	71,900	22,600	25,000	47,600	10,300	14,000	24,300
20-24	29,600	35,700	65,300	20,200	21,600	41,800	9,400	14,100	23,500
25-29	25,800	31,400	57,100	14,800	18,200	33,000	11,000	13,100	24,100
30-34	24,000	26,500	50,400	14,400	16,800	31,200	9,600	9,700	19,200
35-39	20,400	24,200	44,600	11,600	16,600	28,100	8,800	7,600	16,400
40-44	17,600	19,300	37,000	11,600	14,300	25,900	6,100	5,000	11,100
45-49	17,500	17,400	34,800	12,400	13,800	26,200	5,100	3,500	8,600
50-54	16,900	15,400	32,300	13,300	12,800	26,100	3,600	2,600	6,100
55-59	14,000	12,500	26,600	11,700	11,000	22,700	2,400	1,500	3,900
60-64	13,100	12,800	25,900	11,600	11,100	22,700	1,600	1,600	3,200
65+	19,800	18,500	38,200	17,700	16,300	33,900	2,100	2,200	4,300
Total	338,400	358,200	696,500	234,600	247,400	482,000	103,800	110,700	214,500

Note: Totals may not add up due to rounding.

are a number of distinct, but related communities in eastern Bhutan. According to some observers, they are related to similar Indo-Mongoloid groups in the Assam, Himalayas, presumably migrated to Bhutan in the past millennium. A third element in Bhutan's population consists of a number of small tribal groups, such as the Lepchas, Doyas, which are described sometimes as the aboriginal or indigenous inhabitants, to which can be added the families of ex-slaves, often from similar tribal communities of India adjacent to Bhutan. Finally, there are the Nepali Bhutanese, most of whom have been resident in Bhutan for three or four generations, representing a new, still somewhat alien element in the population structure.[7]

The Bhutanese of Tibetan origin commonly called as the Ngalops make most of the social and political elite throughout Bhutan. They are concentrated in western Bhutan. They form a large majority and along the northern border areas from west to east. Agriculture is their main livelihood. They cultivate rice, wheat, barley, maize, etc., among others. In the regions of Thimphu and Paro, apple is also cultivated as cash crop. They are known for Lozeys or making ornamental speech and for Zheys, enacting dances that are unique to the Ngalops.

The Indo-Mongoloid people of Bhutan together known as Sharchops are commonly inhabitants of Mongar, Trashigang, Trashi Yangtse, Pema Gasthel and Samdrup Jongkhar. Besides cultivation of maize, rice, wheat, barley and vegetables, the Tshanglas rear domestic animals to supplement their living. Weaving is popular occupation of women. They produce beautiful fabrics mainly of silk and raw silk.

In Bhutan, the Nepalese people are popularly known as Lhotshampas i.e., the people of south. It is generally agreed that they migrated from Nepal in the beginning of the 19th century, as labourers. They practice Hinduism. One can find various castes of Lhotshampas including Bhawans, Chhetris, Rai's, Limbus, Tamangs and the Gurungs. They essentially depend on agriculture and cultivate cash crops such as ginger, cardamom, oranges, etc.

Apart from three main ethnic categories, there are several small tribal groups, who constitute the population of Druk-Yul.

The Bumthaps, Mangdeps and Khengpas who speak Bumtapkha, Mangdepkha and khengkha, respectively inhabit the central pockets of

Bhutan. The Bumthaps cultivate buck wheat, potatoes and vegetables. A section of this population rears yaks and sheep, and produces fabrics of wool and yak hair. The Mangdeps depend on cultivation of rice, wheat, maize, vegetables besides rearing domestic animals. The khengpas depend on agriculture similar to the Mangdeps. However, they are known for the bamboo and cane craft. Kurtoeps are the other category of people in the east. They inhabit the district of Lhuentse and the villages found spread along the banks of Kurichu. Khoma women are expert weavers, known for their skill in weaving the grandiose Kushithara.

The Brokpas and the Birmis are semi-nomadic community. They are settled in two villages of Merak and Sakteng in eastern Bhutan. They mostly depend on yaks and sheep for livelihood. Living on the high altitude zones, they hardly take up agriculture. They speak different dialect and have their unique dress made of yak hair and sheep wool. They are experts in cane and bamboo crafts.

To the extreme north are the Layaps, who speak the Ayapkha. Like the Brokpas, they are semi-nomads whose source of livelihood is on yaks and sheep— the products of which they barter with the people of Wangdue Phodrang and Punakha in exchange of rice, salt and other consumables.

The Doyas are the other tribal community. They are settled mostly in southern Bhutan. They are considered the aboriginal inhabitants of western and central Bhutan, who settled over the years in the present areas in Dorokha. They have their own dialect and dress in the own unique style.

The Monpas are a small community in Rukha under Wangduephodrang. Together with Doyas, they are considered the original settlers of central Bhutan. They speak different dialect unique to their own, but one that is slowly dying as these people are now being absorbed into the mainstream Bhutanese society.[8]

Lepchas constitute a very small community inhabiting particularly Haa valley. They are of palaeo-Mongoloid stock. The community follows jhum or tseni i.e., shifting cultivation. Some are engaged in horticulture, agriculture, trade and animal husbandry. Lepcha villages are small in size— controlled by the council of village elders with a head at the top. They primarily follow Buddhism of Tibetan variety along with indigenous beliefs and rituals.

The Kochs, who once expanded their rule to several valleys of Bhutan own to a sub-group of the great Bodo community. They are the residents of south Bhutan. Ethnically Koch are Indo-Mongoloid Bodo-group of people and culturally more closer to Mechs and Rajbansis of Assam and North Bengal. Kochs are agriculturists. Tephoos constituted an indigenous group— settled in Spuona-kha of north Bhutan. They were of Indian extraction branched out of Koch tribe. The Tephoos are considered the descendants of Raja of Cooch Behar, namely Padmanarayana.

It seems some Muslim communities from plains had settled in south Bhutan. During Duars war, a number of people belonging to Muslim community were found in the vicinity of the forts of central Bhutan. Some Tibetan Muslims were settled in the towns and urban centres of Bhutan, particularly after Chinese occupation of Tibet. Many Muslims of Indian origin had moved to Bhutan for the sake of trade, business and professional works. The descendents of earlier Muslim settlers, who were the products of marriages between Muslim males and local females continued to live in the country as inseparable part of Bhutanese population. The Drupkas called the Muslims as Kaches, which is a Tibetan term to denote the Muslims.[9]

The word 'Bhutanese' in political parlance includes all groups, who have settled in Bhutan and are its citizens. However, from the cultural point of view, it refers primarily to people, who follow the Drupka sect of Buddhism, popularly known as Drupkas. There has been practically no fusion of the people of Nepalese origin with the Drupkas.

Language

Bhutan represents an astonishing array of linguistic diversity. A large number of languages are spoken in Bhutan. The chief language of Bhutan is the "Dzong language" or Dzongkha, taught in all schools and written in classical Tibetan block letters Ucan for purpose of print. Handwritten script of Bhutan is known as "Juyig". Although Dzongkha may have its origin in classical Tibetan, it varies greatly in pronunciation, prefixes and end-letters, mute in the high Tibetan languages. These are still spoken or heard at least in the Bhutanese pronunciation.

In the South east of the country, the Mon and Khen language of aboriginal inhabitants of Himalayas are still alive. These old languages are a striking linguistic mirror of the rich Bhutanese tradition comprising treasures of the local legends, songs and plays. These are a lively echo in which still resound the voices of sunken prehistoric times. Six of these languages belong to the Dzongkha group. They are as follows;-

1. Dzongkha, the language of the Dzongs, spoken especially in western Bhutan and common language of Bhutan.
2. Tapadamteng, spoken in south west near Buxa.
3. Laya Lingzhi, the shepherd language of the North West in Laya and in Lingzhi.
4. Tshalingpa, spoken in the Tshaili area of the Shongar district and in eastern Bhutan.
5. Dagpakha, a Tibetan dialect of the north eastern border, and;
6. Mira Sagtengpa, Tibetan Dialect of Tashigang in the farthest east of Bhutan.

The following seven dialects belong to the so called Khen languages:

1. Mangdikha, spoken in the Magdi district (Tongsa)
2. Gungdekha; an archaic language of the South, originally without relation to Khenkha, today reluctantly joined to the Khen- group
3. Khenkha, spoken in the khen district south of Tongsa.
4. Bumthangka, spoken in Bumthang and in the whole of central Bhutan.
5. Tsamangkha, spoken in the east and north east on the eastern border of Kurto
6. Kurtopakha, especially spoken in Kurto
7. Salabekha or Yangtsepakha, spoken in Yangtse district as also in Tawang and in southeast Tibet.

The two dialects, which belong to the Mon group, are:-

1. Monpakha in the south and south east; and
2. Sharchagpakha, spoken in the east and southeast, especially spoken in the Tashigang and Dungsam.

Although, many languages are spoken in Bhutan one can safely conclude that there are four main languages in Bhutan today:-

1. Dzongkha, spoken in the western and northern Bhutan, is also the official language of the country.
2. Bumthangkha, spoken in Central Bhutan.

3. Sarchapka, spoken in Eastern Bhutan.
4. Nepali, spoken in southern Bhutan.[10]

While Dzongkha, Bumthangkha, Sarchapka are written in the Tibetan Ucan script, Nepali is written in the Devanagari script. English is the medium of instruction in schools and is extensively used in offices.

Religion

Before the advent of Buddhism in Bhutan, there existed religion, which would always remain somewhat difficult to describe. Bhutan's original religion has been called Bon, and perhaps broadly falls in the category of Animism. One is inclined to believe this original religion must be entirely based on nature worship. Some aspects of nat..re worship which Ponism professed was duly incorporated in the Mahayana Buddhism which Guru Padmasambhawa introduced in the 8th century A.D., The religion of Bhutan today is essentially a sect of Mahayana Buddhism, allowed by the process of evolution to develop and establish as distinct faith of the land.[11]

Je Khenpo, the head of religious affairs in the kingdom, holds a prominent place in the social and cultural life of the Bhutanese people. The two most sacred and historically significant Buddhist temples Kyerchu and Byampsa were built in the 7th century. It was not until the visit of great Indian saint Guru Padmasambhawa (A.D.746) that Buddhism took firm roots in Bhutan. Padmasambhawa converted king (Sendha) reigning in the Bumthang valley to Buddhism, after which the faith gradually spread to the other regions of Bhutan. The religious life of the people of Bhutan is dominated and guided by Lamas. They devote their entire life to prayer and meditation. They live upon charity from people and government. The centre of activity of Lamas is the monastery. Almost every village of Bhutan has a monastery of its own.[12]

As witness to the people's faith in religion stand the innumerable religious monuments in every corner of the tiny kingdom, one find prayer wheels turning and religious flags waving in the breeze— sending the message of Buddha from populated valleys, mountain slopes, bridges and high passes to desolate and remote mountains. The lonely alpine passes have the sacred mantra, Om Mani *Padmae* Hun, carved on stones and hillsides. Every home has a shrine choesham, where the family prays at the altar. The altar has usually statues of three great lamas- Sakyamuni, Guru Rinpoche and Zhabrung Rinpoche. Seven bowls filled with water are placed at the altar, as offerings to deities.[13]

Hinduism is the main religion in south Bhutan.

Women in Bhutan

Bhutan offers an interesting study as far as gender relation are concerned. A close look at society and its social structure compels one to marvel at the positive attitude towards women (The girl child in particular, which makes Bhutan a very different country from other South Asian nations). The participation of women is omnipresent at home and workplace. They are pillars of strength and they enjoy better position than their counterparts in South Asia and gender bias is not a common feature. The monarchs of Bhutan and the government have kept women at the forefront of country's development enterprise. In this country with Buddhist religion, equality seems to be not only in letters but also in reality. A similar view has been expressed by Dutch Anthropologist Reiki Crins. She states, "Social relationship in Bhutan between men and women are marked by gender equality— unique in South-Asia."[14]

Women who constitute 47.7 per cent of the kingdom's population have traditionally held a place of honour in the society. No overt discrimination exists in the country. In general Bhutanese women enjoy a high status in society and have full and complete equality under law. Instances of female infanticide, malnutrition, dowry deaths and other discriminatory social malpractices are virtually unknown and unheard.[15] Overall, parents do not have a preference for sons and give as much care to girls as to the boys. This is reflected in the overall sex ratio which is 110 males per 100 females.[16]

The theme of women development has figured as an integral part of country's Five Year Plans. The government has worked to ensure that equal opportunities are provided to men and women alike. It enables them to participate and share in development. Bhutan has ratified the Convention on Elimination of Discrimination against Women (CEDAW) and has unconditionally accepted all the provisions contained therein.

However, I would like to analyse the current situation and the data which is available in education and training, health, employment, violence against women, ageing mental health and disability and the strategic measures which have been taken to promote general mainstreaming. Gender discrimination may not be visible, even distinctions are seldom relevant but this is not to state that there are absolutely no differences. Nature has made two sexes differently, endowing each with separate attributes and biological functions. It stems from biological and physiological differences men and women have in advancing family and community. Survival and progress has come to specialize in certain roles which are most suited to them.

Bhutanese society is traditional, yet changing— there are common and separate roles for men and women, but there are no rigid agreement. They can be altered depending on the situation. The consensus seems to be unspoken and unwritten between a man and a woman.

Education and Training

The development of modern education started in Bhutan in 1960s. Earlier traditional monastic education was given. Today, there is an extensive network of schools throughout the country. Most of them have boarding schools. The enrolment to Nursery begins when the child reaches the age of four.

In primary schools, the enrolment of girls and boys is equal. In some cases, girls outnumber boys in some of the dzongkhags. Bhutanese parents have taken education seriously, which is free and sponsored by government. Earlier hardships like remoteness of schools are a thing of past when parents found more convenient and safe to keep their daughters at home. Enrolment of girls in early years was very low. Since 1995, the situation has improved. It is continuously showing an incline. More schools have come up. Hostel facilities have been introduced. Improved road communication has enhanced mobility, reducing the mental dread of distance. However, the Government of Bhutan in its Tenth Five-Year Plan has targeted to make the net enrolment in primary level to 100 per cent by 2013. At the time of preparing this manuscript it was 88 per cent.

The proportion of girls attending schools tends to be higher in urban areas than in rural areas. This may be correlated with higher cash income in urban areas, which allow parents to provide girls the opportunity to attend schools. But in secondary education, there seems to be a fall in the number of girls due to reasons which are not attributed directly to the education system. These are, socio-cultural factors such as early marriage, teenage pregnancy (which is in sizeable number in Bhutan), imperatives on domestic and subsistence labour and parents' assumption that girls need more social security.

Table 2: Number of girl students in various Schools/Colleges

Dzongkhag	*School/College*	*Total Students*	*Girl Students*
Mongar	Mongar Lower Secondary School	810	420
	Wangdue Chholing Primary School, Singor	50	26
Bumthang	Lower Secondary School	954	504
	Higher Secondary School	494	243
Punakha	Khuru Middle Secondary School, Khuruthang	1093	554
	Higher Secondary School	673	329
Thimphu	Lungtenzampo Middle Secondary School	1157	650
	Lower Secondary School	1400	701
Paro	Goepel Lower Secondary School	08	06
Chukha	Phuentsholing Lower Secondary School	2023	1143

(***Source:*** Statistics from Schools in Bhutan Collected in a survey by me from 01 June - 26 June 2010.)[17]

Enrolment level for girls is about half of that for boys from pre-primary to grade VI. From grade VII- VIII, it drops to less than 40 per cent and in grade IX and X to roughly 26 per cent and 17 per cent respectively.[18]

The dropout rate at the secondary level is reflected at the higher level. Only when the enrolment at primary and secondary level increases, the figures will go up at the higher level.

Employment

A majority of women in Bhutan are employed in agriculture sector. They are significantly underrepresented in higher skilled and higher paid jobs. Women labour force participation is lower than that of men particularly in urban areas. Similarly, the unemployment rate is very high for females in comparison to males. In 2006, women unemployment rate was 3.8 per cent; however male unemployment rate was only 2.6 per cent.[19] There is a high proportion of females who are employed, but are unpaid family workers. Employment of underage girls as domestic workers is a rapidly growing problem of urban areas.

The disadvantage in the area of employment has been attributed to Bhutan's late starting of modern education for women in particular. Women's traditional ties to the land, prevailing inheritance patterns, cultural stereotypes and perceptions and lack of urban sector skills in an increasingly urbanised society constitute other barriers to opportunities for women for paid and skilled employment.

Here I would like to present a study on what parents feel about the future for girls, which may be useful to understand their preference for daughters.

Table 3: Future for Girls[20]

Dzongkhags	*No Plans*	*Farmer*	*Teacher*	*Administration*	*Health*	*Army*	*Others*
Thimphu Town	4	—	1	—	5	—	2
Thimphu	7	7	—	1	—	—	—
Chukha	3	4	—	4	3	—	—
Shemgang	13	1	3	3	3	—	1
Pemagatshel	—	—	—	—	—	—	—
Samdrup Jongkhar	—	—	—	—	—	—	4
Total	27	12	4	8	11	—	7

The above chart shows the parents' preference of jobs for daughters in 1989. In west and central Bhutan and some parts of the east, family system is matrilineal and land is inherited by daughters. 60 per cent of rural women hold land registration titles. Mother or the eldest daughter may become the head of the household. Earlier, lack of education limited them to homes, but today the scene has changed completely. There is a desire in women to utilise their talents for uplift of society and nation and to help families acquire higher living standard.

The recent survey in June 2010 reverse the trend. Most of the educated girls told me "My mother was a farmer, but she gave me education and helped me in becoming what I am today." This testifies that women have blessings and moral support of elders, who encourage them to seek career in other professions.

Table 4: Job Preference by Educated Girls[21]

Dzongkhag	*Business*	*Government*	*Private*	*Technical*	*Business and Govt. Both*
Kanglung	3	34	—	—	3
Mongar	1	37	—	—	2
Bumthang	1	38	—	—	1
Punakha	4	30	2	2	2
Thimphu	5	24	3	—	8
Paro	6	34	—	—	—
Phuentsholing	13	26	—	–	1
Total	33	223	5	2	17

The chart shows that a large number of women prefer working in government jobs; for it gives them security as well as fixed working hours compared to the private sector, where the working conditions are more severe. The presence of large number of females in the commercial places has not necessarily been their preferred choice of career. In most of the markets, the shops are run by females. Some are independent and others take care of their family business. Technical education is still in its infancy. Women are not much charmed by it. An almost negligible number of women engineers display least inclination towards technical jobs.

Bhutan's newly inducted constitution has given women the right to equality, although there was never discrimination between men and women. Trend shows that development and enlargement in the field of women education has led to increased employment opportunities in urban sector. In Article 7 (8), the constitution provides Bhutanese citizens with equal access and opportunity to join the public service, while Article 7 (6) affirms the right to vote and to exercise adult franchise. These provisions are reinforced for women by Article 9 (17), which outlines the responsibility of the state to take appropriate measures to eliminate discrimination against the exploitation of women in the public and private spheres. Article 25 (4), meanwhile, directs the Royal Civil Service Commission (RCSC) endeavouring *'to ensure that civil servants render professional service, guided by the highest standards of ethics and integrity, to promote good governance and social justice in implementing the policies and programmes of Government.'*[22]

There are some other legislation— such as the Election Bill enacted in 2008, which do not differentiate between women and men. No seats are reserved for women in the National Assembly. The political parties are not required to have certain proportion of women members or candidates.

Women representation in politics at national level is inadequate and low. In the present parliament, there are only four women members in National Council and three in National Assembly. There is not a single woman minister in the cabinet. Till now there has been no female district administrator (Dzongda). During my survey between 1-26 June 2010 when I asked "What stops women from coming into politics?" Out of 250 women 13.5 per cent said— it is because of the family circumstances, 18.25 per cent held the attitude of the political parties responsible for their absence from political arena, 2.24 per cent opined that there were not many opportunities, but overwhelmingly 46.03 per cent said they were not interested in coming into politics.

The Royal Government of Bhutan is giving attention to increasing women's participation in development activities and in public decision making. Here, the women remain under represented.

In Judiciary barely six per cent are women. The data provided by the Royal Court of Justice shows a proportionately higher representation at the lower grades. For studying law degrees, government scholarship is required, which needs high pass marks in Dzongkha. The number of female lawyers is not even 10. There is a lack of interest in women for postings outside Thimphu.

Table 5 (Five)-: Female Representatives in the Judiciary

	Female: Male Ratio	*Proportion of Women*
Drangpon (Judge)	0.03	3 per cent
Drangpon Rabjam (Assistant Judge)	0.04	4.2 per cent
Registrar (includes Registrar	0.30	30 per cent

Although, there is an increase in women's representation in civil services, still it falls short. In 2006, women accounted for 28 per cent of civil servants (40 females for every 100 males). This is up three per cent points from 2002 and 12 per cent points from 1996. Women's representation is lowest at the top levels (Grades 1-3), accounting for only five per cent of civil servants; this partly be can explained by the late participation of women in the education process. At the same time, women's representation in the civil service is highest, 32 per cent in the category of Grades 9-13 appears to indicate that younger women are entering the civil service or are on their way up to higher grades.[23]

Table 6: Proportion of Female Civil Servants by Grade

Grade	*Female: Male Ratio of Civil Servants*	*Proportion of Female Civil Servants*
1–3	0.05	5 per cent
4–8	0.34	25 per cent
9–13	0.47	32 per cent
14–17	0.37	27 per cent
Total	0.40	28 per cent

As on June 2008, women constituted 29.5 per cent of civil service. Women comprise 12.5 per cent in specialist category. To say, 5.3 per cent at executive level, 30.33 per cent at professional and management level and 31.71 per cent in supervisory and support category and 19.86 per cent of the operational category.

In times to come, their talent, labour and competitiveness is going to be an asset to the society. Bhutanese women have emerged self confident and a number of reasons can be attributed for their preference to commercial fields.

Present conditions in society have made it easy for them to step out and sky is now the limit for them. High standard of living and sharing husband's responsibilities have become the propelling force. They want to utilise their time in such way which is productive and economically beneficial. The spread of higher education as well as professional education is helping them hone their talents and materialise ambitions.

Women's household responsibilities and lack of education is becoming a thing of past. They are now entering new areas fully equipped with required knowledge.

In my opinion, three factors stand out for their working outside home -

(a) Family circumstances.
(b) Ambition and self-satisfaction.
(c) Utilization of time.

Economic independence has further enhanced their social status and helped them change environment around themselves. This quest takes them out of security of homes to work places. Earlier, they worked in low-skilled and low paid jobs in informal sectors i.e., at home as weavers, but now they are visible in all spheres. They are in large numbers in teaching, nursing and fine arts.

Working women are entitled to three months of maternity leave with full pay or one month with full pay in case of a miscarriage. On completion of maternity leave, they may resume work without loss of seniority, turn of promotion or any other opportunity. Male civil servants are entitled to five days of paternity leave, which may be combined with other forms of leave. There is a term called flexi-time allowing them flexibility of work hours "to attend to personal needs during normal working day." Scope thus exists for breastfeeding mothers to use the flexible time arrangement after three months of maternity leave.

Table 7: Opinion on Duration of Maternity Leave[24]

Dzongkhag Surveyed	*Maternity Leave Sufficient*	*Maternity Leave Insufficient*
Kanglung	15	18
Mongar	11	28
Bumthang	10	34
Punakha	15	11
Thimphu	20	16
Paro	19	17
Phuentsholing	12	8
Total	102	132

Urbanisation has necessitated educated women to come out and augment the family income, but the joint family system which was deeply ingrained in the social structure of Bhutan is giving way to nuclear families. Most of the working women have to face the consequences how to bring up small children till they go to school. 56.41 per cent women feel the present duration of maternity leave is not sufficient. It will be of great help and an indication of sensitiveness towards women's role as mothers on the part of administration if it be increased to six months. On the other hand, the administration gives its own reason for maintaining the *status quo* on the issue, stating that they do not have replacements easily available and are not in a position to allow long absence of professional women.

Industrial Employment

Very little can be said about the participation of Bhutanese women in the industrial sector, since industries are not highly developed in the country. In 1986, as indicated by the Department of Industries and Mines, there were 349 manufacturing and mining firms licensed, of which 14 were public owned. 285 of these firms employed less than ten workers, 21 had workers numbering about 10-19, 16 employed from 20-49, while 18 had more than 50 workers. Figures indicating the number of female employees in these industries are not available but the number at present is unlikely to be large since the total labour force is still quite small.[25] Even today the scene has not changed much as industries have not yet developed in large number.

Self-Employment

In growing urban centres, women serve in the private sector, mainly as managers of shops and small-scale enterprises. Almost all shops in these urban centres are managed by women, whose husbands are not involved in government service. Occasionally in both urban and rural areas, women who know the art of weaving earn substantial income to supplement the regular income of the family. They either weave materials on their own or arrange for hired labourers in producing traditional materials required for making the national costumes. These woven materials are profitable. Similarly, women who know knitting organise hired labourers in producing woollen sweaters or jumpers for winter. Women also earn from their embroidery and cane basketry expertise. These activities normally keep women busy and bring them additional income. Indeed, these skilled housewives often earn more than their husbands. Government servants' wives are permitted to organise such home-based cottage industries.[26]

Tourism has offered them a lucrative business as many Bhutanese families have turned homes into guest houses which are comparatively cheaper and provide house comfort, for example in Bumthang, there was a small guest house which was owned by a family. It was run by their daughter, while the father looked after farming, mother did weaving and brother was being educated at Geddu College of Business Studies. There are umpteen examples of such cases in Bhutan. Here, the government can provide assistance to unemployed youth, whose number is on rise now, training can be imparted and they can be a part of the professional tourism.

Women in Traditional Sector

Agriculture is the major activity on which rural population is dependent. Except in Lhotshampa group, land is owned by women in both Ngalops and Sharchops who follow matriarchal system. Women inherit agricultural land and associated properties. They have a more central role in the family. They have access to livestock. The control of income is in the hands of women and hence the decision making powers concerning household expenditure. Against a backdrop where women have hold over land and home in rural areas, there is no clear distinction or division between the roles men and women have. Though these views are not shared by Uni Wikan, who says that there is a division of task between men and women, but her observations are largely from western Bhutan.

Females as well as males can weed and transplant, harvest, thrash and winnow, and either can look after the animals. But in practice, it is said to be rare for males to weed and transplant, mainly women do it. But only the male cuts grass, dig the earth and plough and sow, it is said that should women plough, the oxen would cry...... only women, by contrast pluck the seedlings, feed the pigs and cows, milk the animals and perform all operations connected with manure: collecting, carrying and distributing. It is said should a man come into contact with manure his brains would deteriorate.......thus only an uneducated woman can handle manure.[27]

Her discussions with women led her to make the following observations:

The (effective) head of the household should be a man, and the husband will be regarded as the locus of authority even when the farm on which the couple resides is the wife's property......likewise the coordination of task and the allocation of duties to the household members will be in the hands of a stronger and more active male....... This does not mean that women do not participate in family decisions and have no voice....... in some families, a woman may indeed dominate by virtue of her stronger personality or intelligence, but in some cases her dominance is muted and standard role appearances maintain that male is the decision maker.[28]

She acknowledges that gender roles differ in different parts of Bhutan. She agrees that in eastern Bhutan there is greater equality in gender rules— with respect to child care and authority within the household.

Marketing patterns seem to influence the control of income within the household. Women seem to frequent market with poultry, butter, cheese and vegetables. The income generated from these products is generally kept and used by women for their own expenditure as well as to run the household. Men or women who sell milk to local markets generally have control of the income for their own use. Households selling milk to cooperatives tend to use their income for family rather than for their personal use.

The Department of Agriculture has established several training projects for women in various districts. The regular farmer training programmes try to involve women trainees in Khangma of Tashigang district of Bhutan. Several training courses for women focus on child healthcare, improved method of food processing and preservation, kitchen gardening, knitting, tailoring and weaving. Subjects such as personal hygiene and environmental sanitation are also introduced during short term training courses.

The traditional role of Bhutanese women is not different from that prevailed earlier in the world like house keeping, animal husbandry and cotton industries. They worked for survival and contributed in meeting basic needs for food, clothing, housing and health care. Since inception women have contributed in agriculture sector, but education along with new opportunities has worked as catalyst. It has not only developed their personality and rationality but also qualified them to utilise certain economic cultural opportunities thereby improved their socio-economic status.

Marriage

Marriages in Bhutan are more a matter of convenience than conviction. It is the most important institution affecting the role of women. Men and women enjoy freedom to choose partners. Love marriages are common in urban areas but arranged marriages are also visible. In Lhotshampa, ethnic group women join their husband's families after marriage, but in Ngalops and Sharchops there is no rule that women have to move. Often the couple moves to the woman's house, but the increasing trend is that the couple leads an independent life but continues to keep very close ties to his/her natal family. Divorce is socially and religiously well accepted and divorce rate is very high.

The proportion of married population is found to be the highest in the middle age group. The divorced and separated population is found to be the highest among women in the age of 30-34 years followed by 25-29 years at 7.3 per cent and 5.7 per cent, respectively. The widowed population constitutes a small proportion, or 4.7 per cent of the total population consisting of 3.2 per cent males and 6.2 per cent females. Remarriage of divorcees and widows is also common practice. The law prohibits polyandry but there are a few cases among the Brokpas of Mera-Sakten, where if brothers mutually agree they can share one wife among them.

Motherhood and fertility are valued highly. Parents are usually looked after by daughters in their old age in Ngalops and Sharchops ethnic groups.[29]

Table 8: Registration of Marriages and Divorce Cases (1982-88)

Dzongkhags (Districts)	*Registration of Marriages*	*Number of Divorce Cases Referred to the District Courts*
Samchi	23	956
Chukha	301	77
Tashigang	700	150
Mongar	480	44
Lhuntsi	327	25
Pema Gatshel	25	368
S/Jongkhar	Not Available	Not Available

Source: Women in Development: Bhutan, Country Briefing Paper

This table is a clear indicator of how Bhutanese view marriage as an agreement between two individuals and if the relationship is not smooth there is no pressure from the society or stigma attached for living separately. In recent times, the number of divorce cases is on rise and registration of marriage has been made compulsory.

Land Inheritance

Traditional practices of matriarchal inheritance system still apply in most of the families. Many women in western and central Bhutan inherit land. 60 per cent of rural women hold land registration titles. This is based on the belief that women need more economic security to take care of parents and children. The gender pilot study conducted by Family Planning Commission upheld similar views. Mother or eldest daughter becomes the head of the household. One reason which is often given why men are not given land is that they move to monastic establishment and authorities in public place. In these areas, they have predominance. Generally, it is required that at least one male child from each household will enter into monk body, which is their source of livelihood. Buddhist teaching does not discriminate between men and women either in Bhutan or elsewhere; currently in the country there are about 250 nuns.[30] At the monastery level, the life of women is very different.

The monastery was founded by men. Monks occupied it for a long time. At present, it serves as a school for lay religious practitioners (gomchen) where girls are excluded strictly. Outsiders invited to perform ceremonies are invariably monks. The religious dances of the annual festival are traditionally never performed by women, but by men.[31]

The significant presence of women participants in some surviving bon rituals suggest women had prominent positions— either real or symbolic based on religion and ritual.

Bhutan is a Buddhist nation. The religion in this country is not just a means of perpetuating faith. It defines a way of life and enforces the gender-determined role and conduct of its followers. In the tradition of Mahayana Buddhism, male and female are considered equal. The Sutra says "There is no difference between sexes on the road to enlightenment." The doctrine of Karma gives the women an elevated status more so since there are many female deities such as Tara, Saraswati, Dorji Phagmo….. who are worshipped in this religion."[32]

Violence against Women

Bhutan has committed itself to the Vienna Declaration of 1983, United Nations General Assembly Declaration on Elimination of Violence against Women and Beijing Platform of Action 1995. The government is working to remove this social problem. According to National Consultation on

Violence against Children, April 2005, violence is of four types: violence at work places; in schools and institutions; in homes and families like physical beating of domestic servants, violent behaviour amongst parents; and violence in communities such as the issue of night hunting (where men enter village houses at night to have sex with young girls, although this practice is on decline now) and alcoholism (Bhutan has highest cases of alcoholic violence).

According to Kuensel as on December 2008, of 28 victims of sexual abuse in Thimphu 8 were miners, the youngest victim being a three-year old girl (Records from Royal Bhutan Police, Thimphu). The data indicates that the reports of assault against women and children have fluctuated since 2000. Data also reveals a total of 71 reported cases of domestic violence in the capital in 2005, out of which 34 were registered and 37 withdrawn. There are various reasons why women deter from reporting violence against them as police and judicial officials may not know how to deal sensitively with victims of violence. Lack of awareness among women and the limited number of women in police and judiciary is another reason. As on August 2008, there are 170 women in Royal Bhutan Police Force with female: male ratio of 0.05.

Table 9: Royal Bhutan Police Force, August 2008[33]

Category	*Number of Females*	*Number of Males*	*Female : Males Ratio*
Officer	9	126	0.07
Constables	114	1631	0.07
Non-Commissioned Officers	13 (upgraded)	1916	0.07
Recruits in Training	34	94	0.36
Cadets in Training	Nil	4	0
Total Police Force	170	3771	0.05

Senior Citizens

Bhutan, a country steeped in traditions has a healthy attitude towards its elderly, where they are treated with love, care and concern. The longevity is increased with the help of health services being expanded to the nook and corner of the country. It was only recently that the first old age home has been opened at Radhi Gewog (Block) in Trashigang Dzongkhag, opening itself to a debate whether they should be a part of a Buddhist country or not.

From the beginning of planned development, Bhutan adopted a policy of integrated health care delivery service system to its scattered population across difficult mountainous terrain. Since the adoption of the primary health care approach in 1978, Bhutan's health services have achieved unprecedented progress exceeding 90 per cent of the population.

Utmost importance is given to striking a balance between economic growth and the preservation of age-old traditions and culture. Human development continues to remain the highest priority. GNH has been development paradigm. It is thus not surprising that the government has consistently maintained high investments in social sectors. The health sectors in 2004/05 received 11.38 per cent budget outlay.

With the start of the Eighth Plan (1997-2002), the Ministry of Health initiated Community-Based Rehabilitation (CBR) and Mental Health Programmes to address the quality of care services. Examination of some perspectives on gender and its implications vis-a-vis ageing, mental health and disabilities is useful in underlying the common as well as specific challenges related to these areas.

The term 'older' is an arbitrary concept but, according to the World Health Organisation (WHO), it generally refers to age 60 and above. A series of international conferences on ageing has resulted in adoption of three pillars as a conceptual approach toward active ageing, namely, health, participation and security. Bhutan has a very young population, with close to 56 per cent younger than 25 and only 4.7 per cent older than 65; therefore, the issue of ageing is just beginning to receive prominence in national health plans and policies.

Demographic Trends in Bhutan

Sex-disaggregated data and gender-analysis are necessary to form policies on ageing. A discussion on ageing demographic trends takes into consideration factors such as fertility, mortality, life expectancy and related parameters. Currently, however, it is problematic to critically analyse gender-ageing issues in Bhutan because of a lack of demographic data in this respect.

In Bhutan, the average life expectancy at birth of 45.6 in 1980-85 has increased by 2000 to 66.0 for men and 66.2 for women. This increase has been attributed to improvements in immunisation, nutrition, water supply and sanitisation, and control of communicable diseases as well as to higher literacy rates. In Bhutan, the gender difference in average life expectancy is now negligible. Yet worldwide, women have a higher life expectancy than men, which means that women are the majority of the elderly, especially the oldest age group. This trend will need to be monitored in Bhutan in the future, and life expectancy ought to be considered with the quality.

The Population and Housing Census of Bhutan (PHCB) 2005 also indicates not only the overall young population, but also a smaller proportion in younger ages, which may indicate declining births in recent years. The median age of the population is 22.3 years, which implies that half of the population is below the age of 22.3 years. About 29,745 persons are older than 65. If those 60 and older are included, the total rises to 44,319 elderly, of which 51.6 per cent are males and 48.4 per cent females.

As shown in the table below, differences in the ageing aspect of women and men are almost negligible. It is thus important that future health services and facilities available for the elderly consider provisions adequate for both older women and men. At present, the widowed population totals 17,531 persons, of which 70 per cent are females. These findings point out to the need of ensuring female-dominated widowed population with adequate care and financial support.

Table 10: Elderly population age 60 and above disaggregated by age group and gender

Age Range	*Male*	*Female*
60-64	7,564	7,010
65-69	5,999	5,362
70-74	4,493	4,249
75+	4,839	4,803

(**Source**: PHCB 2005, p. 24)

Table 11 below shows that hearing impairments, followed by visual impairments, feature as the major forms of disability for the elderly. However, the proportion of older women with visual and mental disabilities is slightly higher compared to other disabilities like speaking, hearing and moving. This shows that older women and older men are likely to have different ageing disabilities.

Table 11: Distribution of Types of Disabilities for Elderly Population Disaggregated by Age Group and Gender

Disability Type	*60-64 Male*	*60-64 Female*	*65-69 Male*	*65-69 Female*	*70+ Male*	*70+ Female*	*Total*	*Female Proportion*
Seeing	261	285	302	270	730	833	2681	51.8 per cent
Speaking	145	111	108	98	191	151	804	44.8 per cent
Hearing	439	323	425	350	1007	813	3357	44.3 per cent
Moving	220	149	216	136	389	338	1448	43 per cent
Mental	38	41	27	25	47	40	218	48.6 per cent
Total	1103	909	1078	879	2364	2175	8508	

(**Source**: Population and Housing Census of Bhutan 2005, p. 213.)

With declining mortality rates, high birth rates and rising life expectancy, population growth had accelerated to 3.1 per cent per annum by the mid-1990s. However, following the emphasis over the issue during the Eighth plan, the rate came down to a more moderate 2.5 per cent by 2000. According to the PHCB 2005, the natural population growth rate now stands at 1.3 per cent.

Ageing Index

The ageing index is defined as the ratio of population above 65 years of age to the population of children below 15 for every 100 persons. The ageing index for Bhutan stands at 14.2, which implies 14 persons aged 65 and above for every 100 persons younger than 15. This too indicates a young population.

Dependency Ratio

Many ways exist of looking at the extent to which elderly people become dependent on society. The old-age dependency ratio indicates the number of dependents older than 65 relative to the population aged 15 to 64, for every 100 persons. The PHCB 2005 shows that the total dependency ratio (child and old age) is 60.6 per cent, which means that for every 100 population in the working age group 15-64, there are 60.6 dependents. The old age dependency ration exclusively is 7.5 per cent; however, the PHCB 2005 does not disaggregate this ratio by gender.

Care of the Elderly

Because of the country's late start into development and other constraints, gender differences have been documented only in relation to some aspects of health. Attention is yet to be given to understanding gender differences in the health status of older adults. Given the foreseeable rapid ageing population, an urgent need exists to estimate and project changing levels and trends in older health, taking into account any gender differences.

The National Pension and Provident Fund (NPPF) is one national initiative. It extends support mechanism after retirement. Nevertheless, a large proportion of older women are likely to be left out from such pension schemes, without means of independent support, given that the working force is still predominantly male. Social insurance systems are generally based on the assumption that women whose work constitutes mainly unpaid domestic labour will be the beneficiaries of social protection provided to the male breadwinners in the family. Once women reach old age, many are likely to become totally dependent on their husband, if he is still alive, or on other relatives for support. This renders them more vulnerable to poverty and economic insecurity.

Nevertheless, Bhutanese society has been firmly rooted in and guided by the Buddhist philosophy of compassion and filial piety, which accords a highly supportive and informal care giving environment to the old and infirm. Problems of the elderly traditionally have been taken care of by family members, particularly women, who are often responsible for caring for ageing parents.

While this ideal still holds true in Bhutan, issues are increasingly rising that hold implications for the elderly. Erosion of traditional family patterns, with a move toward more nuclear family households, and rapid urbanisation and migration patterns of younger family members, leaving older members to fend for themselves. These trends are eroding the status traditionally enjoyed by elders as the heads of families. It takes away their purposeful economic and social roles and weaken their traditional sources of support. Such trends indicate the needs for the country to take initiative in the matter of elderly care. Securing the health and psychological and economic well-being of the ageing will be challenging for a country like Bhutan. Examination of gender differences in care giving and the elderly, as recipients and as givers of care, will be needed.[34]

With a small population and scarce resources, Bhutan has tried to utilise manpower as well as natural resources judiciously. A country of strategic importance lying between India and China it has been successful in securing the interests of its people and nation. The Drukpas and Sharchops occupy important positions in all the government institutions, but lately the Lhotshampas who basically are from southern Bhutan and Nepalese in origin have raised their discontent about their underrepresentation in higher places in Bhutan. Predominantly agricultural, Bhutan has opted for selective development. The fruits of it are being partaken by all the groups that constitute the country.

Health

The improved health services are reflected in the growing life expectancy. Improved health infrastructure consists of a network of trained doctors, nurses, health workers reaching into the villages. The modern allopathic medicine is being practiced for which doctors are being sent for training to India, Bangladesh and Burma. The Jigme Singye Wangchuck Referral Hospital in Thimphu provides for good, modern facilities and complicated cases from adjoining areas are also treated. A new hospital has been made in Mongar, but, Bhutan is yet to come up with an independent Medical College. Indigenous health care is also given importance. Buddhist healers including lamas, monks, nuns, tsipas and gomchens as well as traditional healers like pawo, phadjo, nendjum and pamo practise the traditional medicine.

The Royal Government of Bhutan's commitment to the provision of free and accessible health care to all women and men in Bhutan is reinforced by Article 9 (21) of the Constitution, which states, '*The State shall provide free access to basic public health services in both modern and traditional medicine.*'

Since 1961, when the first hospital came up, an all round effort to improve health care and to reach to the remotest area was made. Today, the number stands as 29 hospitals, 178 Basic Health Units (BHUs), 519 Outreach Clinics (ORC) in the country.[35] Medical care is provided free-of-cost and those, who required to be sent abroad for treatment are also sponsored by the government. As a result, life expectancy at birth in Bhutan has increased significantly since 1950s, from 36.1 years to 66.1 in 2000 and 66.3 years in 2011 (66.8 years for females, 65.6 years for males). Total population in 2011 is 695,819 out of which 34,000 are old people.[36]

Some of the figures from the Dagapela Hospital, a remote place in Dagana Dzongkhag in southern Bhutan show that the rising number of people avail the medical facilities.

Table 12: Annual Report of Year 2009 and 2010 [Dzongkhag Hospital Dagapela, Bhutan[37]]

Outpatient Services	*Total Number of Patients in 2009*	*Total Number of Patients in 2010*
New Cases seen	15069	15306
Total number of Repeat Cases-attendance	3038	5544
Total number of Lab Test	5640	9436
Total number of eye patients	962	2215
Total number of Dental patients	927	1787
Total number of X-ray patience	162	231
Total number of Physiotherapy patients	320	557
Total number of Indegenous patients	839	1128
Total number of OPD morbidity cases	18136	21756

Source: Statistics collected during my visit to Bhutan in October 2011

Table 13: Statistics Dzongkhag Hospital Dagapela, Bhutan Year 2011[38]

Particular *Cases*	*Jan*	*Feb*	*Mar*	*Apr*	*May*	*June*	*July*	*Aug*	*Sep*
Total number of new cases	1137	954	1589	1683	1657	1361	1483	1565	1615
Total number of old cases	144	178	345	411	636	565	491	548	502
Laboratory Test	556	589	785	464	1225	1099	1301	1672	1321
Dental cases	147	110	144	329	155	101	158	166	152
X-ray cases	39	24	38	49	54	36	30	Nil	46
Physiotherapy	0	0	79	56	49	70	83	92	72
OPD morbidity	936	937	1601	1892	2247	1857	1912	2053	1987
Eye cases	96	92	152	153	211	93	155	111	N/T
Indigenous cases	83	56	48	57	122	95	104	124	117

(**Source:** Statistics collected during my visit to Bhutan in October 2011)

Table 14 below shows that the government effort to check the birth rate is gaining momentum while the death rate is declining due to improved medical facilities and people are availing medical facilities by the government. Even rural areas now have access to health services.

Table 14: Statistics of Tsirang General Hospital, Bhutan

S. No.	*Vital Statistics*	*2005*	*2006*	*2007*	*2008*	*2009*
1.	Total Births	348	441	321	258	269
2.	Total Live Births	345	433	320	253	263
3.	Total deaths	34	91	59	55	38
4.	Total Deaths less than 28 days	02	0	02	05	05
5.	Death under 1 year	11	03	02	05	03
6.	Total death less than 5 years	14	03	05	0	03
7.	Maternal deaths	0	01	0	0	01
	Others	*2005*	*2006*	*2007*	*2008*	*2009*
1.	Total laboratory Examination	3619	1754	2096	6546	8248
2.	Total disability (Physical Impairment)	680	450	422	347	441
3.	Total T.B. cases	19	06	16	14	16
4.	Total T.B.	02	0	05	03	06

	Pulmonary Positive cases					
5.	Plasmodium Falciparium (B50)	14	18	06	02	08
6.	Other Malaria (B51)	07	14	11	01	05

Source: Statistics collected during my visit to Bhutan in October 2011

Development of Traditional Medical Services

It was the third Druk Gyalpo Jigme Dorji Wangchuck, who in November 1967 directed the Health department to establish traditional medicine system. Accordingly, an indigenous dispensary was opened on 28th June 1968 at Dechencholing, Thimphu. The first batch of persons to work in the dispensary were Drungtsho Pema Dorji and Drungtsho Sherab Jorden both of whom were trained in Tibet.

The training programme for Menpa commenced in 1971 as on-the training. As per the resolution No.11 of the 32nd National Assembly held on May 29th 1970, His Majesty the fourth king Jigme Singye Wangchuck commanded to introduce training programme for the Drungtsho. The training programme for Drungtsho was started in 1978 with an appointment of Ladakh AMCH as the Principal. The indigenous dispensary was upgraded to national indigenous hospital and shifted at Kawajangsa in 1979. It became the National Institute of Traditional Medicine (N.I.T.D.) in 1988 and, upgraded as the Institute of Traditional Services (I.T.M.S.) in 1998.[39]

Currently, there are 39 Traditional Medicine units in all 20 districts and there is a plan to establish traditional medicine units in all the Basic Health Units as enshrined in the Constitution of Kingdom of Bhutan. The district Traditional Medicine Unit is manned by 01 Drungtsho (Traditional Physician) and 01 Menpa (Clinical Assistant). The Traidtional Medicine Unit in the Basic Health Unit is manned by 01 Menpa. For the benefit of rural communities, religious centers and secluded areas, the outreach services for traditional medicine is introduced in all districts, where Drungtshos and Menpas visit the places on a monthly basis.

Establishment of Dzongkhag Traditional Medicine Units[40]

Dzongkhag	Year of Establishment	Dzongkhag	Year of Establishment
Trashigang	Nov 1979	Trongsa	July 1981
Bumthang	Mar 1982	Haa	Nov 1987
Punakha	Jan 1988	Mongar	Mar 1993
Sarpang	Nov 1993	Pemagatshel	Mar 1996
Zhemgang	Mar 1996	S/Jongkhar	Apr 1996
Paro	Dec 1998	Lhuntse	Oct 1999
Dagana	July 2000	Samtse	July 2000
Tsirang	Nov 2000	Wangdue	Nov 2000
Gasa	Nov. 2001	Chukha	Jan 2002
Reserboo	Nov 2004	Phobjika	Dec 2004
Dorokha	Apr 2006	Rang Jung	Sep 2008
Ura	June 2006	Daga Pela	Sep 2008
Daksa	May 2006	Zhemgang	Sep 2008
Korphu	July 2007	Pan Bang	Sep 2008
P/ling	Sep 2008	Samdrup Choling	Sep 2008
Kanglung	Sep 2008	Lhamoi Zhingkha	Sep 2008
Kengkhar	Sep 2008	Jomotsangkha	Sep 2008
Drametse	Sep 2008	Gedu	01 Jan 2010
Nganglam	Sep 2008		

Conclusion

The health service in Bhutan has to overcome many challenges to expand its facilities and to deliver a good standard. They need to have more doctors as most of the hospitals have one doctor and sometimes no district officials with much experience. The reason is that Bhutan has to send its medical students to be trained abroad. The numbers trained there is not enough. There is need to increase the staff in the Basic Heath Unit and the number of female health workers. The Health Assistants should increase awareness for HIV/AIDS. The risk factors related to pregnancy and child birth have decreased and the family planning programme introduced in 1971 has helped women play a more deciding role in families and in overall improving health standard in Bhutan.

References

1. Statistical Yearbook of Bhutan 2009, National Statistics Bureau, Royal Government of Bhutan, p. iv.
2. Mehra G.N., 'Bhutan: Land of Peaceful Dragon', New Delhi, 1974, p. 20.

3. White, John, Claude, 'Sikkim and Bhutan: twenty- one years on the North-East Frontier 1887-1908', Published by Edward Arnold, London, Publisher to India office 1909, pp. 247-248.
4. Singh, Nagendra, 'Bhutan: a Kingdom in Himalayas- a study of the land its people and their government', S. Chand & Co., New Delhi, 1988, p. 15.
5. Population and Housing Census of Bhutan, Office of Census Commissioner, Royal Govt. of Bhutan, Thimphu, p. 17.
6. Labour Force Survey Report, 2010, Labour Market Information Division, Department of Employment, Ministry of Labour and Human Resources, Royal Government of Bhutan, p. 29.
7. Rose, Leo E, 'The Politics of Bhutan', Cornell University Press, Ithaca, 1977, pp. 44-45.
8. http://www.tourism.gov.bt/bhutan/about-bhutan/people-and-society
9. Mondal, Sekh Rahim, 'People of Bhutan: A Study of its Society and Culture in Bhutan: Dilemma of Change in a Himalayan Kingdom', B.C Upreti (ed.), Kalinga Publicatios, Delhi, 2004, pp. 33-34.
10. Singh, Nagendra, *op. cit*., pp. 65-67.
11. *Ibid*. p. 69.
12. Dasho Rigzin, Dorji, 'A Brief Religious, Cultural and Secular History of Bhutan', Asia Society Galleries, New York, 1989, pp. 16-17.
13. Kohli, M.S, 'A Kingdom in the sky', Vikas Publishing House, 2004, pp. 76-77.
14. Crins, Reiki, 'Religion and Gender Values in a Changing World', The Spider and Piglet, Proceedings of the First International Seminar on Bhutan Studies, ed. by Karma Ura & Sonam Kinga, Centre for Bhutan Studies, 2004, p. 581.
15. Tenth Five Year Plan 2008-2013, Main Document, Vol-I, Gross National Happiness, Royal Government of Bhutan, p. 80.
16. Bhutan at a Glance 2009, National Statistical Bureau, Royal Government of Bhutan.
17. Collected during my survey in Bhutan from 1- 26 June 2010.
18. Women in Development: Bhutan by Lhadon Pema, November 1, 1989, pp. 6-7.
19. Labour Force Survey 2006, Ministry of Labour and Human Resource, p. 1.
20. Education and Gender in Bhutan: A Tentative Analysis, Joke Buringa and Lham Tshering, Thimpu, July 1992, p. 41.

21. Collected during my survey in Bhutan from 01- 26 June 2010.
22. National Plan of Action for Gender 2008-2013, Gross National Happiness Commission, National Commission for Women and Children, Royal Government of Bhutan, p. 18.
23. *Ibid*, p. 20.
24. Collected during my survey in Bhutan from 01- 26 June 2010.—
25. Lhadon Pema, 'Women in Development: Bhutan', November 01, 1989, pp. 6-7.
26. *Ibid.*
27. Uni Wikan, 'The Situation of girl child in Bhutan', mimeo, Thimphu, Bhutan 1990, p. 19.
28. *Ibid.*
29. Lhadon Pema, 'Women in Development: Bhutan', November 01, 1989, *pp.* 16-17.
30. Francoise Pommeret, Introduction to Bhutan (Hongkong: The Guidebook Company Limited, 1990).
31. Martin Brauen, 'A Village in Central Bhutan', in Christian Schicklgruber and Francoise Pommaret (eds), Bhutan: Mountain Fortress of the Gods (Delhi: Bookwise (India) Pvt Ltd, 1997), p. 93.
32. Upreti, Sonia, 'Status of Women in Bhutan, Bhutan: Society and Polity', ed. by Pamakant, Ramesh Chandra Misra, Indus Publishing House, 1996, p. 53.
33. Gender Focal Point, Royal Bhutan Police (RBP), Thimphu.
34. National Plan of Action for Gender 2008-2013, Gross National Happiness Commission, National Commission for Women and Children, Royal Government of Bhutan, pp. 109-112.
35. *Ibid.*, p. 85.
36. Key note address delivered by honorable Health Minister of Bhutan on World health day 2012.
37. Statistics collected from Dzongkhag Hospital Dagapela, Dagana Dzongkhag, Bhutan during my visit to Bhutan in October 2011.
38. *Ibid.*
39. Information collected from a display in Dagapela General Hospital, Dagana Dzongkhag, Bhutan during my visit in October 2011.
40. Wangchuck Dorji, Introduction to Traiditional Medicine Services in Bhutan, Third edition, March 2010, Institute of Traditional Medicine Services, Ministry of Health, Royal Government of Bhutan, Thimphu, pp. 16-17.

4

Bhutanese Culture and Education System

Life of every Bhutanese is governed by religion, especially Buddhism which is also the State religion. A deep influence of religion can be seen in their daily lives, festivals, dances and traditional arts. Every Bhutanese family earlier used to devote one child to the monastic order.

The concept of culture is synonymous with the ancient civilisation. It has grown with time in terms of art, human excellence and festivals. Deriving inspiration from Buddhism, ethnical concepts of Buddha, Dharma and Sangha, it lays emphasis on inner and outer spiritual living. In short, the entire cultural and social fabric of Bhutan is weaved around Buddhism. Its geographical isolation helped this country to build rich cultural heritage which is of interest to academicians, laymen and tourists, endorsing a special position in the world community.

Culture is one of the four pillars of socio-economic development goals of Bhutan today. Bhutan does show signs of accelerated modernisation, evident during my visit in 2008, 2010 and 2011. The middle class shows signs of change. Educated in English medium schools with increasing exposure of youth to western influence may lead to new styles, different from the country's rich cultural heritage. Like other countries of the world, Bhutan will have to see to the revitalisation and reinterpretation of values in the light of modern scientific advancement to improve the lives of people, enhance the happiness and ensure overall development of the country.

The change is evident not only in the urban areas, but also in rural as well as semi-urban areas. Youth has access to internet and trends in fashion which was not available to the previous generation. Thimphu appears today an ever-expanding city as a hub of fashion, technology and knowledge. The change in habits of Bhutanese is apparent. Though, they were primarily rice eaters, now they includ more cereals in meals. Even Pizza outlets are popular. Archery is still the national game and on week-ends one may see Bhutanese playing for amusement or competitions, but football is liked immensely. The matches are followed on television reli-giously. For a society where simplicity was associated with marriage, mar-riage remains a question of personal choice of adults. The role of family still remains to put an approval on the already agreed decision, but now the rich in society are opting for grand receptions.

As the Bhutanese society allows external influence on traditional one, the need is to promote Dzongkha language, for a language is a means of communication and Bhutan can undoubtedly boast of many languages, which change with just a few miles. The third king His Majesty Jigme Dorji Wangchuck while recognising the importance of national language had initiated the process of committing the language to script. Dzongkha is still a developing language and the Dzongkha Development Commission has a big role to play.[1]

According to C.T. Dorji, Bhutanese culture can be divided into two parts which are very closely related to each other. Tangible culture is visible and touchable which concerns public services, covering all properties and structures including:

—Sculpture
—Painting
—Tailoring and embroidery
—Black-smithy
—Gold-smithy
—Silver-smithy
—Food and beverages
—Weaving
—Wood works including carpentry
—Wood-carving and wood turning
—Paper making
—Masonry

—Stone and slate-carvings
—All kinds of casting work
—Pottery making
—Writing

The bio-deterioration is one of the major causes in respect of cultural properties and extensive studies have been done worldwide in the area of bio-deterioration. Tangible culture must be conserved with traditional as well as latest methods.

Intangible culture is not visible and touchable but thinkable, audible and vanishable which entertains public. It covers the following entertainment:

—Dances (both folk and masked dances)
—Music (folk and religious)
—Songs (classical and modern)
—Ballads and elocution
—Drama and play
—Sports (traditional and modern)
—Language and linguistics
—Literature (written and oral version)
—Legends
—Stories (fiction and non-fiction)
—Proverb and sayings
—Habits and customs
—Etiquette
—Ceremony
—Festivals and tshechu
—Anniversary and new year celebration
—Social system
—Marriage system
—Birthday celebration
—Death ceremony
—Promotion ceremony
—Inauguration
—Law and order
—Medication and treatment
—Worship, rituals and religious practices
—Belief and faith
—Astrology
—Daily life

As a matter of fact, intangible culture is under a great threat. It must be preserved immediately for the benefit of future generation. It must be documented and recorded because it is an oral tradition. It will vanish when the old and knowledgeable people die.[2]

Dzong

Dzongs form an integral part of Bhutanese life. The word Dzong means a 'castle' or a 'monastery'. In earlier times, dzongs were used for defensive purposes. Now, these are used for administrative as well as religious purposes. They were built on a cliff or ridge. The whole population of the valley under attack would take refuge in the dzong. They were also used for stocking food grains in times of emergency. The dzong was the seat of religious Head, which continues till today. Inside the dzong, there is a monastery where monks reside, study and pray. In Bhutan, they symbolised the power centre of administration and religion. The functions of the dzongs are the same except their defensive uses.

Construction Style of Dzongs

The dzongs are designed in enclosed courtyards with an internal division between areas dedicated to monastic body and centres for civil administration. Deviations from standard, square-unit patterning were generally due to the physical characteristics of the terrain. The structure of the dzong consists of heavy-load bearing walls made of stone masonry, which gently taper from the foundations to the roof. Construction materials of mud, stone, and timber comprise other features of the dzong including windows, doors, flooring, and roofing.

The habitable rooms are normally found on the upper levels of a dzong, where the outer wall consists of timber and mud construction that allows more leeway in construction due to lighter weight and plasticity of form. The vertical emphasis reflected in overall size and decoration serves the purposes of both defense and aesthetics. Windows and cornices form the main decorative elements in the white outer wall, though sparsely decorated windows at the lower levels are small and modest, sober wooden frames set the heavy stonewalls. The higher one ascends, the larger and more ornamented the window become.

A tower-like structure, or *utse*, is located in the center of the courtyard, forming the core of the dzong and containing the main temples. It is the most important space within the dzong and is usually a multi-storey structure, square or oblong in plan. The most sacred space within the utse is the *lhakhang*, which means 'house of god', rendering an overall equivalent of 'temple'. Statues of Buddha, Guru Rinpoche, *Bodhisattvas*, and other saints are placed in the *lhakhang*.

In order to reach the *lhakhang*, one has to cross the *tshokhang*, more commonly known as *kunrey*. Kunrey is the large hall where the monks gather several times in a day for prayers and other religious activities. In most of the dzongs, the *tshokhang* is flanked by one or more smaller shrine rooms, which are devoted to a variety of deities and saints. In all of these spaces, the walls are richly adorned with murals.

Before entering the *tshokhang*, one has to pass through the *gorakha*, which literally means "mouth of the door". This is a half open space, with walls on three sides, whose open side faces the courtyard. There are no statues in the *gorakha*, but rich murals adorn the walls. These are normally devoted to the guardian kings of the four directions or are of different types of mandalas.

Almost without exception, there is a path for pious circumambulation around the *utse*, marked by a continuous row of prayer-wheels set into the niches at the base of the building. These prayer-wheels are cylindrical with mantras painted on the outer surface and are filled with prayers written on paper. In order to pay respect to the temple and its deities, the pilgrims circumambulate the *utse* clockwise and turn the prayer-wheels. Every turn of the prayer-wheel carries the religious message painted on the surface and written on the pieces of paper inside, over the world. The prayer-wheels are usually placed in their niches in front of slates with carved images of Buddhas, the *Bodhisattvas*, saints, *mahasiddhas* or lamas.

Rough but beautiful large flat stones flank the courtyard called the *dochen* enclosed by outer walls of a dzong. As there is a division between the monastic body and civil administrative center, usually there are more than one dochen. Along the sides of the dochen, the outer structure of the dzong generally consists of two or three stores with inward-facing decorated arcades. These structures house the living quarters and classrooms for the monks in one part of the dzong and the administration offices in the opposite part.[3]

Dzongs across the country vary in size, although their basic structure remains the same. Some of the important dzongs are as follows:

—Dogar Dobji Dzong,
—Byakar Yulgyel Dzong,
—Gasa Tashi Thongmon Dzong,
—Zhongar (Mongar) Dzong,
—Paro Ta Dzong,
—Trashigang Dzong,
—Zhemgang Dechen Yangtse Dzong,
—Simtokha Dzong,
—Tango Dzong
—Trongsa Dzong
—Lhundrup Rinchentse Dzong
—Trashiyangtse Dzong
—Druk Gyal Dzong
—Tashichho Dzong
—Punakha Dzong
—Haa Dzong
—Wangdue Phodrang Dzong

Dzongs, lhakhangs and chortens are unique examples of architecture introduced by Tibet to Bhutan. Dzongs were mainly built on sites overlooking valleys.

Simtokha Dzong (Sanga Zabdoen Phodrang)

Simtokha Dzong was the first dzong to be constructed by Zhabdrung Ngawang Namgyal, the greatest builders of Dzongs in Bhutan. He undertook the constructions of six Dzongs to consolidate his newly acquired domain in western Bhutan and defend from the internal foes and external enemies.

The location of the dzong has a great historical significance. The present place, where the Dzong stands was the crossroads of three prominent western regions of Sha (Wangduephodrang), Wang (Thimphu) and Pa

(Paro). The intersection was marked by three stones that belonged to the people of Punakha, Thimphu and Paro. In the middle of stones was a piece of land known as Sem – tokha or Sem – Dokha with a temple on it. This temple was later gifted to Zhabdrung by Lam Pangka Shong. History says that a prophecy was made by one Tibetan Lama known as Lama Zhang that Zhabdrung Ngawang Namgyel after his arrival to Bhutan would build a Dzong at the junction of three western lands. As a gesture of fulfilling the prophecy and soliciting the offer of Lama Pangka, Shong, Zhabdrung decided to build the Dzong.

The area was inhabited by many demons and legend has it that the particular place where Zhabdrung decided to build the Dzong was occupied by a demon harming travelers who stayed overnight. Zhabdrung visited the place and subdued the demon, banishing her into the rock on the hill, where the present Dzong is located. The Dzong was constructed enclosing the rock ensuring imprisonment of the demon. Hence, the Dzong derived its name as *Simtokha* from the word *sinmo* (demon), *Do* (stomach), *Kha* (on) – the Dzong on top of the demons stomach.

At the age of 36, in 1629 corresponding to the 11th Rabjung and Earth Snake Year of the Bhutanese calendar, he laid the foundation of the Dzong. The construction of the Dzong was undertaken by Tango Chhoje Mipham Tshewang Tenzin with assistance from Zhabdrung's devotees and disciples.

The Dzong was successfully completed in 1631 corresponding to the Iron Sheep Year of the Bhutanese calendar two years leter. The Dzong was named as "Sanga Zabdhoen Phodrang" (Palace of the Profound Meaning of Secret Mantras).[4]

Punakha Dzong

One of the oldest is Punakha Dzong. Situated on a stretch of land where two rivers – the Phochhu and the Mochhu converge, Punakha Dzong was the second Dzong to be built in Bhutan. Zhabdrung Ngawang Namgyel built it in 1631. It was named punthang Dechen Phodrang Dzong or 'the Palace of Great Bliss'.

Punakha became the capital of Bhutan, where the successive *Desis* administered the country through the Dual system of government. It served as the seat of government until the reign of the second king Jigme Wangchuck. The negotiations with the British envoys took place in this Dzong. It was also the place where Ugyen Wangchuk, Bhutan's first hereditary king, was crowned in 1907. The first session of the National Assembly of Bhutan was held here under King Jigme Dorji Wangchuk in 1952.

Disasters have struck Punakha dzong repeatedly. It had to be rebuilt several times to the original specifications. It was damaged by fires in 1780, 1789, 1802, 1831, 1849, and in 1986. There was a massive earthquake in 1897 and a devastating flash flood in 1994 when the Dzongchhung, housing the images of the Lord Buddha and Dupthob Ngagi Rinchhen was nearly washed away. According to a common folklore, the then Zhabdrung disliked Punakha; therefore in 1835 he summoned a flood upon the area, damaging the Dzong. The *Desi* repaired the Dzong in 1849. Another fire in 1986 caused considerable damage to the south-west corner of the Dzong, the home of the Je Khenpo.

In 1969, Tibetans attacked Punakha to recover the relics of Ranjung Kharsapani, but were defeated. In honour of the protective deities that is deemed to have played a key role in the victory over the Tibetans, Zhabdrung had an additional chapel built in the Punakha Dzong. The Punakha Damchoe is held to commemorate this famous victory every year.[5]

The latest edition to the Dzong is the wooden bridge (*Bazam*) built in May 2008, with the German assistance. The only wooden bridge, with the longest unsupported span worldwide, considering the applied structural methods, the 55 m long Puna Mochhu bazam at Punakha was opened to the public on May 28 2008 by Prime Minister Jigmi Y Thinley and executive chairman of Pro Bhutan Association, Harald N Nestroy.

A sleek creation of Walt+ Galmarini AG, a renowned engineering company specialised in designing bridges, the bridge is the prototype of a hybrid construction, using a mix of medieval traditional designs and innovative modern technology.

Since the Dzong and the bazam come under the "red area" of potential danger from glacial lake outburst floods, the new concrete foundation has special protection with thousands of boulders and concrete blocks placed into the riverbed.

For the security of the people using bridge in future, invisible steel elements have been incorporated to stabilize the high bridge arch and prevent it from twisting or falling sideways.

Construction began in mid–2006, two years after the Pro–Bhutan Association was approached by the then Prime Minster Lyonpo Sangay Ngedup. The completion of Puna Mochhu bazam marks the close relationship between Bhutan and Germany celebrating 100 years of monarchy in Bhutan.[6]

Tashichho Dzong

Known as "The Fortress of the Glorious Religion", Tashichho Dzong is the most impressive building situated on the banks of the Wangchu (Thimphu River).

Tashichho Dzong was built in 1641 by Zhabdrung Ngawang Namgyal and reconstructed in 1962, by the late king, His Majesty, king Jigme Dorje Wangchuck. The Taschichho Dzong was built in the late 1700's and also serves as the home of the Central Monastic Body.

In 1216, Lama Gyalwa Lhanangpa built the Dho-Ngen (blue stone) Dzong on a hill above Thimphu, where Dechenphodrang now stands. When Zhabdrung Ngawang Namgyal came to Bhutan in the 17th century, the lhapas were completely crushed and the Dho-Ngen Dzong fell into the hands of Zhabdrung. In 1641, Zhabdrung the Dho Ngon Dzong was rebuilt and named as Tashicho Dzong (Fortress of the Glorious Religion). In 1694, it was enlarged by the fourth *Desi* Tenzin Rabgye. During the reign of the fifth *Desi* Gedun Chophel in 1698 the Dzong caught fire and was restored. The tenth *Desi* Mipham Wangpo built the Kagyu lhakhang inside the Tashichodzong. In 1747 the Dzong was enlarged at the initiative of the thirteenth *Desi* Chogyal Sherab Wangchuk.

During the reign of the sixteenth *Desi* Sonam Lhendup and the 13th Je Khenpo Yonten Thaye the Dzong caught fire for the second time. The two proposed to then build the Dzong at the site of its current location. In 1777 during the time of the eighteenth *Desi* Jigme Singye the Kunre of the Dzong was renovated as it was totally dark. It was further renovated by the twenty fifth *Desi* Pema Cheda. The thirty second *Desi* Phurgyal installed many new statues.

In 1869, the Dzong caught fire and afterwards was extensively repaired. The late king Jigme Dorji Wangchuck had the Dzong rebuilt between 1962 and 1969 and made the building into the new capital.[7]

Paro Ta Dzong

One of the picturesque dzongs is Paro Ta dzong, built centuries ago and does not have any written available source. Paro Ta dzong is located about five and a half kilometres from the Tshongdue town. It is built in between the palace of the Hungrel Ngonpa and famous ancient Donam Dzong. The Ta dzong is situated near the ancient Gonsakha temple, 500 meters above Rinpung Dzong.

All the material used in the construction of the dzong was locally available. The dzong is seven storied and is divided into many cells within its building and sizes. Ta Dzong being a war fortress had a security system within. There was also a hidden path connecting the main Rinpung dzong with the river below, used for fetching water through the tunnel in times of war.

The builder of Ta Dzong was La Ngonpa Tenzin Drugdra, who was the second temporal ruler in 1656 and ruled for twelve years. 1649 is the ascertained year of construction of Ta Dzong. Its foundation has been laid on the right side of the holy syllable Hung and main entrance facing west and back of the dzong faces east. The round passages inside Ta Dzong are designed and constructed to trap and halt the ambush of enemies.

Ta Dzong lay dormant and unused for a long time which resulted in a gradual decline in stability. His Majesty the third king Jigme Dorje Wangchuck commanded the Ministry of Development to renovate the dilapidated Ta dzong in 1966. The Ministry took great interest to renovate Ta dzong and further constructed a motorable approach road and developed infrastructure around.

Conversion of Ta Dzong into Museum

After renovation of the Dzong, the third king commanded the collection and display of significant cultural artifacts, establishing the National Museum of Bhutan in 1968. Geshe Tshewang was the founding director. Mr. Kunzang Rigzin became the curator and custodian of the valuable artifacts. The museum became a separate entity within itself from 1969 and continued to collect artifacts from the government and private donations to form full time exhibits. In 1974, electricity was installed in the museum and were built standard exhibit showcases. The museum is restoring and preserving the valuable and irreplaceable objects for future generations of

Bhutanese, while offering a venue for cultural interface with visitors to the country. Today, there are over 3,000 artifacts in the museum.

Temples and Exhibits of the Ta Dzong

Ta dzong consists of seven floors, the uppermost of which is the *Utse,* which gives a majestic view over the valley, however, it is not open to the public. On the sixth floor is the major attraction, a tree of assembly, or Tshogshing which displays the unique masters and traditions of four sects of Tibetan Buddhism. Mr. Damcho, a renowned clay master from Hephu Gonpa in Paro, built the Tshogshing. Philately dominates the upper floors of the museum, chronicling the highly sought-after products of the Department of Posts and Telegraph since 1962. Fifth floor has the Namtse Lhakhang in the central part. Consists of eight different images of the *Namtse*, including stone, rhinoceros horn; vajra and bronze images are on display in showcases. Ancient scroll paintings, called *thangkas*, as well as sixteen *arhats* made of bronze, and a segment of iron chain made by the fifteenth century spiritual master Thangtong Gyalpo are on display.

Fourth floor has the main entrance, model of Ta Dzong, Dawn of Bhutan. It has related exhibits and evolution of Bhutanese scripts. The third floor displays brass, bronze and clay containers manufactured prior to the fourteenth century. It stores a traditional Bhutanese water clock, traditional lamp and jewelry, numismatics, wooden cups, consecutive king's crowns, historical clothing from various regions, and arms and munitions. Works from Zhabdrung's era are exhibited in the central part of the gallery on the third floor.

Second floor round corridor has exhibits of religious items as well as an era dedicated to the flora and fauna of Bhutan. The innermost portion of the second floor, which has two rooms, are not utilised and though it has a tiny entrance door, it is not used at present. They are believed to be the dungeons used in ancient days.

First floor has a rotating exhibition space. Its permanent exhibits include cane and bamboo products, farming implements and drills. Ground floor has exit door with dungeon in the central part. Exhibits ancient spears, guns, canons and the palace of serpents. Eighteen and nineteenth century works appear alongside old, including a porcelain cup belonging to the first *Desi*. Urns and copper containers are exhibited in the front side of the ground floor. Two Mani Dungkhors are at the exit where merits can be gained through turning them. Slate carvings of guardian deities are fixed on the wall. It seems this was the only entrance door to Ta Dzong.[8]

Haa Wangchuk Lo Dzong

Because of its location, being near to the border of Tibet, the dzong has a strategic importance. The Dzong as any other in the country had a Ta Dzong (watch tower) for the purpose of detecting enemy approaches from afar. This Dzong was built in a place called Dumchog. It was also called Haed Dumchog Dzong. In addition to its military and secular purposes, the Dzong became a reservoir of grains, which could be distributed to the people should any natural disaster in the region cause famine.

Another oral tradition has reason that the Dzong was built in this place to hold back the evil influences of the serpent deities upon the lives of the people and their livestock. This place, where the Dzong was built, was well known for abundance of serpent deities. People say there were about hundred and eight such serpent deities in and around that place. Some of the stupas which were built in order to appease these deities can still be found. Unfortunately, in 1913, during the tenure of Haa Drung Kazi Ugyen Dorjee, the Dzong caught fire and was left as a pile of ashes. The devastation was so huge that the Drung, who otherwise had the authority to summon people for reconstruction decided it was easier to build a new one than to revamp the burned Dzong. Thus, Dumchog Dzong met with its end in a futile fire incident. It was finally abandoned and a new Dzong erected.

All that is left today of the Dzong are ruined wall worn out by weather and time, and some scattered boulders. Sadly, a marvellous and significant artifact was once and for all lost to the power of nature.

In the same year that Dumchog Dzong was reduced to rubbles by fire, Gongzim Ugyen Dorjee took charge to build the new Dzong. The people of the four Geogs were summoned to contribute labour tax during the entire renovation period. The new Dzong assuming the functions of the ruined Dumchog Dzong was built about a kilometer away from the debris of the

Dzong. A prefix, *Dzongsar* meaning the new Dzong, was added to the new name of the Dzong. Hence, the Dzong was called Dzongsar Wangchuk Lo Dzong.[9]

At present, the dzong has been given to the Army, the indian army where imparte military training to the Bhutanese soldiers .

Wangdue Phodrang Dzong

Wangdue Phodrang Dzong was founded by the Zhabdrung in 1639. Zhabdrung Ngawang Namgyal was supposedly at Chimmi Lhakhang in Punakha, when he met a decrepit old man, who described a ridge in present day Wangdue Phodrang as a 'sleeping elephant'. He told him he would unite the country by building a Dzong on the 'neck' of the ridge. The Zhabdrung, surmising the old man to be Yeshey Gonpo (Mahakala), took his suggestion and sent forth a noble to scout the area. As the emissary drew close to the area, he saw four ravens circling above the ridge. Upon reaching the ridge, the birds flew away in four directions, north, south, east and west. When returning to Chimmi Lhakhang, he made his report. Zhabdrung Ngawang Namgyel took this as a good omen and immediately set forth in 1638 to construct a Dzong overlooking the convergence of Dangchu and Punatshang chu. The people of Wang and Shar Dar Gyad were involved in construction along with the people of Rinchen Gang, who were skilled masons.

The Dzong consisted of three doorways and three courtyards. The first gate is the entrance; the second leads to the inner sanctum of the Dzong; and the third contains the deep interiors of this historic structure.

Years later, the Dzong was enlarged by the fourth *Desi* Tenzin Rabgye. In addition to the four storied *Utse* built by Zhabdrung, he added another two storied *Utse*. The construction was looked after by the Dzongpon Gedun Chophel. The seventh Dzongpon of Wangduephodrang Sonam Lhendup added new structures to the Dzong. He also installed a statue of Lord Buddha.

Much later with the passage of time a powerful local lord known as Kawang Sangye, extended the Dzong towards the present town. Another Wangzop, Acho Boep, ordered further construction, modifying the Dzong to the form which it holds today. In 1837, the Dzong was destroyed by a great fire and rebuilt later. During the time of Lam Neten

Pelden Singye, the Dzong was damaged by severe earthquake which was rebuilt later. Dzongpon Domchung seems to have also restored the Dzong though at an unknown time. During the reign of the late king Jigme Dorji Wangchuck, the Dzong was renovated supervised by Dronyer Pema Wangdi.

The rabdey was first instituted by Zhabdrung after the completion of the Dzong which was increased during the time of tenth Desi Khenpo Tenzin Chogyal.[10]

The 374 -years old Wangdue Phodrang Dzong was completely destroyed by recent fire in June 2012. Since the Dzong was under renovation before the fire, most of the relocated, sacred relics, were saved. The loss has been termed as a national tragedy by the acting Prime Minister Lyonpo Yeshey Zimba.

Festivals in Bhutan

Bhutanese culture is characterized by religious celebrations. Its people love socializing, attending festivals, joking, playing, and doing things that help them in the spirit of celebration. Religion and social life are so intrinsically linked in the culture that some festival appears to be taking place somewhere in Bhutan throughout the year. Among the festivals, one of the most recognized and attended by the masses is the *Tsechu* festival ('*Tse*' means 'date' and '*Chu*' means 'ten'; i.e. ;10th day'). This festival is celebrated to commemorate the great deeds of the eighth century Tantric Master Guru Padmasambhava.

'Guru Rimpoche' or simply 'Guru' as he is referred to introduced the Nyingma school of Buddhism into Tibet and Bhutan. Each tenth day of the lunar calendar is said to commemorate special event in the life of *Padmasambhava*. Some of these are dramatized in the context of a religious festival. Most of the festivals last from three to five days - of which usually one day falls on the tenth day of the lunar calendar. It is not just the time for people to get together, dress up and enjoy a convivial light hearted atmosphere, but also a time to renew one's faith, receive blessings by watching the sacred dances, or receive 'empowerment' from a *lama* or Buddhist monk.

The main festival during spring season is the Paro festival. Monks as well as laymen dressed in brilliant costumes and wearing masks of wrathful as well as peaceful deities re-enact legends and history of Buddhism in the Dragon kingdom. The festival culminates in the spectacular showing of the four-storey high, 350 -years old *Thangkha* (Buddhist religious scroll), celebrating the deeds of *Padmasambava*, who is credited with introducing Buddhism to Bhutan.

Wangdue and *Thimphu Tsechu* are the major festivals during winter season. The festivals of Bumthang and eastern Bhutan exhibit the true flavour of Bhutanese culture.

Apart from religious implications, the *Tshechu* is an annual social gathering, where people dress in finest clothing and jewellery. A small fair may be organized outside the Dzong for those looking for variety entertainment. Locals attending the festival enjoy a picnic lunch with an abundance of locally brewed alcohol.

Life in Bhutan year round offers a riot of colours in the form of festivals. It takes in almost all the parts of the country which is the precious and rich legacy imparted from one generation to another. These festivals attract the locals and foreigners alike in large numbers.

The Annual-Black-Neck Crane Festival

The annual-black-neck crane festival is celebrated in the courtyard of Gangtey Gonpa, in Phobjikha valley. It is an occasion for the locals to rejoice and celebrate the arrival of heavenly bird which becomes part and parcel of their daily lives during winter months. However, the annual black-necked crane festival is organized with the following objectives:

- Generate awareness and understanding among local communities and visitors on the importance of conserving the endangered black necked cranes
- Institute economic incentives (payment) for the festival to strengthen linkages between conservation and economic welfare and sustainable livelihoods
- Provide avenue for local community to renew commitment to conserve the black-necked cranes, and showcase their cultural heritage and skills.

The festival generally includes cultural program such as folk songs and dances (some with black-necked crane themes) and mask dances performed by local people, crane dance and environmental related drama and songs by school children. The festival was first initiated by Royal Society for Protection of Nature (RSPN) in 1998. It has now become a part of the local culture in Phobjikha valley.

Gomphu Kora Festival

Gomphu Kora lies in the heart of the agrarian belt of eastern Bhutan. It is 23 kilometers from Trashigang Dzong, the headquarters of Bhutan's most populous district, and two kilometers from Duksum, a quaint hamlet consisting of a few shops.

Gomphu means "Meditation Cave" and *Kora* means "Circumambulation". The name is derived from a cave formed out of rock-face next to temple, built as a tribute to this sacred site.

The story of *Gomphu Kora* goes back to the Eighth century AD. Legend has it that an evil non-human spirit named *Myongkhapa* escaped from Samye in Tibet when *Guru Padmasambhava*, the progenitor of the *Nyingma* strand of Buddhism, was spreading *Dharma* in the Himalayas. *Myongkhapa* followed the course of present-day *Kholongchhu* stream and concealed himself inside a rock, where *Gomphu Kora* stands today. The *Guru* followed the evil, mediated for three days inside the rock cave and finally vanquished it.

Several prominent religious personalities have undertaken pilgrimage to *Gomphu Kora* and the earliest was *Gongkhar Gyal*, grandson of Lhasay Tsangma. He built a small shrine at *Gomphu Kora* around the Tenth century A.D. In the Fourteenth century, Terton Pema Lingpa, visited Gomphu Kora and enlarged the existing shrine. It was renovated and enlarged in the Fifteenth century by Yongzin Ngagi Wangchuk, the grandfather of Zhabdrung Ngawang Namgyel. He also inscribed murals on the walls of the temple.

The biggest attraction of *Gomphu Kora* is the circumambulation. "Go around *Gomphu Kora* today for tomorrow may be too late", so goes a local song that entices devotees to visit *Gomphu Kora*. The place comes alive, once every year from 23rd to 25th March, when people all over eastern Bhutan descend upon the narrow valley, dressed in finery, to partake in the festivity, worship and reunite themselves with illustrious past.

The sanctity of the three day religious festival equally draws the *Dakpa* tribe in neighboring Arunachal Pradesh (India), who endures days of travel on foot amid rugged environs with entire families in tow. Some say the *Dakpas* have done this for more than a millennium, beginning shortly after *Guru Padmasambhava* sanctified the place in the Eighth century AD.

The Guru is attributed to have said that devotees will flock to *Gomphu Kora* for eons to celebrate the triumph of good over evil. There couldn't be a more accurate prophesy.

Paro Tshechu

The Paro *tsechu* in spring is a major attraction in Paro district. People come from neighbouring districts to participate in the festivity. On the final day, the best time is go to in the early morning as monks of the Paro *Dzong* prepare to display a giant appliqué *thangkha*, the Guru *Throngdel*, inside the *dzong*.

Day 1: (Inside the *dzong*)

Lord of Death and his Consort (*Shinje Yab Yum*)

Bodhisattva Manjusri – representing the wisdom of all Buddhas – takes on the appearance of terrifying Lord of Death (Shinje). His wrathful buffalo face guards the four continents.

Lord of the Cremation Grounds (*Durdag*)

A dance that takes place in cremation grounds. The dancers wear skull masks and represent protectors of the religion who, live in the eight cremation grounds on the periphery of symbolic Mt. Sumeru.

The Black-Hat Dance (*Shanag*)

The black-hat dancers assume the role of yogis with power to subdue and create life. The dancers wear brocade robes, wide-brimmed black hats and aprons with the face of protective deity. This is an important dance, used in purification ceremonies during the construction of *dzongs*, temples, *chortens*.

Drum from Dramitse (*Dramitse Ngacham*)

A dance inspired in meditation. The dance is a vision of *Guru Rinpoche* and his celestial palace, *Zangdopelri*. Here, *Guru's* attendants are transformed into hundreds of peaceful and terrifying deities. The dance originated in Dramitse Monastery in eastern Bhutan and is considered a Bhutanese heritage.

Eight Kinds of Spirits (*Degye*)

A dance of gods of three worlds (sky, earth, underground). The gods protect the doctrines of Buddha and subdue spirits who make the world unhappy. Endless happiness is recovered. The dance is performed by gods (believed to be incarnated in the dancers themselves) to renew faith and wisdom.

Religious song (*Chhoeshay*)

This commemorates the opening of gateway to pilgrimage site of *Tsari* in eastern Tibet by the founder of the Drukpa School of Buddhism, Tsangpa Jarey.

Day 2: (*Outside the dzong*)

Lord of Death and his Consort (*Shinje Yab Yum*)

Bodhisattva Manjusri – representing the wisdom of all Buddhas – takes on the appearance of terrifying Lord of Death (Shinje). His wrathful buffalo face guards the four continents.

Dance of the Black Hats with drums (*Shanag Nga Cham*)

A dance to signify the victory of religion over enemies. The sound of drum represents the religion .

Three Kinds of Ging with Sticks (*Gingsum*)

A dance signifying subjugation of demons that are obstacles to religions. It takes place in Zangtopelri, the heavenly palace of *Guru Rinpoche*.

Lords of the Cremation Grounds (*Durdag*)

A dance that takes place in cremation grounds. The dancers wear skull masks and represent protectors of religion, who live in eight cremation grounds on the periphery of symbolic Mt. Sumeru.

Three Kinds of Ging with Drums (*Driging*)

After the demons are vanquished, the *gings* with drums dance with happiness. They beat the drums of religion and the dance is performed to usher good luck to all beings and to wish them happiness. This dance brings blessings to all who watch it.

Stag and the Hounds (*Shawa Shachi*) – 1st Part

The dance tells a favourite tale of *Milerepa*, who converts a hunter to Buddhism.

Day 3: Lords of Cremation Grounds (*Durdag*)

A dance that takes place in cremation grounds. The dancers wear skull masks and represent protectors of the religion, who live in the eight cremation grounds on the periphery of symbolic Mt. Sumeru.

Terrifying Deities (*Tungam*)

Dressed in beautiful brocade and terrifying masks, this is a deeply symbolic dance— where a sacrificial murder is performed. *Guru Rinpoche* appears in a wrathful manifestation to save the world. The dance is meant to show all beings the way to salvation.

Heroes with Six kinds of Ornaments (*Guan Drug Pawo*)

The heroes hold six ornaments – five rings of bone ornaments and a small drum and bell in hands. By their gestures and sound of their melodies, the heroes lead sentient beings from the wheel of reincarnation along the path of liberation.

Kyecham is an accompanying dance to the next dance. The *kyecham* dancers wear knee-length yellow skirts, and animal masks.

Noblemen and Ladies (*Pholeg Moleg*)

A comical play that depicts the life of king Norzang. The play is full of bawdy and rustic humour as two princes and two princesses, and old couple and clowns enact a story of misbehaviour, deceit, and mistrust. The story ends happily with the princes marrying the princesses and reconciliation takes place as a lesson to life.

Dance of the Stag and the Hounds – 2nd Part

This is a conclusion of the dance begun on the second day. The saint *Milarepa* appears in a long white dress and converts the dogs, the stag and the hunter with a song. The conversion is symbolised by the hunter and his dogs jumping a rope.

Day 4:

Lord of Death and His Consort (*Shinje Yab Yum*)

Bodhisattva Manjusri – representing the wisdom of all Buddhas – takes on the appearance of terrifying Lord of Death (Shinje). His wrathful buffalo face guards the four continents.

Four Stags (*Sha Tsam*)

A dance that depicts Guru *Rinpoche* subduing the God of Wind is who believed to have created unhappiness on earth. Dancers dress as stags in yellow knee-length dress and deer masks. The stag represents the mount of the God.

Judgement of the Dead (*Raksha Mangcham*)

This dance is based on the *Bardo* (Book of the Dead). When beings die, they wander in an intermediate state known as the *bardo*. They cross the *bardo* to meet the judgment by the Lord of Death. Also present is the white god and black demon, who have been with every being from birth. The dance is like a play which depicts the judgment of a sinner and a virtuous man who goes to heaven. The *rakshas* are the helpers of the Lord of Death.

Drums from Dramitse (*Dramitse Nga Cham*)

A dance inspired in meditation. The dance is a vision of *Guru Rinpoche* and his celestial palace, Zangdopelri. Here, Guru's attendants are transformed into hundreds of peaceful and terrifying deities. The dance originated in Dramitse Monastery in eastern Bhutan and is considered a Bhutanese heritage.

Day 5:

The great thangkha (*thongdrel*) is shown early in the morning followed by the *Shugdrel* ceremony.

The Heroes (*Pacham*)

A dance to lead believers in the human world into the presence of *Guru Rinpoche*.

The Ging and Tsholing

Guru Rinpoche initiated this dance during the consecration of ancient Samye Monastery in Tibet. It is a purification ceremony. People whistle to chase bad spirits away. The *ging*, dressed in orange skirts and a terrifying mask, use drumsticks to hit everyone on the head to drive impurity out. The *tsoling* represent protectors of religion and are dressed in long colourful dresses and terrifying masks.

Eight Manifestations of Guru Rinpoche (*Guru Tshen Gye*)

This dance is one of the highlights for Buddhist practitioners. The Guru appears in eight different forms in a dance that is also a play.

The Sixteen Fairies

After all eight manifestations, sixteen fairies sing and perform two dances in front of the Guru. The fairies are Goddesses of Offerings, who perform dance to bring happiness. They are dressed in brocade dresses with carved bone ornaments. After these final songs, the manifestations go out in a long procession.

Religious Song (*Chhoeshay*)

This commemorates the opening of the gateway to the pilgrimage site of Tsari in eastern Tibet by the founder of the Drukpa School of Buddhism, Tsangpa Jarey.

Punakha Festival

Punakha is located in the western part of Bhutan. It is the winter home of chief Abbot of Bhutan, the Je Khenpo. Punakha played great importance in the history of Bhutan during Zhabdrung Ngawang Namgyel in 17th century. Zhabdrung Ngawang Namgyal is known as the unifier of Bhutan as a nation state. He was the one who gave Bhutan and its people the cultural identity that identified Bhutan from the rest of the world.

In 17th century, Bhutan was invaded several times by the Tibetan force to seize a very precious relic, the *Ranjung Kharsapani.* Zhabdrung Ngawang Namgyal defeated the Tibetan army and to commemorate the victory, he introduced the Punakha Drubchen. Since then Punakha Drubchen also known as Puna Drubchen became the annual festival of Punakha district. In addition to Punakha Drubchen, another festival known as Punakha Tshechu was introduced by the 70th Je Khenpo Trulku Jigme Choedra and the then Home Minister His Excellency Lyonpo Jigme Yoedzer Thinley in 2005, on the request made by Punakha District Administration and people for upholding Buddhist teachings and keeping alive the noble deeds of Zhabdrung Rimpochhe.

Punakha Drubchen is a unique festival due to a dramatic recreation of the scene from the 17th century battle with Tibetan army. The 'pazaps' or local militia men, dressed in battle gear showcase a battle scene of this distant past. They recall the days when in the absence of a standing army, men from the eight Tshogchens or great village blocks of Thimphu came forward and managed to expel the Tibetan forces out of the country ushering in a new-found internal peace and stability.

Punakha Drubchen and *Tshechu* not only play an important role in preserving Bhutan's rich cultural and tradition but is also an event where devout Buddhists has a place and time for prayer and pilgrimage. These festivals reflect the richness of everything that is Bhutanese and are very special in the eyes and hearts of tourists, who visit Bhutan.

Thimphu Festival

One of the biggest festivals is the Thimphu Tshechu, held in the capital city for three days starting from 10th day of the 8th month of lunar calendar. Before the actual *tshechu* that is being witnessed by thousands of people from the capital city and the nearby Dzongkhags, days and nights of prayers and rituals are conducted to invoke the gods.

It was first initiated by the 4th Desid, Gyalse Tenzin Rabgay in 1867. It had only a few dances being performed, that too strictly by monks. These were the *Zhana chham* and the *Zhana Nga chham* (dances of the 21 black hats), *Durdag* (dance of the lords of the cremation ground), and the *Tungam chham* (dance of the terrifying deities).

Thimphu tshechu underwent a change in the 1950s, when the third king Jigme Dorji Wangchuck, introduced numerous *Boed chhams* (mask dances performed by lay monks). The additions has added colour without compromising spiritual significance. Mask dances like the *Guru Tshengye* (eight manifestations of Guru), *Shaw shachi* (dance of the stags) are enjoyed, because they are like stage theater.

Equally important are the *Atsaras*, who are more than just mere clowns. The *Atsaras* are the *dupthobs* (acharyas), who provide protection. The dances and the jesting of the *Atsaras* are believed to have entranced the evil forces and prevented from causing harm during *tshechus*. Modern *Atsaras* also perform short skits to disseminate health and social awareness messages.

To farmers, the *tshechu* is also seen as a break from the drudgery of farm life. It's an occasion to enjoy, get blessed and pray for health and happiness. The festival lasts for three days.

Thimphu Dromchoe

Besides the annual three day tshechu, Thimphu also celebrates oneday festival known as the *Thimphu Dromchoe*. The day long festival dates back to the 17th century. It was first introduced by Kuenga Gyeltshen in 1710, who was recognized as the reincarnation of Jampel Dorji, son of Zhabdrung Nawang Namgyel. The *dromchoe* is celebrated three days earlier to the *Thimphu Tshechu*.

The *Dromchoe* showcases the sacred dances dedicated to the protecting deity of Bhutan, *Palden Lhamo*. Legend has it, that the deity *Pelden Lhamo* appeared before Kuenga Gyeltshen and performed the dances while he was in meditation. Based on these dances, Kuenga Gyaltshen initiated the dance ceremony.

Trashigang Festival

Trashigang is the largest district in the country and the bastion of Tshanglas, the aboriginal inhabitant of the district. The dzong that sits majestically on a ridge overlooking the Dangmechu and the Gamrichu was built in 1651. Over the years, it has played crucial roles as the Administrative headquarter of the district. It also withstood some of the prominent Tibetan attacks launched in the 17th century from Tawang in Arunachal Pradesh.

While every village has their own *tshechus* to celebrate annually, however the highlight is the three day *tshechu* that is held in the dzong from the seventh to eleventh of the tenth month of the Bhutanese calendar that corresponds to the month of December. The *tshechu* is witnessed by the *Brokpas*, a semi-nomadic community of Merak and Sakteng, the *Khengpa* community, and people from as far as *Samdrup Jongkhar*, *Pema Gatshel* and *Trashi Yangtse*.

On the seventh day, the monks take the thrue or the bath and on the eighth have their rehearsals. On the ninth day, the *tshechu* begins. On the tenth day is unfurled the thongdrol of *Neten Chudrug* (Sixteen Arhats) together with different mask dances. On the final day, the old thongdrel of Guru Tshengyed is displayed with Guru Tshengyed Chhams.[11]

Taktsang Monastery

Taktsang Monastery, also known as Tiger's Nest Monastery, is located in Paro, Bhutan, about 10 kilometres north of Paro city. It hangs on a precipitous cliff at 3,120 metres (10,240 ft), about 900 metres (3,000 ft) above the Paro valley, on the right side of the *Paro Chu* ('chu' means "river or water". The monastery is one of the most venerated places of pilgrimage in the Himalayan region.

Taktsang Monastery was built in 1692 by Gyalse Tenzin Rabgye. Gyalse Tenzin Rabgye is believed to be the reincarnation of *Padmasambhava*. Legend believes that Padmasambhava (**Guru Rinpoche**) flew to this location from Khenpajong, Tibet, *on back of a tigress*. Guru Rinpoche meditated for three months in the cave at Taktshang. He also subjugated the eight categories of Evil Spirits and converted the valley to Buddhism.[12]

The monastery buildings consist of four main temples and residential shelters–ideally designed by adapting to the rock (granite) ledges, the caves and the rocky terrain. Out of the eight caves, four are comparatively easy to access. The cave where *Padmasambhava* first entered, riding the Tiger, is known as '*Tholu Phuk*' and the original cave, where he resided and did meditation is known as the '*Pel Phuk*'. He directed the spiritually enlightened monks to build the monastery here. The main cave is entered through a narrow passage. The dark cave houses a dozen images of *Bodhisattvas* and butter lamps flicker in front of these idols. An elegant image of *Chenrezig* (*Avalokitesvara*) is also deified here. In an adjoining small cell, the sacred scripture is placed; the importance of this scripture is that it has been scripted with gold dust and the crushed bone powder of a divine Lama. It is also said that the monks who practice *Vajrayana* Buddhism (the formal State Religion of Bhutan) at this cave monastery live here for three years and seldom go down to the Paro valley.

All the buildings are interconnected through steps and stairways made in rocks. There are a few rickety wooden bridges along the paths and stairways also to cross over. The temple at the highest level has a frieze of Buddha. Each building has a balcony, which provides lovely views of the scenic Paro valley down below. The monasteries have ancient history of occupation by monks, as hermitages.

On April 19, 1998, a fire broke out in the main building of the monastery complex, which contained valuable paintings, artifacts and statues. The fire is believed to have been caused by electrical short-circuiting or flickering butter lamps lighting the hanging tapestries. A monk also died during the fire. The restoration works were undertaken at an estimated cost of 135 million ngultrum. The

Government of Bhutan and the then king of Bhutan, Jigme Singye Wangchuck, oversaw the restoration of the damaged monastery and its contents in 2005.[13]

Taktsang monastery holds an important place in every Bhutanese spiritual life. Along with the religious significance, the location makes it a natural paradise where nature is at its best. The sound of Pachu River mingles with the beautiful landscape. This unmatched beauty allures the nature lovers and trekkers to climb the challenging route to the monastery. Bhutanese throng the monastery on *Guru Padmasambhava's* birthday. It is an occasion to pay their respect as well as treating them with an outdoor activity, mostly with their families. I caught a glimpse of this overweening spirit, when I visited Taktsang Monastery in 2010.

The 2-3 hours steep trek to the Taktsang monastery gives a deep insight into Bhutan's pristine nature and a masterpiece of Buddhist architecture, along with the spiritual fervor embedded deeply in the inhabitants of this mountainous country.

Conclusion

In the document Bhutan 2020: A Vision for Peace, Prosperity and Happiness, by GNH Commission, Royal Government of Bhutan, the need for a culture and heritage act and fund has been emphasised as follows:

- Elaborate objectives in respect of cultural preservation, conservation and promotion;
- Specify priorities in respect of the objectives formulated;
- Specify the responsibilities and duties of different institutions and bodies at different levels in respect of the priorities;
- Identify new mechanisms required to promote an understanding and appreciation of culture and heritage;
- Specify incentives consistent with the preservation, conservation and promotion of our culture and heritage;
- Specify fines and punishment for crimes committed in relation to culture and heritage.[14]

The Bhutanese culture remains vibrantly alive in the everyday life of people it is the outcome of the care and far-sighted policies taken by the rulers and the religious community. The culture is evolving and dynamic, therefore, with modernisation, globalisation and the impact of other cultures cannot be overlooked. The new challenges which will come have to be taken in its stride. The need to emphasise and strengthen the old traditional values and institutions among the youth of the country will help in the promotion, preservation, development and sustainability.

Education System of Bhutan

With the development and modernisation in Bhutan, one area which has seen expansion and growth is education. The Ministry of Education has articulated the vision in its *Education Sector Strategy: Realising the Vision 2020: Policy and Strategy* as "to maximise the happiness of all Bhutanese and to enable them achieve their full and innate potential as human beings" (RGoB, 1999, p. 47). The twin aims of education are to acquire knowledge and to build character. In Bhutan an effort is being made to achieve both these aims through education. Since the beginning of modern education in 1960s during the reign of the third king, the message was clear that the system of education should be such that Bhutan should be able to overcome the infrastructural problem. The schools should be established in the remotest villages and with teachers, who have knowledge of English as well as local languages and customs.

The Planning Commission's Bhutan 2020 (RGoB, 1999) sets out parameters for the development of broad sectors of Bhutanese life over twenty years. The document presents the tension between cultural traditions and development in this way:

We have built unity out of diversity....we take quiet pride in our independence...unity and development would have been impossible without the continuity and vision that have been bestowed upon our nation by the beliefs and values of the faith we have held for more than 1,000 years. Firmly rooted in our rich tradition of Mahayana Buddhism, the approach stresses, not material rewards but individual development, sanctity of life, compassion for others, respect for nature, social harmony and the importance of compromise...our approach to development has led us to emphasise the importance of institutions that are able to guide and manage the process of development as well as foster participation....The values underlying our approach to development have meant that we, unlike many of other developing countries stand on the threshold of a new country with our natural environment largely intact....We have been assisted by others in our efforts to modernise and transform our nation. (RGoB, 1999, pp. 20-24)

At present, education in Bhutan can be categorised in three streams- the monastic system, Dzongkha medium education and modern education. All the three aim at the development of society. The monastic stream is the oldest traditional form of education, aimed at preserving Bhutan's religious traditions and Buddhist culture. Dzongkha education is developed for the population, which was far flung and whose needs were not served by either the monastic or modern education. This aims at preserving Bhutanese cultural traditions. The modern education based on European and post-colonial Indian model aims at producing globally competent Bhutanese, who have access to scientific knowledge and are well-versed in English. They are being fully equipped to go for higher studies in international institutions. In short, an effort is being made to improve the quality and relevance of education.

Structure of Modern Education

Bhutan's current formal education structure consists of seven years of primary schooling (classes pre-primary [admission age: six years] to VI), six years of secondary education comprising two years of lower secondary (classes VII-VIII), two years of middle secondary (classes IX-X), and two years of higher secondary (classes XI-XII) schooling. This is followed by three years of undergraduate programmes provided in the country's tertiary institutes with smaller numbers of students going abroad for professional and postgraduate studies. The recent establishment of the Royal University of Bhutan is expected to cater to Bhutan's higher education needs and aspirations. (Thakur Singh Powdyel "From Innocence to Passion: Bhutan's Tryst with Education").[15]

Development of Education in Bhutan

According to the Honourable Minister of Education and Chairman Commission of Women and Children Thakur Singh Powdyel:

- Education is the bottom line. Any nation that aspires to do anything good and succeed has to make education its foundation and especially for small systems like Bhutan.

- Education in Bhutan has come in terms of waves, the first is the Monastic Education Wave that would have started somewhere in Eighth century. That wave still continues but somewhere in the early 1960's was started the big Modern Education Wave and today's professionals, bureaucrats, administrators, managers, diplomats, members of parliament, civil servants, all belong to the second wave.
- The third wave is the Non-Formal Education Wave. This programme was meant for people who missed their opportunity when they were young. It was felt that they must be given a second chance in life, so the Non-Formal Education Programme was started for housewives, the villagers and farmers who could not go to school early on. This caught on very well and today a lot of local leaders are graduates of the Non-Formal Educational Wave.
- There are lot of people in the civil service, who started working after finishing Grade VIII, Grade X, because there was a need for educated people in system. They got into jobs even before they were able to complete their education that they would have wished to, so now to upgrade their qualification and knowledge, was started the fourth education wave which is called the Continuing Education Wave.
- The fifth wave he feels will be the Digital Education Wave.
- The enrolment especially at the primary level is close to 98 per cent and in the next couple of years, the government wants to make sure that every single child is in school, who should be in school. The constitution of kingdom of Bhutan provides for eleven years of schooling. Class X is supposed to be the basic education level, so the government is required to provide basic education to all the children of Bhutan.
- The government launched a massive education reform programme in 2010 when the new academic year began in February 2010. This education reform initiative is called Education for Gross National Happiness. Gross National Happiness being the developing goal of this country, the long term vision of this country, the education system has to take ownership of the dream, cater to advance the dream, so was began the programme called Educating for Gross National Happiness.
- Today, education is meant only as an entry into the job market, prepare people for employability. People are not talking even about employment, today they are talking about employability which means the system makes big schools, colleges and universities only to

prepare people for the job market, to be employed, to serve a certain end but that is not the only purpose of education. Education has a bigger role. It has a bigger responsibility, that's why education is called the 'Noble Sector'.[16]

In the Tenth Five Year Plan, the national goal is to achieve near 100 per cent enrolment in primary education. Primary education has seen enormous expansion with the net enrolment ratio reaching 88 per cent. It has been possible through the community primary schools and the provision of boarding facilities in rural and remote areas. The following factors which previously were a hindrance in expanding education in the remote mountainous kingdom are no longer an obstacle:

(a) The number of schools was few and sometimes it would take hours to reach the institution. Now schools are provided within one hour of walking distance.
(b) Special emphasis is being laid on women's education. Earlier, boys got preference for going to school, as it involved travelling long distances and girls were kept at home for security reasons.
(c) Now boarding facilities are provided. Mid-day meals and free stationary and for children for poor family stipend, clothes and other necessities are also provided.
(d) The changed attitude of parents' who may not be educated themselves but are opting for educating their children is a major shift and boosting factor.

The success of primary education has increased pressure on the secondary education level, where more educational institutions have to be opened to accommodate the large number of students willing to be admitted. One major development in recent years has been that women who used to drop out at secondary stage are now opting to finish schooling and move to higher education and professional courses.

In the tenth Five Year Plan, the targets for the education sector are:

(a) Enhance Primary Net Enrolment ratio to near 100 per cent.
(b) Enhance Basic Net Enrolment ratio near 90 per cent.
(c) Enhance Enrolment of girls in tertiary institutes to 80 girls for every 100 boys.
(d) Enhance adult literacy rate to 70 per cent.

The proportion of girls attending schools tends to be higher in urban areas than in rural areas. This may be correlated with higher cash incomes in urban areas, which allow parents to provide girls the opportunity to attend the schools. But in secondary education there seems to be a fall in the number of girls due to reasons, which are not attributed directly to the education system like socio-cultural factors such as early marriage, teenage pregnancy (which is in sizeable number in Bhutan), imperatives on domestic and subsistence labour and parents' assumption that girls need more social security.

Table 1: Enrolment of girls at various levels in Dzongkhags (Districts)

Dzongkhag	*School*	*Total Students*	*Girl Students*	*Boy Students*
Mongar	Mongar Lower Secondary School	810	420	390
Wangdue	Chholing Primary School, Singor	50	26	24
Bumthang	Lower Secondary School	954	504	450
	Higher Secondary School	494	243	251
Punakha	Khuru Middle Secondary School, Khuruthang	1093	554	539
	Higher Secondary School	673	329	344
Thimphu	Lungtenzampo Middle Secondary School	1157	650	507
	Lower Secondary School	1400	701	699
Paro	Goepel Lower Secondary School	08	06	02
Chukha	Phuentsholing Lower Secondary School	2023	1143	880

(***Source:*** Random Statistics from Schools in Bhutan Collected from 01 June - 26 June 2010.)[17]

Expansion of education in Bhutan was supported by international community such as World Bank, Asian Development Bank, UNICEF, Save the Children (US) and India has been the main benefactor. Although, initially the government of Bhutan was reluctant to appoint Indian teachers but due to shortage of staff, most of the schools in Bhutan are predominantly staffed by Indian teachers. But, this trend is witnessing a change in present times as was evident during my visit to Bhutan in 2011. I was told that in Arts subjects, now most of the teachers are Bhutanese, trained at the Paro College of Education and Samtse College, Samtse. In science stream Indian teachers remain in large number, but an effort is being made to train as many Bhutanese as possible. The same can be said of the higher education where along with Indians, many foreign nationals are employed. But, the figure of Bhutanese teachers is rising.

Bhutanese initially relied on Indian curricula (Thinley, 1999). An attempt to install a progressive-style primary curriculum in the late 1980s was only partially successful (Dorji, 1999). By the mid-to-late 1990s, local Bhutanese curricula had been developed and implemented for all levels up to Class X. Similarly, Class XII curricula had been constructed by Bhutanese educators for 2005. The comprehensive system of examinations is now entirely controlled by the Bhutan Board of Examiners.[18]

The Advent of the University

The country's desire for a place in the intellectual sun came to fulfilment on June 2, 2003 when the Royal University of Bhutan was born, coinciding with the celebration of the 48th birth anniversary of His Majesty Druk Gyalpo Jigme Singye Wangchuck, the fourth hereditary monarch of Bhutan.

The founding of a nation university is the culmination in the transition of an education system, which had the most humble beginning, evolving steadily over the years, and gaining a profile which is a story of success by all counts.

Designed on a distributive model, comprising the existing colleges and institutes, which are expected to grow into centres of excellence, the major functions of the university include knowledge development, personnel development and provision of services among others. More specifically, the university is called upon to serve the following functions:

- Instituting of programmes of studies, and granting of degrees including postgraduate and doctorate.
- Creation of qualified manpower to serve the professional sector of the fast expanding economy.
- Monitoring course quality and teaching effectiveness in member institutions.
- Establishing criteria for and providing accreditation to member institutions.
- Coordination of exchange and sharing of resources among member institutions.
- Overview of development and delivery of relevant curricula.
- Guiding the direction, dimension and quality of higher education in the country.[19]

Although education in Bhutan has been developed and nurtured by the government, but the recent trend is private investment with many posh private institutions coming up in bigger cities like Thimphu and Paro. Teaching in Bhutan, is still not the first career choice. The reasons may be that they may have to work in rural or remote parts of Bhutan which may require walking for a longer period. In comparison to the work, the payment is not that high. Although, government is trying to improve the conditions as reflected in His Majesty's address at the third convocation of the Royal University of Bhutan on February 17, 2009, "Our education system built and nurtured with your hard work and dedication has served us well. But, we must understand that the times have changed here in Bhutan and all around us in the world. We cannot face new challenges with the same tools. The private sector is adjusting itself to new challenges and opportunities; the bureaucracy is finding its place in a new system of governance; the entire country is adapting to new roles in our young democracy. Thus every person and institution must evolve to meet the aspirations of our people and the changing needs of our nation."[20]

During the Ninth Five-Year plan, vocational education and training was improved and was made available to every Bhutanese citizen. Six vocational training institutes which are directly under the administration of Ministry of Labour and Human Resources have been established in important areas such as carpentry, auto mobile engineering, electrical engineering and traditional arts and craft. Though, this is dominated by males, the number of females has also started increasing.

The non-formal education programme was given an impetus in the Ninth Five-Year plan. It offers a one-year basic literacy and nine month post-literacy course in Dzongkha aimed at providing functional literacy to those who have either missed or dropped out of formal education system. Some of the subjects are agriculture, health, sanitation, culture and tradition, forestry and environment and use of smokeless stoves. These centres are in rural areas where 70 per cent of learners are women.

The Ministry of Education had also started a pilot continuing education programme in collaboration with a private school in Thimphu in 2006. At that time, there were 70 women and 78 men enrolled in classes IX and XI and while women made up a higher percentage of Class IX students enrolled (17 women out of 32 enrolled), the reverse situation was observed for Class XI (64 men out of 117 enrolled). As of 2008, the programme has expanded to two other private schools in Paro and Chhukha and the gender balance has changed with 311 women and 266 men enrolled in classes IX-XII. In fact, there are now more women enrolled in Class XII while more men are enrolled in Class IX unlike in 2006.[21]

Conclusion

Being a mountainous country with scattered population, it may not be easy for Bhutan to have schools at the remotest places, where it takes days of walk to reach, but the herculean effort being put by the Royal Government of Bhutan needs to be admired. The primary schools which have the basic infrastructure, dedicated teachers and staff are amazingly sufficient to ensure overall development of a child. An effort has been made to try to narrow the teacher-student ratio. The target was to enhance primary net enrolment of children aged 6-12 in classes PP-VI to near 100 per cent by 2013. Extended classrooms are to be established to provide education in areas far and remote. The poor will have education fully financed by the government, which includes stipend, clothes and other essential sources.

Along with the efforts of the government, the noticeable feature is the overwhelming cooperation of the people. The importance of education has dawned on parents, who now want the best for their children. Girls are being enrolled in big numbers, equal to that of boys and sometimes even more.

I had the privilege of visiting twelve out of twenty Dzongkhags and most of their primary schools. It will not be an exaggeration to say that overall development and holistic approach is adopted for imparting education. As children sit facing each other in friendly environment with charts and hand-made illustrations, the raw minds do not see learning as a painful exercise, but something to be practically enjoyed.

Lessons in sports and environment preservation are emphasised upon. The gardens are maintained by the children; so are the trees planted by them. They are the proud owners as the names written in front of the trees proudly proclaim.

Children are the future of the country. They should be left only in trained and dedicated hands. Most of the teachers whom I met had the opinion that teaching kids is highly challenging, but equally satisfying and they enjoy it. It may be difficult but is a fruitful exercise. Encouraging the children in the direction they enjoy will see them emerging as masters and champions in chosen fields as they grow older.

It is rightly said that we reap what we sow. Let the prayers they say be answered, as they grow into confident, educated and enlightened citizens of Bhutan.

The spirit is best reflected in the letter written by Lyonpo Thakur Singh Powdyel, the Education Minister, to the schools dated June 11, 2008, "Education is a process of gently turning the human mind to look for and to love what is true and good and useful." He further reinstates, "the principal goal of our schools is to provide quality wholesome education and building knowledge that is useful and at the same time good, knowledge that makes the scholar both smart as well as graceful".

References

1. Bhutan 2020: A Vision for Peace, Prosperity and Happiness, Planning Commission, Royal Government of Bhutan, p. 41.
2. Dorji, C.T., Proceedings of the 5th Colloquium on "Tangible and Intangible Culture of Bhutan", National Museum of Bhutan, Paro, Bhutan.
3. Dorji, C.T., *A Brief History of Dogar Dobji Dzong*, Fortress of the Dragon, National Museum of Bhutan, Paro, Second Edition, 2009, pp. 12-13.
4. www.bhutan2008.bt
5. *Ibid.*
6. www.kuenselonline.com, 12 May 2008.
7. www.bhutan2008.bt
8. Namgyal Dorji, *The History of Paro Ta Dzong*, Fortress of the Dragon, Proceedings of the 4th Colloquium, The National Museum of Bhutan, Paro, Second Edition, 2009, pp. 170-173.
9. Op.cit, ref 7.
10. www.bhutan2008.bt
11. http://www.bhutanmysticbliss.com/bhutan-travel/festivals-of-bhutan.html

12. http://www.lonelyplanet.com/travelblogs
13. http://en.wikipedia.org/wiki/Paro_Taktsang
14. Bhutan 2020: A Vision for Peace, Prosperity and Happiness, Planning Commission (now GNH Commission), Part-I, p. 44.
15. Thakur Singh Powdyel, Honourable Minister of Education, Bhutan, 'From Innocence to Passion- Bhutan's Tryst with Education' in the book 'Education Reform in Societies in Transition: International Perspectives, Ed. by J. Earnest, D. Treagust, 2006, Chapter 4, p. 57.
16. In an interview of Honourable Minister of Education and Chairman, Commission of Women and Children, Thakur Singh Powdyel taken by self on 20 Oct. 11, in his office at the Ministry of Education, Thimphu, Bhutan.
17. Collected during my survey in Bhutan from 1- 26 June 2010.
18. Baker David P., Wiseman Alexander A., Education for All: Global Promises, National Challenges, Emerald Group Publishing, 2007, p. 187.
19. Thakur Singh Powdyel, Honourable Minister of Education, Bhutan, 'From Innocence to Passion- Bhutan's Tryst with Education' in the book 'Education Reform in Societies in Transition: International Perspectives, Ed. by J. Earnest, D. Treagust, 2006, Chapter 4, p. 57.
20. Educating for GNH, Nurturing Green Schools for Green Bhutan- A Guide to School Management, Education Monitoring and Support Services Division, Department of School Education, Ministry of Education, Thimphu, Chapter 3, p. 13.
21. National Plan of Action for Gender 2008-2013Gross National Happiness Commission, National Commission for Women and Children, Royal Government of Bhutan, p. 60.

5

Advent of Democracy

In South-Asia, Bhutan was the only country without a codified constitution. This was taken care by commanding the drafting of a Constitution. On December 17 2001, King Jigme Singye Wangchuck declared:

I would like to inform our people that the government has decided to draft a Tsa-Thrim (Constitution) for the Kingdom of Bhutan. Drafting Committee, which is headed by the Chief Justice, comprises 39 members and includes the speaker of the National Assembly along with 20 people's representatives, one from each dzongkhag, all the members of the Royal Advisory Council and representatives of the government. While drafting the Tsa-Thrim, it is of utmost importance that we safeguard the security and sovereignty of our nation, ensure the well-being of our people and establish a democratic political system that will best serve the interest of our country for all time to come. One of the most important responsibilities of a king is to enable the people to govern and look after the country through the establishment of a dynamic political system. To achieve this objective it is very important for us to bring forth the best possible Tsa-Thrim, when we have the time and opportunity to do so today, to serve the present and the future interest of our country. Once the new Tsa-Thrim has been drafted, it will be distributed to all the 20 dzongkhags, and the government and people will hold close consultations before the written constitution for the Kingdom of Bhutan is passed by the National Assembly.[1]

The Constitution which was prepared envisages Bhutan as a 'Democratic Constitutional Monarchy', declaring Bhutan to be a sovereign kingdom with powers vested in people. It talks about the role of monarchy, stipulates fundamental rights and duties, provides for two-party parliamentary system and outlines provisions for citizenship. Article 2 of the Constitution declares the king to be the upholder of religion and politics. He is to protect and uphold the constitution in the best interest and welfare of people. The Druk Gyalpo is not answerable in the Court of Law. Article 20 of the Constitution requires the executive to be responsible to the legislative as well as the Gyalpo. Leaving space for the role of monarch will not depend on the constitutional provisions, but on the way it is implemented in the coming years. The role of the National Assembly and the Supreme Court becomes very important.

In all, the Constitution has 35 Articles and the final authority to amend the Constitution is vested with the people through optional or mandatory conduct of *national referendum*. The Constitution is supposed to be the final law, but judicial review is conferred to the High Court and the Supreme Court. The Constitution contains the spirit of good governance and equal development. There is a provision of checks and balances among the various branches of the government. Principals of human rights and international law are recognised. No state force will be used against a foreign state accept in self-defence. The Constitution of Bhutan has the vision of His Majesty to give his country a political system, which will fulfil the aspirations of his people and provide good government. As His Majesty always said, "I have been saying for 30 years, that the destiny of the nation lies in the hands of people," he further added, "I have always made it clear that the people are more important than the king. We cannot leave the future of the country in the hands of one person, these are not mere words. The constitution will be the fulfilment of our country's destiny being placed in the hands of our people."

The document was a product of a careful study of merits and demerits of the political system of other countries and has tried to absorb the best for the present and future of the Bhutanese people.

The king's vision was materialised with Bhutan's first ever National Elections, held on March 24 2008. Elections portrayed there a very unique phenomenon. While people voted to elect their representatives, they considered these elections as a gift from monarchy. In history, such examples are few.

In a Kasho issued on this 30th Day of the 10th Month of the Wood-Bird Year (December 31 2005), the fourth king Druk Gyalpo Jigme Singye Wangchuck instructed:

The draft constitution of the Kingdom of Bhutan that was framed to ensure the present and future interests of the country has been distributed nationwide and consultations with our people in the 20 Dzongkhags on the Constitution are already taking place.

Once the constitution is adopted and the introduction of parliamentary democracy takes place, it is of paramount importance to ensure that elections are conducted properly. As it is necessary to make full preparations to carry out this important task before parliamentary democracy is established, Auditor General Kunzang Wangdi is hereby transferred and appointed as the Chief Election Commissioner until the new parliament is formed after the adoption of the constitution. The office of the Election Commission is a very important Constitutional post and it is imperative to build a strong foundation for implementing the functions of this post while we are in the process of establishing democratic practices and norms in our country. The Chief Election Commissioner must carry out his responsibilities with the highest level of loyalty and dedication to the government and the people without any distinction or discrimination between regions, dzongkhags and gewogs, and establish a strong electoral system for the present and the future interest of the country.

In keeping with the provisions of the Constitution for a minimum of two and a maximum of seven members in the National Assembly for each dzongkhags, on the basis of population, the Chief Election Commissioner must finalise the constituencies for the election of National Assembly members. Towards this end, the Office of the Election Commission must review and finalize the boundaries of the dzongkhags and gewogs together with the concerned ministries and departments.

The Office of the Election Commission must also finalize the electoral rolls and election schedules as well as make full preparations for the supervision, direction, control and conduct of elections to the Parliament and local government. The Election Commission must conduct training and familiarisation for the people in the electoral process during the next two years in 2006 and 2007 so that the first general elections in the country can be successfully carried out in the year 2008.[2]

An Election Commission was established in January 2006, with the Chief Election Commissioner as its head and two Election Commissioners as the members. It is an independent body responsible for the overall conduct of elections. The secretariat employees are civil servants, who are appointed for a five-year term. The ECB shoulders a broad range of responsibilities, which consist of issuing electoral rolls, delimiting election boundaries, giving directions to prepare electoral rolls, registration of political parties, voter education, oversight of the parties, financial regulation and adjudication of election- related complaints.[3]

For administration, it was a task which they had to carry out for the first time. The 20 Dzongkhags of Bhutan had to be educated, rules had to be made and implemented in such way that transparency was maintained. In each of the 20 districts, the governor was designated as the Chief Election Co-ordinator during the election period. The ECB designated civil servants as Returning Officers for election period. The Returning Officer was to decide on the candidates' nomination, receive complaints, issue postal ballets and had the overall responsibility for the counting process.[4]

Before the elections, two rounds of mock elections were conducted in April and May 2007. National Council elections were held on December 31 2007 and January 29 2008. The two main parties which emerged after the multi-party elections were the Peoples Democratic Party, registered in September 2007 and the DPT in October 2007. All registered political parties were eligible to participate in the National Assembly elections. For these elections the two registered political parties submitted letters of intent to ECB by 22 Jan 2008. The PDP was led by former Agriculture Minister Sangay Ngedup and DPT known as the party of blissful harmony, was led by the Foreign Minister and Prime Minister Jigme Thinley.

The election campaign in Bhutan was a very interesting affair. Though formally it started on January 2208, both the parties were active across the country even before, seeking to recruit members and familiarising electorate with their candidates. It included strategic village gatherings of 20-30 individuals, house-to-house canvassing, special focus on promotion of Gross National Happiness, the improvement of health sector of the rural areas, of the road system, of the education quality and the preservation of environment and culture. While PDP tried to present itself as the party of new generation politicians, the DPT insisted on the proven experience of its senior candidates.[5]

Both political parties nominated minority candidates from the ethnic Nepalese minority Lhotshampas from the southern part of the country. DPT nominated 9 Lhotshampa candidates and PDP nominated *six*. Nine Lhotshampas were elected all from DPT. The practice of allowing voter education, campaign and election material to be printed only in Dzongkha and English added to the difficulty of minority candidates. But candidate meetings and voter education sessions were permitted to be conducted in minority languages.[6]

On March 24, 2008, National Assembly elections were conducted in Bhutan which converted tiny kingdom into newborn democracy in South Asia. It was a big leap forward for Bhutan. In the electoral process the voting age for Bhutanese citizens was 18 years. It excluded members of monastic community from voting based on the constitutional provision that religious figures should remain above politics. The number of voters for National Assembly election was 318,465. This was an increase of 568 over the National Council elections which had 312,817 total registered voters. This number varied because of 1,000 transfer cases, people changing their place of registration since the previous elections.[7]

Voter education for the elections was an important task for the Election Commission. For, this would be the key component for the success of the process. In November 2006, Bhutan Electoral Education and Training Strategy (BEETS) was established. Its main work was to educate Bhutanese citizens throughout the country to ensure the conduct of free and fair elections.

The voter education was carried out through the media-radio and television. Local songs were composed, CDs were shown of electronic voting machine and their operation. Election advertisement boards were set up in each constituency, where the candidates could put up their posters for public viewing.

Civil society organisations were forbidden by law from engaging in activities directly related to elections. There are very few civil society organisations in the country and none of them deals with women issues.[8]

Participation of women was in large number as the Bhutanese legal framework prohibits gender discrimination. Women remain clearly under-represented in public life. Unlike in other fields where they work in large numbers, only four women were elected for the National Assembly. In the National Council elections the number is four again. Although one of the Election Commissioners is a woman, yet no woman was represented in Dzongkha in the category of election officers and Returning Officials, though there were few women registration officers and delimitation assistants. Women in large number participated in election process, attending candidates meetings but most of the party workers and representatives were men.[9]

It can be said, to the credit of Election Commission that the first exercise which they undertook was very successful. This is evident from the large turnout and the result of the final elections and the fact that the result of the final election was made known to the country within a span of two hours. These elections saw the old and the young, the privileged and the non-privileged, all making use of their ballots. And the king's faith in his people when he exhorted them to come out and vote in large numbers was fully indicated by the voting percentage of 79.4 per cent, which was indeed awe-inspiring. Women voters outnumbered men being a whopping 56 per cent out of the total 76.4 per cent.

People's reaction about the process is varied in nature. They are happy, excited and worried at the same time. People walked over long distances to vote even at the age of 85. Many decided to brave odds to cast their vote. For instance, a woman of 65 years trekked six hundred kilometres with walking stick and rubber slippers to cast her vote. Tshewang Dema took 14 days to reach the eastern district Trashiyangste, from where she passed through six districts, daring cold and rough terrain. 'I have a disliking for cars' she said. 'and since I didn't want to lose my vote, I walked."[10]

During my stay in the country June 09-22, 2008, I saw that for the common Bhutanese people, governance was identical with a person or a system that was responsive and catered to the needs of the people. They wanted stability in their country. At the same time, the age-old institution of monarchy continued to be the most respected institution. They said it is sad to see the king stand aside. The people were slowly warming up to the idea of democracy.

Democratic process involves participation of people in governance at all levels. What will emerge in Bhutan is still unfolding. For there are also concerns and misgivings in Bhutanese people over the negative impact of introducing such political reforms, when the nation was enjoying an era of peace and prosperity. The people are still not sure about the wisdom of introducing a constitution and changing a stable, time-tested system. But, the king is sure of his decision. He says "The constitution of our country must fulfil the aspirations of our people.It must be relevant and beneficial for the best interest of the nation."

White Ross says "The debate in the National Assembly will be a key part of the process, as it will not only scrutinise the document, but develop general public awareness about its meaning." The constitution was debated in the National Assembly and was sent to the king for the final approval in July 2008. It will be adopted, if approved by a simple majority of the people in a referendum.

Bhutan presents the world's most peaceful transition to people's rule. It also presents a rare example, which cannot be easily figured in any other country. The Director of the Election Commission Pheuntsho Namgyel brought out some salient features during discussion. He pointed out that the first challenge was to frame the election bill; second to delimit the constituencies and then to prepare the voting list. But the most daunting task was to educate and enlighten the Bhutanese voters about the elections and to prepare them for the final day. Two mock elections were held primarily to educate them. In this process, they were helped by the Election Commission of India. Besides, preparing for the ground work for elections, Indian legal experts also proved to be indispensable in preparing Bhutan's new constitutional framework. Lyonpo Sonam Tobgay, who was Bhutan's Chief Justice for 17 years said that for the formidable task of drafting the country's constitution, he sought the assistance of two Indian legal luminaries with whom he had interacted during his several visits to India.

The Indian Election Commission's legal advisor, S. K. Mendiratta was asked for assistance in drafting Bhutan's Election Bill and Indian

Constitutional expert K. K. Venugopal was asked to go through Bhutan's draft constitution with a fine toothcomb.

"Their help has been immense. Venugopal took almost a year with the draft constitution and did all this pro bono. The Indian legal luminaries provided us with sound constitutional advice and several of their suggestions have been incorporated by us," said the Chief Justice.

He added, "We are hoping Bhutan will be a multi- party democracy like India one day. But for the moment, we have settled for a two-party system like the USA. We do not want the new government to be taken hostage by too many political parties and fragmented votes."[11]

The two party system has come in for criticism, but Bhutanese officials have defended it. When I met the Election Commissioner Aum Dekhi Pema, she explained that they were not against multi – party system, but the country could not afford the kind of situation that India faces. At the preliminary stage, multi-party system is followed. It is only after these elections that the winning candidates of the majority parties will form the two National Parties. Any candidate, who does not belong to either group, is free to join one of these parties. It ensures that a deserving candidate is not stopped at the primary stage only.

Another striking feature of Bhutan's political system has been to decide the retirement age for the members of National Assembly and Council as well as making graduate degree mandatory to stand for elections. All the newly elected members are graduates. The Election Commissioner Dekhi Pema said, "This is responsible for the good standard of debate in the National Assembly."

The parties DPT and PDP have heavily drawn their leaders from ministry, bureaucracy and various professional groups. Most of the candidates are from every possible professional group. Another factor that has drawn professionals into politics is the absence of any political movement in Bhutan. Bhutan's constitution seems to have drawn heavily from the constitution of India and other South Asian countries. It prohibits participation of people related to religious institutions in the electoral process. They are not given even the voting right.

Democratic process in Bhutan presents a paradox as with jubilation there is lot of scepticism among its people. Still the people of this kingdom are not ready to forego their loyalty to the throne. At one place, we may hear a voice which says frankly "I did not vote in the council polls. Let them have any kind of system here, but we want the king." Another opinion "We cannot right away tell whether democracy is good or bad for Bhutan but, the king is, without any doubt, the most revered person here." Most of the Bhutanese hold this point of view. The people have made their decision but only after a lot of appeals and exhortations by both the kings, specially the fifth king, who said "My father has handed over his responsibilities to the people and now it is our turn to take the country forward by following his legacy."[12]

The fourth king Jigme Singye Wangchuck's firm belief in the people of Bhutan is the unique example of a ruler; whose every move is for his people, as he is confident that Bhutan can face the challenges of future. The Bhutanese people have integrity, the perception and capability to carry out the important responsibility of shaping the destiny of the nation."

Bhutan's elections were largely peaceful. This is unlike the other neighbouring countries Nepal, Bangladesh and Pakistan, where people are getting killed in the name of democratic elections. Even India is not above that. Overall the picture has been of dedication, commitment and cautious approach to what will happen to the new system introduced in politics. Election Commissioner Dekhi Pema said "It may have been a new phenomena and a mammoth exercise to conduct the first ever elections, but it was a privilege we have enjoyed." Same views were expressed by the Director, who said that from laying the infrastructure for election to conducting the process it had been a team effort. Right from the kings to the Chief Election Commissioner and the entire team of the Election Commission had worked to make their first ever elections—a reality in Bhutan.

The success of democracy in Bhutan is evident at the level of making elections a success as the old, the young, the privileged and the people living in the remotest area voted in large number. It is only in Bhutan that we can see such commitment, where an Election Officer has to walk for three days to reach his place of work but he performed his task. There is another constituency, where there were only nine voters and the equal number of officials to conduct it. However, what has been achieved till now and whatever efforts have been made will only yield result if entire Bhutanese society gets its due. The democratic beginnings, of Bhutan should be based on development, equality and security for all.

At present, it seems that the fourth king His Majesty Jigme Singye Wangchuck's vision of vesting sovereignty in the people of Bhutan has borne fruits. But, the tree which has been planted and nurtured by the king, only time will tell as to how its fruits will taste in time to come.

Democracy is a new phenomenon for Bhutan. It is not merely holding elections, but an endeavour to educate its people for strong commitment, self-determination, tolerance and working for public benefit. It will require an establishment of proper infrastructure for good governance, respect for each other's views and deep commitment towards a new political system.

A UNDP-sponsored study of elections, which was first of its kind, sheds light on how Bhutanese feel about their electoral exercise. About 84 per cent of Bhutanese felt that National Assembly elections were free and fair. five per cent had reservations and another 11 per cent had no opinion. Around 80 per cent were pre-decided a month ago and only 10 per cent decided at the polling station. In National Council Elections, the turnout was 53 per cent, while in National Assembly it was 80 per cent. One of the key finding is that the party leadership had a major impact on the popular voting patterns. It was also found that 10 per cent voters did not know how many parties were involved and another 40 per cent did not know that there would be an elimination round in case more than two parties received considerable votes.

It was also found that PDP ended up spending more money than DPT. The study was conducted in nine Dzongkhags and 18 constituencies of all regions.[13] Gembo Sithey who worked on the UNDP project, and now has a 'Centre for Research Initiative', a private research organization, said "I have limited my analysis to the data". His report does not contain the detailed opinion of national and international media which examined the various reasons for DPT's victory.[14]

In 2008, Bhutan got the most educated parliament in South Asia. The last two years seem to be the learning years how the power has to be shared between the elected members and people of their constituencies. There are high hopes that people will have more crucial role to play in the developmental process. No doubt that all the rules of the book are not applicable as far as Bhutan's democracy is concerned, but once again the holding of local elections to choose Mayors in four Dzongkhags Thromdes (town) of Gelephu, Phuentsholing, Samdrup Jongkhar and Thimphu on January 21st 2011 confirms the desire to involve people more and more into democratic process. It was identical with National elections wherein women voters played a vital role. Out of 4,269 people who, cast their votes 53.85 per cent (2,299 voters) were women while the rest 46.15 per cent (1,970 voters) were men.[15]

During the Thromde elections, 37 candidates contested the elections for the position of Mayor (Thrompon). The number of registered voters for the elections of Thrompons was only 8,462. The constituency size varied considerably between 6,226 and 614 voters for Thrompon elections, but for Tshogpa constituencies (Demkhongs) remained vacant, another 16 constituencies went uncontested, leaving voters with the choice to accept or reject the lone contender. Overall turn out was 50 per cent.

During the local government elections, a total of 2,185 candidates were nominated to contest 1,475 positions in the local governments, of which only 1,102 positions were filled, and 371 local government positions still vacant.

Nationwide, 347,938 people were eligible to vote of which 194,952 (56 per cent) turned out on polling day.[16]

When the four first elected Thrompons (Mayors) met His Majesty the fifth king Jigme Khesar Namgyel Wangchuck, he said that elected representatives and officials have a special commitment, purpose.They have to be just and good for the society. He further added that Bhutanese planners should not make mistakes which have occurred in the past. The lessons of growing towns in Bhutan are abundant in the challenges facing so many cities around the world, and in the immediate neighbourhood. He reminded them that they have got elected through people's support; therefore, in office, their dedication should be to the welfare, convenience and comfort of the people.

This reassures that democracy should not be mere elections, but about valuing human values and offices are just instruments to fulfil people's expectations. Effective local governments are a firm foundation on which an astute nation can be built.

Even after the onset of democracy, the monarchy is still omnipresent in Bhutan. For people do not want to forget what invaluable changes it had brought in their lives. It still is a symbol of unity for them. The drastic changes may not be overtly conspicuous. But slowly, the idea of empowering common man is seeping in, as Churchill said, "At the bottom of all tributes paid to democracy is the little man walking into a little booth with a little pencil making a little cross on a little bit of paper". Surely as Bhutanese vote for their elected representatives, they have a big responsibility for what decisions they are taking today will shape the destiny of Bhutan.

As Bhutan got ready for its second general elections in 2013, the Election Commission armed with the experience of the first general elections was hopeful of making the "election system technically sound for the elections in 2013". In an interview on October 2011 in the new Election Commission Office in Thimphu, the Chief Election commissioner Dasho Kunzang Wangdi told me that they want to introduce the system in checking, which exists in Nigeria where fingerprints of voters can be taken so that the voters can vote even if they have no document . He also said in keeping with the general elections, by July and August 2012, Capacity Building Programmes will be completed. Training Programmes such as the "BRIDGE" (Building Resources in Democracy, Governance and Election) will be implemented. The idea comes from U.N. and Australian Election Commission. In the process, they will have international level facilitators who will train the election officers who in turn will train the people. There were also plans to have a meeting with all the stake holders in BRIDGE policy, such as media on November 21-24 2011 and invite them for lasting four-five days session for discussion.

About the nature of election in 2013, he said, "It's not going to be smooth. We know that people know about the system now, they know the tricks. We are aware of it. We have to match up to that expectation".

He added, "Earlier we did not have access to other systems, we did not have the luxury to go to India. Now, we know how the world is doing it. We know the Indian system better now. We have our own system in place. So, we are better prepared." "In Bhutan, elections are same as in any other country. As nature is same everywhere, even India has natural challenges such as Siachen Glacier, Jammu and Kashmir, various rivers, but the election officers are doing a good job. We have tremendous respect for Indian election system. It is well managed. If we compare it to other countries, even America does not have such a good system."

"We have renewed our Memorandum of Understanding with India. There is a plan under way to establish an International Training Centre at New Delhi to train Election Officers. We are thinking of running bilateral programes with India", he added.

"We were able to implement that candidates, who stand for elections are graduates; because democracy was introduced in our country during peace time—while India had to do it after freedom struggle and they had to give place to their freedom fighters." He further added that the emphasis on two-party system has been because the country is still not ready to have a coalition government. Bhutan's constitution assures a sustainable government, but let's see what happens."

Responding to the question as to why women hesitate in joining politics in large numbers, he said, "Everything has to be done for the first time, even when our fourth king ascended the throne after his father's death, he was very young, he also must have thought that he had a great responsibility of leading a nation; then when the fifth king was crowned, he must have felt the same. So women also have to make a start. Earlier, because the infrastructure was not in place, we had no roads, one had to climb mountains, women could not compete in this field, but now I think they are making their mark." He reminisced, "Our fourth king travelled extensively throughout the country and he used to especially address girls and women to motivate them. He would always say that we must take advantage of this section of more than 50 per cent of our population."

Elaborating on the position of women in Bhutan, he said, "Bhutanese women are still dominant in traditional sphere. Women are the head of the families and in entire Bhutan—most of them, either elder daughter or wife inherit land. We don't have those dehumanising practices, we are more flexible in marriage system, household chores sharing, but we are adopting western culture and laws. For example the Tobacco Law, I remember as children, our parents and relatives used to smoke. We took tobacco leaves as gifts for our friends and relatives, but now you put innocent people, who are trying to make two ends meet behind bars. Another example is marriage age. If someone gets married young, they are put behind bars, while earlier people had married young and they contributed towards society. We must understand that our society is evolving, changes are automatically coming. The two of my colleagues (the two Election Commissioners) don't even touch meat. So, we must educate our society and tell people that tobacco is bad for health, that early marriage is not good rather than making laws blindly. Nowadays we are adopting "Fashionable Democracy" that we should do because someone else has done it.

On being asked that how educated Bhutanese electorate are, he responded, "We see in media reports that when people are asked whether they know about the election process; only few say that they don't know, most of them tell that election commission people had come and had explained to them about elections. We are employing each method to reach out to people. We are accessing young people to motivate their parents to vote. They should tell them that it is for their future and if the parents do not vote children should tell them that they are not doing enough for their future".

"We are planning to have a Resource Centre to educate people regarding election process. So, whatever the other institutions are not able to do, this Centre will fill the vacuum."

2013 elections also had many challenges which the Election Commission foresaw, such as ",vote Buying" which is rampant in many neighbouring countries including India and Thailand. This leads to the question 'Can a Bhutanese be bribed for his vote or will their religious and cultural background be strong enough to reject it?' The Chief Election Commissioner feels; whether future elections in Bhutan can be free and fair. Some controversial issues such as Constituency Development Grant and the state funding of parliamentary elections, campaigns of political parties and candidates being pushed through are the cause of concern. The second parliamentary elections will test the spirit of Bhutan's newly adopted constitutional institution.

General elections in 2013 were conducted in two rounds, the first ended on May 31, with four contesting political parties . The two parties with the biggest vote share –the Druk Phuensum Tshogpa, which received about 40 per cent of the vote, and the People's Democractic Party, which received just over 30 per cent contested the poll on July 13.[17]

The People's Democratic Party (PDP), led by Tshering Tobgay swept the elections to the General Assembly of Bhutan. It won 32 out of 47 seats, while the outgoing party, the Druk Phuensum Tshogpa (DPT), managed to retain the remaining seats. The results were declared on the website of the Election Commission of Bhutan.

The PDP which made huge gains in Nepali-speaking southern Bhutan, won only 12 seats in the May primaries. It secured 32.5 per cent of the votes, against outgoing DPT's 44.5 per cent.

Much of the credit for the PDP's victory was attributed to the dynamic and vocal Mr. Tobgay, a former civil servant who, even with just two seats in the outgoing assembly, put up a formidable and vocal opposition in the last five years. The focus of the party's election campaign in the last few days was the "strained India-Bhutan relations," where it laid the blame for withdrawl of subsidy on LPG and kerosene among other things, on the mishandling by the DPT.

Mr. Tobgay also did some smart informal mergers with the Druk Nyamrup Tshogpa (DNT), which lost the primaries by fielding seven of their strongest candidates. He crafted his party's campaign around exposing what he described as "the DPT's hollow claims on Gross National Happiness" aimed more at an international audience, which he alleged, did not deliver tangible benefits to people.

All except two of the cabinet ministers, who contested the elections retained their seats. The DPT won in Thimphu and Paro towns.

The polls were witnessed by India's Chief Election Commissioner VS Sampath, who was a special invitee and visited several polling stations. India provided some logistical support by gifting 4,130 electronic voting machines to Bhutan.[18]

Since the successful conduct of first democractic elections in 2008, Bhutan's experiment with democracy has seen a remarkable rise in the living standards of people, road connectivity, internet connectivity and basic health indicators. However, the political scene has been marked with corruption, which is on an upward swing. The Home Minister and the Speaker of Parliament were convicted on March 8 2013 on the charges of corruption. The High Court had upheld the verdict and the accused appealed to the Supreme Court as on June 15 2013.[19]

The apprehensions and misgiving in the minds of the people of Bhutan toward democracy are natural. A strong, stable and upcoming nation is their dream. It can come true, if the hard work undertaken eventually produces the desired results. But, the ultimate reality is that Bhutanese experiment with democracy has just begun. How it develops and takes shape, only time çan tell; whether it is the sharing of responsibility or simply acquiring political authority. The path is long and exhausting, but with sincere efforts, the people are likely to deliver and deliver fast.

References

1. Speeches by the fourth King compiled by Bhutan Times, p. 174.
2. Nishimizu Mieko, 'The Portrait of a Leader', The Centre for Bhutan Studies, 2008, p.113.
3. Election Bill of Kingdom of Bhutan, pp. 5-12.
4. European Union Election Observation Mission, The Kingdom of Bhutan 2008, Final Report, p. 25.
5. *Ibid*, pp. 10-13.
6. UNHRC General Comment, Number 25, Point 12, 'Information and Material about Voting should be available in minority languages'.
7. Ibid., pp. 25-26.
8. Civil Society Organisation Act.
9. *Ibid.*, p. 23.
10. PTI
11. Indian Express, New Delhi, February 07 2007.
12. *Ibid.*, December 17 2006
13. Kuensel, August 6, 2008.
14. *Ibid.*,
15. www.bhutantimes.bt, Tenzen Karma, Article 'Female Voters Dominate LG Elections', January 23 2011.
16. The Journalist,October, 02 2011, Dorji Tshering, 'The Journey Ahead', p. 32.

17. Ahmad Omair, 'Experiments With Democracy in Bhutan', India Ink, June 15, 2013.

18. 'Opposition scores handsome win in Bhutan', The Hindu online, Thimphu, July 13, 2013.

19. *Ibid.*, Ref 17.

6

Gross National Happiness

In today's world where materialistic achievements are preferred by nations and individuals alike, the victor may have been the economic growth; but moral life has seen a grave decline and is a matter of concern for those who care for man's development in terms of spiritual enhancement. An effort is being made to work upon new paradigms in development, so that the overall development is achieved, not partial. As the Gross Domestic Index soared, the Gross Human Index was a big casualty. Before the destruction could be beyond control, efforts are on to take care of the human resources. One such effort is made by a tiny South-Asian country Bhutan, where the inevitable development process was initiated in 1961 by the third king Jigme Dorji Wangchuck and hastened by the fourth king Jigme Singye Wangchuck. For him, the well being of the Bhutanese subjects was paramount, neither could development be ignored nor their well being. The result was the origin of the concept of Gross National Happiness- a philosophy which has its roots in the Buddhist Middle path Way.

This experiment attracted interest from world over and even today the debate continues whether happiness can be achieved along with materialistic development. What can be the ingredients which may help a citizen or state to develop the full potential of the individual and the nation?

Without the development both economic and moral, the society cannot progress, but in modern times, stress has always been on economic development—as nations which had supremacy through economics dominated the world. Example- USA and Japan. The effects of this mad race are evident to all and hence, an effort is being made to develop parallel parameters for development. And, in Bhutan this idea came to fore during the time of His Majesty Jigme Singye Wangchuck, who says that the ultimate purpose of the government is to promote the well being of its subjects. In his speeches, he stresses on prosperity and happiness. It was him who said, "Gross National Happiness is more important than Gross National Product".[1]

Gross National Happiness provides a holistic paradigm for social and economic transformation of the country, paying attention to selected, conventional aspects of development as well as non-conventional areas considered key to collective happiness and quality of life.

To enable the government to mainstream GNH into its development plans and policies, UNDP supported the Centre for Bhutan Studies (CBS) in the development of the GNH Index. The GNH Index comprised 72 indicators covering nine domains, which are: Psychological Well-Being, Time Use, Living Standard, Culture, Health, Education, Ecology, Good Governance, and Community Vitality. The nine domains were selected on normative grounds, because they are crucial to happiness and holistic development. Analysing the index allows GNH to be measured in policies and plans enabling grassroot change.[2]

Bhutan is one of those few countries, which were never colonised; hence they were spared the direct interference in culture. As a result, their cultural and spiritual life developed unevaded from external factors. But, a time came, when it could no longer carry an isolated life and the country was opened for modernisation and industrialisation. But, the Wangchuck dynasty took full care to minimise the influence on the Bhutanese society. They were also willing to learn lessons suffered by nations, which have whole-heartedly gone for change without thinking of its outcome. The immense benefits of science and technology could not be ignored. Hence, the need was to develop a strategy, which could balance spirituality with modernisation. With this, the concept of preservation of environment, sustainable development and preservation of culture came into being. These could only be achieved through good governance.

With modern education which lay emphasis on English and Dzongkha, spiritual and monastic education was also emphasised. Efforts are also being made that the curriculum blends Buddhist philosophy with scientific study. Buddhist monasteries and retreats strongly advocate the development process taking place and also contribute to the development of the new curricula.

The fourth king His Majesty Jigme Singye Wangchuck not only promulgated this theory to his nation, but also popularised it in international forums. His policy of decentralising power and emphasis that Bhutan is not a concern of one person but all its citizens reflected his desire to get the full support of his people.

Good Governance

Good governance was one of the main objectives of GNH. It was done through decentralisation and democratisation. The people of Bhutan were exhorted to become part of the decision-making.

In the words of the Honourable Ambassador of Bhutan to India—Lyonpo Dago Tshering, "The fourth pillar is strengthening the good governance. This we call the golden pillar. We believe nothing could be achieved unless we have good governance; unless we have transparency; unless we entrust the needed responsibility on the administrators and unless there is total revolution of total decentralisation of power. This is the part and parcel of strengthening of good governance."[3]

Bhutan aims to establish "a system of governance that promotes well-being and happiness of its citizens." Good governance is characterised by the pursuit of integrity, efficiency, accountability and transparency as well as people's participation in the decision making process.[4] The ongoing process of decentralisation and the devolution of power from the king has been identified with good governance and the king himself acknowledged the importance of creating a democratic political system and institutions to allow for increased popular participation. It strives for equitable access to public services and goods.[5]

In 1991, His Majesty said again that we have reached the district level, but most of the people live in rural areas, so we have to reach them now and he established a Block Evaluation Council, that is essentially Block Development Council. So, what happens is that at the block level they elect their own representatives, their own council and determine their own priorities of development. They determine what needs to be done in and around their village. Is it water supply they want? Once they have listed it, the job is distributed and the central government is to provide the support and raise the needed resources to enable them implement the programme they have enlisted and approved at the level of district authority and thereafter at the national level by the National Assembly. So, ultimately what happens is that they are responsible for planning, for implementing, for maintenance of own programmes at the rural level. This is initial part and parcel of the devolution and evaluation of democracy in Bhutan.[6]

General elections were held in March 2008. The government was constituted and met for the first time. The king's response was:

"The introduction of democracy is not for the benefit of a few political parties and politicians. It is for Bhutan and it must serve the nation long after we are gone. We must keep this in mind and begin the work of ensuring its success."[7]

The king further added that democracy in Bhutan was not based on any other country, but designed to fulfil the aspirations of Bhutanese people. He told them that general elections were successful. "In democracy, there are no winners and losers. If democracy succeeds, the nation wins."[8] The constitution of Bhutan was discussed in the Parliament and signed on July 18, 2008. As parliamentary democracy opens up opportunity for political power, monarchy will remain the national institution that transcends all divisions and functions as the most powerful unifying force. This is Bhutanese uniqueness. The king's ability to establish personal relationship with the people and view them as members of his own family is another unique part. This was rightly said by the king Jigme Khesar Namgyal Wangchuck during his coronation address:

"Throughout my reign, I will never rule you as a king. I will protect you as a brother and serve you as a son. I shall give you everything and keep nothing; as the king of Buddhist nation, my duty is not only to ensure your happiness today but to create the fertile ground from which you may gain the fruits of spiritual pursuit and attain good *karma*. This is how I shall serve you as king."[9]

As governance in Bhutan is evolving an effort is being made to involve local communities in decision-making. The role of private sector cannot be ignored, neither can the role of religious institutions be sidelined, which have till now been means of spiritual and cultural development. The role of NGOs needs to be expanded, so that social development to groups which need special attention be given, for example old people, women and children.

The development process now includes the Dzongkhag and the Gewog administration. In this way, people are able to assume greater responsibility for development of their communities and to take care of the questions and problems which affect their lives and their families. The new system calls for high professionalism from civil service as the managing process and future planning is becoming more challenging.

Human society is synonymous with corruption. Bhutan had to fight with the growing corruption through the Anti-Corruption Commission. Lyonchhen Jigmi Y Thinley, Prime Minister of Bhutan put the stance of the government on corruption very strongly, "We cannot and must not allow the cancer of corruption to destroy our democracy in its infancy... It is important for those who have profited from corruption till now to know that this government is serious about 'zero tolerance' on corruption and that it is sharpening its tools."[10]

Preservation of Cultural Heritage

Bhutan believes that preservation of rich cultural heritage is critical to its very survival as a nation state. King Jigme Singye Wangchuck emphasized on many occasions the significance of culture to Bhutan's identity; particularly in view of its location between the two most populous and powerful nations.

In a *Kasho,* he issued to the Special Commission (established in 1986), the king commanded, "I am saddened that our people copy the culture of other countries despite the existence of our distinct culture and etiquette. If we do not think now, we cannot show our religion and culture to the world in the future. This, as you know will affect our sovereignty."[11]

From the time of his kingship, budget was allocated for preservation of ancient monuments, temples and dzongs. Hundreds of monasteries were renovated including Punakha Dzong and Taktshang Lhakhang after fire outbreaks and saw their original splendour restored and surpassed. Cultural preservation was a conscious effort undertaken in view of the impact of modernisation.

Today, culture is developing into an industry by itself—be it architecture, bridge engineering, thangka and thongdrel works, sword making and pottery. Cultural industries have a great potential for generating income through the utilisation of cultural assets and production of knowledge – based goods and services. Bhutan's rich cultural resources provide a major opportunity for the creation of employment and poverty reduction. The promotion of cultural industries has been accorded high priority by the government and is expected to generate substantial social and economic returns as well as contribute to the preservation of the country's rich cultural heritage.[12]

Effort is being made to impart education and make educational curriculum in such a way, which blends Bhutanese point of view with scientific study, for the younger generation is the product of the education that is imparted to them. In today's time, where they are growing up with higher value of material goods and possessions, it is imperative that the negative aspects of modern development are checked through right information and emphasising the need to conserve and protect the historical and religious sites in the country.

Promotion of Dzongkha—the national language, which is still developing in Bhutan is done through the Dzongkha Development Commission. More and more translations of literary works should be done from other languages to Dzongkha.

Sustainable Environment

The natural environment, particularly forest was not considered just a resource base; it's a living entity. The Forest and Nature Conservation Act was passed in 1995. National Forestry Master Plan 1996-2010 was formed, National Environment Commission was set up, National Bio-diversity Action Plan was made operational and Environment Assessment Act was passed in 2000. The largest logging organisation, Geddu Wood Manufacturing Corporation was closed down in 1995 owing to serious environment consequence. Its operation in the form of 'slash and burn agriculture' known as Tseri cultivation was also abolished. The National Forest Policy of 1974 stated that Bhutan must maintain 60 per cent of forests for all times, the present cover is about 75 per cent.

Bhutan's indigenous conservation ethic provided a major input for "Gross National Happiness" and was perhaps the most consistently applied aspect of the concept. As early as 1961, the National Assembly resolved that trees in the ground should be exempted from taxation to discourage felling "in keeping with the Government's conservation policy." The same rationale led to legislation such as the Forest Act of 1969 (and the Land Act of 1979), which contains the peculiar provision that the government owns all trees, including those growing on private land. In 1974, the preservation policy was underscored by declaring vast sanctuaries, parks and forest reserves as protected areas. Today, protected areas constitute about 26 per cent of Bhutan's territory. Elsewhere, Bhutan never exploited its natural resources on grounds of commercial profitability.[13]

Bhutan figures on the ten global hot-spots of the world. In 2005, the United Nations Environment Programme awarded 'Champions of the Earth Award' to the king and people of Bhutan.[14] In order to minimise the problems of uncontrolled tourism, the number of tourists had been managed through a policy guideline regulated tourist tariff. A tourist can only travel in groups and through a registered tour operator. From 20 people in 1974, the number of tourists crossed 21,094 in 2007 generating record revenue of USD 29 million. Today, it is one of the highest earners of foreign exchange.[15]

Through the Royal Society for the Protection of Nature (RSPN), UNDP supports the implementation of a targeted programme on conservation, education and advocacy through a network of 100 school nature clubs and local support groups. As part of this programme, a nature club activity handbook and a nature club management handbook have been published to assist clubs and local support groups to initiate conservation activities and enhance environmental education. Through action grants, schools and communities across the country have implemented activities that address local environmental problems such as protection of drinking water sources, sustainable land management and solid waste management.

Access to sustainable modern energy services for all is an important goal that the RGoB (Royal Government of Bhutan) aims to achieve by 2013. However, a significant number of rural households (12 per cent) will still remain off-grid given the rugged terrain and scattered settlements. It is therefore, important for RGoB to ensure this segment of the population has access to clean, sustainable energy sources. Through GEF (Global Environment Facility) financing, UNDP supported the establishment of a pilot community micro-hydro project for Sengor community under Saling Gewog in Mongar. The micro-hydro plant, commissioned in May 2007, provides electricity to some 57 households benefiting 300 people in Sengor and represents an innovative community micro-hydro delivery model, that is currently being replicated in two other remote areas of the country.

Bhutan is one of the very few countries in the world with net greenhouse gas sequestration capacity largely due to vast forest cover and use of clean renewable energy. However, the negative impacts of climate change can easily undermine the development gains achieved so far and compromise with Bhutan's prospects of achieving the Millennium Development Goals (MDGs) by 2015. While Bhutan is well on track to achieve the environmental targets, conservation is becoming increasingly challenging as the country opens up to meet the new development needs of a growing and modernising population. Sound environmental management is therefore critical for poverty reduction and achievement of the MDGs.[16]

Although Bhutan wants to preserve its forests, the recent trends have shown the topography of Thimphu and Paro to have changed due to unrestrained construction being carried out in the valley. Such changes can be observed in Wandgue Phodrang district also where the major Punatsangchu Hydro power projects are underway. Development cannot be used as an excuse to change the topography, which in turn will result in the change of environment. Bhutan cannot opt for unplanned development, which may cause some of its areas being deprived of natural cover.

The question now arises- will the government be able to take decisions against the developmental activities which violate the basic policy of forest conservation? And to what extent?

Happiness-the Desired Goal

The concept of self happiness as practised in Bhutan stems from the Buddhist philosophy. To quote His Holiness the Dalai Lama, "If in day to day life you lead a good life, honestly, with love, with compassion, with less selfishness, then automatically it will lead to *nirvana*." At the individual level, we should practise the ten positive deeds and the sixteen human values/moral disciplines and try to contribute towards the gross happiness, and at the same time help ourselves. To want happiness at the individual level, these are some of our responsibilities.

His Majesty the fourth king Jigme Singye Wangchuck has often mentioned in his speeches that the future of Bhutan lies in the hands of younger generations. In short, he has always emphasised the role of every individual Bhutanese in the everyday life. At the family level, Bhutanese have a very strong joint family system, where they live in extended families and share the responsibilities and love both. It's a collective effort of each member, which binds sometimes three generations together.[17]

Even in rural Bhutan emphasis is on togetherness and the value of education is appreciated. Even if one member of the family is educated or migrates to a city, they always help other members of the family to get educated. In Bhutan, people take pride that at least one member of the family is related to monastic order. Bhutanese are reserve people but amongst themselves they are fun-loving, easy going and visit each other on holidays and festivals. It is a common sight for large Bhutanese families along with the head of the family having picnics or outings on a public holiday. I witnessed such gathering, when I was in Paro at *Guru Padmasambhava's* birthday in June 2010 and in Tsirang in October 2011 when the Buddhist relics arrived in the district from India. Nearly every Bhutanese made it a point to pay obesience to them.

Although, the urban migration is leading to the disintegration of joint family system, the elderly in the family are considered as an asset and are given a respected place and treated with compassion. The social problems which ail the society such as drug abuse, teenage pregnancies, alcoholism, HIV AIDS, can be controlled, if the family can give an atmosphere of security, understanding and love. Till now, the basic unit of families have contributed positively, but now the challenges they face are both new and varied.

The next level is the community-level co-operation, where many developmental projects are being taken up, such as schools, rural roads and electrification. Bhutan is a country sparsely populated. The distribution of population is also very uneven. Some areas may be in fertile land, others fall into barren and unproductive land. Life may be difficult under such circumstances. An effort is made to survive under the limited resources available to develop and share within the community. The dependence on each other is a reason why one sees the kind of helpfulness they have for each other; especially at the village level, where it is not what you give that counts, but the intention with which it is given. Community tea and meals are the common sights in Bhutan. Even the Royal family members, when they travel, share meals with villagers and villagers in turn pay their respect in organising a grand welcome.

At the regional level, people are made aware of responsibilities and the plans and strategies are drawn after taking suggestions and knowing what the particular region requires. The government in Bhutan calls for positive contribution from its population for the development as well as fraternity feeling amongst them.

Karma Gayleg, in his paper 'The Characteristics and Levels of Happiness in the Context of the Bhutanese Society' [Gross National Happiness and Development, Centre for Bhutan Studies, p. 551] says, "In Bhutan, at the Dzongkhag level, we have the *Dzongdag* and his team of officials who guide the people in the communities in shaping their future. Unlike the past, the development process is now fully decentralised, which is due to the selfless vision of His Majesty. The management concept is bottom-top planning and execution with minimal intervention from the centre. The communities set their own priorities, targets, and goals according to needs and have more chance of influencing their own happiness/ or unhappiness."

In Bhutan, looking from every angle, we see the ingredients for true happiness are always present. The people have faith in leadership and leaders have altruistic attitude towards people. This tradition has been deeply rooted as a direct result of precious *Buddha Dharma* over the past centuries. For example, Bhutanese fondly refer to "*Tha Damtsi* and

Ley Jumdrey," which loosely translated means the regard and respect for the elders, leaders, neighbours and others and '*Ley Jumdrey*' means the unshakeable faith in the cause and effect or the *karmic* consequences. So, the people strive to achieve happiness as an effect, not only in this present life, but in the future lives to come. This is why even at the lay person's level, Bhutanese try to practise the *Dharma* or the positive attributes."

At the national level, the policy of GNH is the guiding parameter towards the government and the people. All the policies and decisions have to cater to what is good for people and the country at large. The welfare of all is taken into account and emphasis is laid that while the government makes people-friendly programmes and policies which will make easier and healthier environment, the people should also do their duties and should have respect for traditional values. Any new decision should be judged by its short and long-term gains. The policy is to adopt the middle path and not rush for development, which may not have the desired result as envisaged for the nation.

At the global level, Bhutan has always promulgated the idea of a global village with co-operation. It has played a positive role in the South-Asian Association for Regional Co-operation. The country has strived for good relations with neighbouring countries. Its effort is always to play a constructive role in the development process.

The GNH Index

In keeping with the result based planning approach of the Tenth plan, efforts were undertaken to develop an appropriate development measure that will capture the essence of GNH and help in tracking national progress towards meeting this overall long-term development objective. The GNH Index is that critical evaluation tool for the result based planning framework of the Tenth plan and future plans to ensure that development truly contributes to the achievement of GNH.

The GNH indicators considered were those designed to be measures of specific dimensions, which make up the GNH model. For instance, demographic indicators allow an analysis of the distribution of GNH dimensions across different social and demographic groups in the country. This includes various age and gender groups, occupational and employment clusters, educational backgrounds, types of households, language groupings and geographical areas. The casual indicators considered were those factors affecting the performance of GNH status indicators. For instance, the general ratings of central government performance were broken down into more specific components allowing detailed analysis of factors affecting general government performance ratings.

These indicators are broadly classified into various domains relating to the areas of psychological well-being, cultural diversity and resilience, education, health, time use, good governance, community vitality, ecological diversity and resilience and economic living standards. These areas and their various indicators/indices were determined based on a pilot survey and a National GNH Survey conducted between 2006 and 2008.

The composite GNH Index is to be aggregated from these indices and indicators from among the nine domains with appropriate weighting. These indices and indicators include a wide range of factors with a significant bearing on individual and collective happiness and include the mental health index, family relationship index, financial security indicator, healthy days per month indicator, body mass index, education level indicator, local air and water pollution indicators, house ownership indicator, human rights indicator and government performance index.

Given the nature of human happiness and well-being, the evolution of GNH policies and strategies and the index must follow necessarily a dynamic, inclusive and open-ended process that consider the relative importance of different variables and factors of happiness and well-being that may or may not be relevant to Bhutanese society at a particular point of time.[18]

Bhutan in the Year 2020

Bhutan 2020: A vision for Peace, prosperity and happiness is a twenty-year perspective strategy, which sets the preferred direction where Bhutan wants to be in the year 2020 starting from the base year —2000. To reinforce the guiding direction for the Tenth plan, it would be useful to recall briefly some of the desirable long term outcomes for the

Kingdom envisioned in the Bhutan 2020 vision. The Tenth plan period straddles after all the critical half-way point on to the year 2020 and presents an opportune time to refresh and recollect that special vision and assess—what needs to be done to accomplish the milestone goals targeted. In particular, the *Vision 2020* development targets set to be achieved by the end of the plan period are highlighted in the later section on Tenth plan targets.

The *Vision 2020* projects that Bhutan will emerge to become a respected and active member of the international community and a country recognised for its role in promoting peace and stability in the region. It envisages that Bhutan's sovereignty and borders will be firmly secure, based on constructive and mutually beneficial relationship with neighbours rather than on military capability. The vision further anticipates that Bhutan will have demonstrated to the world that it is entirely possible to embrace the benefits of modernisation without being overwhelmed by accompanying negative influences, while proudly maintaining a well recognised distinct identity, valued and respected. In terms of societal outcome, the vision visualises the emergence of a compassionate, tolerant, self-confident and egalitarian Bhutanese society with its people living in harmony and unity preferably imbued with a common sense of purpose and destiny.

Economically, the vision pictures that hydro-power led development and growth will have helped the country achieve a high degree of self-reliance with much of the responsibility for financing of development in its own hands. Bhutan by 2020 is expected to sustain rising social-sector investments, meet growing physical infrastructure development requirements and stimulate further expansion and growth in economic activity to continually raise the standard of living and quality of life.

The availability of low-cost hydro-power energy and resource endowments deriving from electricity export revenue are anticipated to help transform the industrial landscape in Bhutan with the development of wide range and host of clean industries and high-technology enterprises. Exports to international markets of high-value Bhutanese niche and eco-based products are projected to contribute significantly to the national economy and gain notable prominence for the quality.

In terms of the natural environment, the *Vision 2020* is optimistic that the natural environment and resource endowments will still be richly intact, with 60 per cent of the country forested and sizeable tracts of protected national parks and reserves harbouring an incredibly rich bio-diversity, the envy of many nations. The vision anticipates the environmental conservation approach will be dynamic rather than static and will not merely treat natural resources as something to be preserved but as an immense asset that can also be sustainably and wisely utilised for socio-economic development.

Bhutan in 2020 is expected have to not only its rich culture still vibrant, alive and clearly visible in Bhutanese lives, but will be richly infused with contemporary relevance and meaning. The vision perceives the latter to be particularly important for young people. It envisages that country's rich traditions, values, ideals and beliefs ideally live on in the minds of Bhutanese youths-referred to appropriately in the vision as cultural custodians, and become a positive force and source of inspiration for them. In terms of activities, the vision placed a high priority towards the active promotion of traditional arts and crafts, architectural styles and national language and the conservation and protection of historical monuments, sites and artifacts, while improving accessibility to rich legacy. The inventorying and recording of cultural legacy, including the rich oral traditions and folklore were viewed as being very important.

In terms of good governance outcome to be attained by 2020, the *Vision* anticipated full development of country's governance and legal institutions and the emergence of a system of jurisprudence based on a body of law respected by all. It also foresaw that these developments ultimately would give rise to new dimensions of existing traditional concepts of representation and democracy in the country. The *Vision* however did not quite anticipate that it would happen as early as this, the vast extent or the noble manner of its initiation through the ongoing democratisation processes and the formulation and adoption of a written constitution. *The Vision* further envisaged the ongoing decentralisation processes would be completed by 2020 with local governments fully and effectively empowered and responsible for many of the development planning and management functions. Through this, it is expected that the

Bhutanese people would genuinely "own" the development process, helping thereby fulfil both long term national goals and local aspirations and priorities.[19]

Conclusion

In Bhutan, the desire to change has given birth to unique situation, where traditional values remained at the cost of modern development. The third king, who envisaged the developmental process in Bhutan where life as described by Thomas Hobbes was considered "solitary, poor, nasty, brutish and short", he weighed the short and long-term gains of policies, which were to be unfolded for the people of Bhutan. In the late 1960s, Bhutan opted for a developmental policy which was considered on conventional patterns with rapid modernization. The third king had described his goal as "making the people prosperous and happy."

His son-the fourth king Jigme Singye Wangchuck declared in the first year of his reign, "Our country's policy is to consolidate our sovereignty to achieve economic self-reliance, prosperity and happiness for our country and people".

The people and their well-being became a matter of concern for the ruler, who thought it his duty to take care of the children's education, health and even the spiritual well-being of the people. The four pillars of GNH- the promotion of environmental preservation, cultural preservation, equitable economic development and good governance do include virtually the developmental and administrative activities, which are taking place in Bhutan. In placing the developmental activities under the umbrella of GNH and even naming the Planning Commission as the Gross National Happiness Commission, the effort is to have a balance and harmony and a country which can manage its assets judiciously and fully keeping in tune with the predominant Buddhist philosophy.

Although Bhutan has offered to the world an alternative development paradigm, there are certain areas which need to be focused upon. Is development directly linked with happiness, for, material prosperity does not guarantee bliss? Individual happiness is linked to the security, mental peace, health and a sense of belongingness. While development has an entirely different end, it does not certainly assure human well-being. The disintegrating joint family system is going to be a big challenge as the children growing up in nuclear families may not be able to understand the essence of their past. Life in Thimphu and Paro has already undergone a change in the last few years.

Even the environmental preservation will be a daunting task. To resist encroachment in the areas, which may offer lucrative gains in the form of hydro-electric power would be challenging. The unemployment problem in the youth may today assume big proportion in coming time and it would be difficult to sustain without giving them proper work. Some time back, most of the Bhutanese were the products of traditional social system, but in today's time, the situation is different. The access to television and internet is certainly changing their perception.

An effort to weave intricately the traditions, values and modernisation can succeed only if both intermingle honestly. There should not be any scope for rigidity for the outer influences will be inevitable, but it will be up to the government and the people to adapt themselves to the changes, striking a balance between tradition and modernity.

References

1. Michael, Rutland, Bhutan: From Medieval to the Millennium, London, 1999, pp. 284-294.
2. Towards Gross National Happiness: A Journey with UNDP, Annual Report, 2008-2009, p. 7.
3. Inaugural speech of Ambassador of Bhutan to India His Excellency Lyonpo Dago Tshering as delivered on 24th Oct 2008 in Malviya Hall, University of Lucknow on the occasion of National Seminar on Bhutan.
4. Royal Government of Bhutan, 9 five year plan, Thimphu, 2000, p. 22.
5. Bhutan Times, 2nd April, 2008.
6. Op. cit., ref. 3.
7. *Ibid.*
8. Bhutan Today, November 8, 2008.

9. Tenth five year plan, 2008-13, Vol. I, Main document.

10. The speech of Lyonchhen Jigmi Y Thinley, Prime Minister of Bhutan, at the National Consultative Meeting on National Anti-Corruption Strategic Framework, March 26, 2009.

11. Kinga, Sonam, Polity, kingship and democracy, Thimphu, 2009, pp. 266-67.

12. Towards Gross National Happiness: A Journey with UNDP, Annual Report, 2008-09, p. 22.

13. Quoted in Gross national Happiness, Centre for Bhutan Studies, p. 38.

14. Op. cit., ref. 9.

15. Royal Government of Bhutan, Nineth Five Year Plan, Thimphu, 2000, p. 95.

16. Towards Gross National Happiness: A Journey with UNDP, Annual Report, 2008-09, pp.16-18.

17. Tenth Five Year Plan 2008-2013, Volume 1: Main Document, Gross National Happiness Commission, Royal Government of Bhutan, p. 18.

18. *Ibid,* pp.19-21.

19. 25 Years of Enthronement, Gross National Happiness, Centre for Bhutan Studies, p. 28.

7

Civil Society and Laws of the Land

PART-I

Man's efforts to organize himself gave birth to the concept of civil society. Till the end of the 18th century, this term was referred to the state or political society. In 18th and 19th century, civil society has served many purposes. While activists in several countries have used civil society to fight against military regimes and totalitarian states, policy makers included in development agendas made it the main focus of society. According to Gordan White, who wrote in 'Democratisation' journal in 1994, civil society is: "An intermediate associational realm situated between the state and the family, populated by organisations, which are separate from the state, enjoy autonomy in relation to the state and are formed voluntarily by members of the society to protect or extend their interests or values".[1]

According to Havel, "Though state has certain social responsibilities in areas such as social welfare, public health, education or the protection of environment, its role as the guaranteed custodian of such functions does not mean that it should be the only one to carry them out directly. Schools, hospitals, environmental offices, and other similar institutions could have the status of non-profit organisations, and while not part of the state as one of its formal agencies, the state could merely possess certain rights and commitments to these kinds of institutions. In this manner, civil society would also include the existence of a system whereby the state delegates certain functions that it would normally carry out to other entities, accompanied by an appropriate system of controls and support for such entities."[2]

The most appropriate definition is of CIVICUS[3] which states that civic society is, "the sphere of institutions, organisations, networks and individuals (and their values) located between the confines of the family, the state and the market, in which people associate voluntarily to advance common interest".

In Bhutan, civil society may not have developed in terms of what it is understood in western countries, but Bhutan has its own unique historical, social and political circumstances which have led to its indigenous development. In present context, when the country is witnessing a rapid social, political and economic transformation, the concept of civil society gains more importance. In its official document *Vision 2020*, it has reflected, "Our development has been able to draw upon strong tradition of self-reliance, self-sufficiency, self-help and self-organization. Our highly dispersed population developed over centuries into tightly-knit and self-regulating communities, bound together by unwritten laws, practices and customs that governed kinship and community relations and the use of such shared resources as irrigation water and grazing land. Without this tradition of cooperation and compromise, communities would have been unable to cope with threat and adversity or, indeed, to have survived in the harsh conditions that characterise most parts of our nation. While development agencies emphasise the importance of local self-reliance, it has been a basic fact of life in our mountain kingdom for centuries."[4]

Bhutan, before the 17th century was dominated by small rulers, who were constantly at war with each other. It was under a theocratic rule, which ended with the foundation of hereditary monarchy in 1907 by the Wangchuck dynasty. During the theocratic regime, there was a close association between monastic community and common people. It was the ordinary people (peasants), who furnished the monastic life. According to Dasho Rigzin Dorji, "Monasteries (met) their expenses from their assets and estates and the support of the general public, who apart from donations in cash and kind, handed over the first produce of their crops to the monks of their locality".[5]

1907 saw a new phase in state-people relationship. Ordinary people could look forward to stability, justice and protection from the state, while they served the monarchial institution with loyalty, dedication and gave their constant support to the dual system of state through taxes and customary work force contribution. A well developed civil society in industrialised countries take into account six key characteristics: independence and autonomy, immunity from excessive state interference, self consciousness, strong middle class with economic liberty, alienation from states' belief system or ideology, and rationality and civility.[6]

If the above parameters are applied on Bhutan, the picture of civil society in Bhutan can be considered as poor, but Bhutan has developed its own social, cultural and economic institutional network which includes the autonomous local institutions. According to Karma Galay, "Individuals in any particular village share many interests simply by virtue of the fact that they are inhabitants of the same village. Consequently strong sense of cooperation and independence among households or individuals historically prevails in the villages. Although, it is often said that this sense of solidarity is due to Buddhist beliefs, and other factors determine their solidarity. The way in which the village resources are managed and the way the festivals and ceremonies are organised also determine their solidarity".[7]

The practices and entities of civil society can be broadly characterised under two sections:

(i) Village and Community-Based Self-Help Practices and Institutions: This section basically covers traditional practices that continue to be carried out within the community; other local level initiatives that receive some form of support from local government sectors and their continuity in relation to community initiatives receiving local government support; and some other initiatives taken 'privately'.

(ii) Formal Non-Governmental Entities: This section covers the various formal institutions that may be associated with contemporary civil society institutions, which have developed in relation to increasing needs and changes taking place in Bhutanese society.

His Majesty the fourth King, in his speech on his Coronation Day, Jun 3, 1974, emphasised the importance of civil society in the development of the nation:

> "As far as you, my people, are concerned, you should not adopt the attitude that whatever is required to be done for your welfare will be done entirely by the government. On the contrary, a little effort on your part will be much more effective than a great deal of effort on the part of the government. If the government and people can join hands and work together with determination, our people will achieve prosperity and our nation will become strong and stable.[8]

Civil society in Bhutan is seen as a relationship in which common interests of people and government can be achieved. The Royal Government of Bhutan visualises the role of people as central to bring about effective development:

> No *development effort can succeed without people's cooperation and commitment and effective development can not be only top to down process. While the government would give the lead in the overall direction of development and provide resources and technical inputs, which are beyond the capacity of the people, plans would have to be formulated in consultation with the people in order that these plans reflect felt-needs and execution is within the capabilities of people. It is the government's conviction that only when these conditions are satisfied and effectively pursued that the benefits of development would actually reach all the sections of population leading to an increased distributional equity. (Planning Commission, 1981)*

Related Social Networks and Social Help System

Before 1961, Bhutan consisted of self-reliance and self-subsistence communities possessing well defined community-based rules and institutions to facilitate the use of common resources.[9] Because of geographical constraints and lack of transport infrastructure and absence of market economy, Bhutan had to rely on social networks and communal self-reliance to build up socio-economic system. Cooperation was related to farming and harvest practices. In two seasons, it is common to see members of each household spend a number of days helping families in the field. This help is extended from house to house. In spring, which is the fourth month of Bhutanese calendar, it is common to hear that members of the household have gone for *Chola* (paddy plantation), either in their own fields or own people's fields. And then in autumn, (9th month of Bhutanese calendar), it's time for harvest. These people are out again in fields for *Jala* (paddy harvest). The host usually gives breakfast, lunch and dinner for those who help from within the same village.

Dependence in times of Hardship

During times of sickness or death, every household in the village helps in same way, be it with supply of labour or in form of cash or other resources such as food and grains. In most villages of Haa, everyone would mourn and care for a death of someone in a village. Even the most significant community event would come to halt, if it coincides with such sad happening. As a way of paying respect to the dead soul and consoling the mourning family, a member from every household would go to see the bereaved family taking two drey (measure of Volume, equivalent to 1.6 kg) of rice and a bottle of ara (home-made whiskey). Nowadays, fellow-villagers would also donate money (Nu. 100-200) to reduce the financial burden of the bereaved family. Material contributions are substantiated by free labour service from the fellow-villagers in organizing funeral and other death rituals. Man help in collecting firewood, passing message to relatives of the deceased living outside the village and making logistic arrangements for the ritual performers, while women would help the bereaved family in several domestic works. Even old people would come to chant prayers near the corpse and its effigy for days and night.[10]

Religious Activities

Bhutanese culture is based on Buddhist principle of inter-dependencies, therefore development of human being with compassion and help to others is important. Dalai Lama has said, "Human happiness is interdependent. Once own successful or happy future is related to that of others. Therefore, helping each other or having consideration of their rights and needs is actually not only for one's own responsibility, but a matter of one's own happiness."[11] Ordinary people interact with local monastic communities to organize religious activities. They build and renovate temples and support spiritual pursuits. There is a tradition of *Sonam* (by which Gomchen and monks living in their mountain hermitages come to villages for alms) in practice even today. Seasonal Buddhist rituals and ceremonies are organised in different villages through collective sponsorships. In Bhutan, a society is judged as good or bad based on the tendencies and capabilities to organise the religious activities. 'The idea of a good society is based on a communitarian philosophy. It assumes social definitions of the good and that a well-functioning (good) society requires a core of substantive (rather than merely procedural) shared values which define not only the public sphere but also private proper behaviour'.[12]

Community Resource Management

Bhutanese have been managing natural resources and other common property successfully through their traditional institution of community resource management. These give people a sense of ownership, identity and laid the foundation to several new community-based organisations.

Forest Resource Management

Rural communities have been collectively managing their forest. The local procedures made along ensure the proper use of natural resources such as timber, firewood, pasture and non-woods products. They also resolve intra-village conflicts over resource use. Some years before the introduction of the Forest Act of 1969 and the Nature Conservation Act of 1995, traditional management of forest and sustainable harvest of natural resources was strong and effective in Segye. Many elderly people claim that rural people were adequately conscious of the importance of preserving forests surrounding their village. There existed an institution of *resungpa* (*re*-forest and *sungpa*-guard) – a person appointed by the community to look after the forest and the one who would also ensure sustainable use of forest resources like firewood, timber, fodder and bamboo. He was responsible to control activities like exessive extraction of wood, bamboo and grasing in the forest.

A system of *mesungpa* (*me*-fire and *sungpa*-guard) in which a person would be appointed to protect the forest from fire and mobilise the community labour in case of fire accident was so common. *Mesungpa* would be appointed from among the villagers every year. He was not entitled to any kind of remuneration, but exempted from tax and obligatory community labour contribution. People in this village claim these institutions of self-management were weakened after trained foresters took away the roles of looking after forests.[13]

Contemporary Associations

The first such association to be formed was National Youth Association of Bhutan.[14] It was formed by a group of young civil servants in 1973. This association was intended specifically to provide a radio broadcast in English on the weekends. It became a part of The Department of Information and Broadcasting in 1979 and thus was absorbed into mainstream government organisations.

The second contemporary association was formed in 1978 by a group of civil servants.[15] They made contributions and conducted a *tshechu* (religious ceremony performed on auspicious days) at the Memorial Chorten in Thimphu on the 15th day of the 4th month of the Bhutanese calendar. The first tshechu stimulated the group to decide to make the *tshechu* an annual event. As the group was engaged only in organisation of *tshechus*, it came to be known as *Tshechu Tshogpa* (an association or a committee).

There are several non-government organizations (NGOs) and semi-government organisations in Bhutan interacting with the state as well as society in designing and implementing development projects. Their participation is more in areas such as environmental protection, women's development, social health and well-being, cultural preservation and youth development. They work through parallel or supportive projects, although they work according to the laws made by the state. The following are the examples of NGOs playing a major role in Bhutan:

National Commission on Women and Children an autonomous agency was established in 2004, and aims to fight for the rights of women and children. In 2004 during the first National Assembly a Women and Children Committee was established as one of the standing committees of National Assembly. It is headed by Hon. Karma Lhamo. It aims to empower women by scrutinising existing policies, legislations directly affecting women and children. The key functions of this organisation are to co-ordinate and monitor periodic country reports to treaty bodies 'Convention on Elimination of Discrimination against Women' (CEDAW) and 'Convention on the Rights of the Child' (CRC), build and strengthen relationships with organisations working for women and children within and outside the country, monitor implementation of activities under CRC and CEDAW and other international and regional conventions signed by Bhutan and assist in the mobilisation of resources for agencies working for women and children in the country. The current projects include ending violence against women, protection and promotion of rights of women and children in Bhutan and moving forward on gender empowerment and protection. The motto of the organisation is "Working together, Working Better" for women and children.[16]

Youth Development Fund established in 1999 by Her Majesty Ashi Tshering Pem Wangchuck, aims to enable Bhutanese youth to realise their full potential as productive citizens of this world through sustained financial support.

Tarayana Foundation established in 2003 by Her Majesty Ashi Dorji Wangmo Wangchuck aims to help the poor rural communities become self-reliant and self-sufficient through the initiation and establishment of income generating activities.

RENEW which has been mentioned above means Respect, Educate, Nurture and Empower Women and was established in 2004 by Her Majesty Ashi Sangay Choden Wangchuck. It deals with violence and tackles major issues facing contemporary Bhutanese women. Its aim is to provide relief and empowerment to disadvantaged women and girls. They have established Happy Homes for women who have no place to go.

All these organisations' goals are to support vulnerable individuals and to achieve greater social equality.

Handicraft Emporium in Thimphu

The Handicraft Emporium was established in 1971 with the command of the third King of Bhutan. In the beginning, it functioned as an extension of the Cottage Industry Division under the Department of Trade and Industry. One of its main objectives was to conserve and promote the traditional arts and crafts of the country by setting up an organised marketing channel for various cottage industry products. It was named Handicrafts Development Corporation under the National Council for Social and Cultural Affairs. It became an independent commercial, self-supporting and semi-autonomous organisation in 1975. It operated under the administrative control of the Department of Trade and Industry.

The Ministry of Trade and industry took it over in 1985 and the board of directors managed its affairs. In 1986, the board of directors was dissolved under the directives of the government and reverted to its status as a semi-autonomous corporation subject to the government financial and service rules. It was also registered under the Companies Act of the kingdom of Bhutan, 1989. A new board of directors was constituted to run the affairs of the corporation. The National Women's Association of Bhutan (NWAB) overtook the organisation in 1991 and became a full Non-Government Organisation in August 2002.[17]

Royal Society for the Protection and Care of Animals

RSPCA was established as Non-Government Organisation in 1999 under the Royal Patronage of Her Majesty the Queen of Bhutan Ashi Tshering Yangdon Wangchuck to look after the care of animals. It works in close collaboration with the Ministry of Health and Education, Ministry of Agriculture, Ministry of Communications, municipalities and Dzongkhags in areas of environment, health and hygiene and other common related societal interests. It is responsible to protect and care for animals in Bhutanese society from cruelty and negligence. It helps authorities to render the streets safe from canine related health hazards like rabies and other infectious diseases.[18]

Voluntary Artists Studio Thimphu (VAST)

A group of working artists formed the Voluntary Artists Studio Thimphu (VAST) in 1998. The VAST was set up to promote, guide and assist young artists to explore their full potential in the field of art and painting. Through the VAST, artists are provided with the opportunity to develop their creative and productive use of their free time on voluntary basis. It also provides them vast opportunity to participate in national, regional and international art competitions, thus widening their scopes and potential.

Classes in developing skills on drawing, sketching, painting and designing, using new materials and techniques are conducted. In addition, it also organises art talks, exhibition and trips for the artists to some relevant institutions within the country. It also aims to participate in art exchanges and art camps outside the country and set up a local artist network in all the districts of Bhutan.[19]

Bhutan-India Friendship Association

It was founded to promote friendship between people of the two countries. It was a voluntary organisation, which initially raised funds from private donations. The fifth king set up a working group to reorganize and strengthen the institution as well as to raise the profile and achievements to a much higher level. The main objectives are— to act as a central unifying body for Bhutan-India friendship, to promote youth and students' participation and to exchange knowledge on both traditional and modern values and developments. The organisation was established under the Memorandum of Association adopted on November 11, 2003. Its activities include organising and sponsoring number of social and cultural projects with active participation from members towards promoting peace and friendship. Its primary source of funds is from grants, from governments and donations and sponsorships from corporate entities.[20]

Role of Community Leaders

Since 2002, when the devolution of power to the people took place, the responsibilities of *tshogpa* have increased considerably. Besides conveying and facilitating the instructions from the *gup*, they also look out for the cleanliness of the village including water problems and advising people in the village on how to take care of animals. He also arranges a weekly clean up of the village with the participation of villagers. Along with the regular post of village *tshogpa,* there are other *tshogpas* such as *zhabto tshogpa* and *zimchung tshogpa,* who look after the maintenance and renovation of village schools. They also discuss issues related to schools and teachers. Each *tshogpa* in the village is given a copy of the relevant *chathrim* (Act), which he/she has to use in order to pass instructions and guidance; this may be seen as how a person appointed by the people without remuneration from the government, supports and aids the government in fulfilling certain local tasks and activities.[21]

Co-operatives exist in the country to execute various functions at national and local level. According to the Cooperative Act of Bhutan 2001, cooperative is defined as "an association of persons united voluntarily to meet their common economic needs and aspirations through a jointly owned and effectively governed enterprise". State is directly involved in development of civil society to meet the demands of new socio-economic changes in the country. All the farm-based cooperatives receive positive intervention either in the form of funding, policy and legal framework from the government or donor agencies. There are mutual agreements and partnership between the government and the cooperatives. The government sees strong cooperatives as an important development partner of the government in developing the private sector. "The purpose of the Cooperative Act is to provide quality products and services to satisfy the economic need of members and their communities.

There are various modern associations such as water users association, seed cooperatives, potato grower associations, mushroom grower associations, bee-keepers, and milk and handicraft associations all of which are aimed at fulfilling the common socio-economic goals. However, one of the drawbacks of Cooperative Act is that it is restricted to voluntary associations concerned with the fulfilment of members' economic needs and aspirations. Volunteer programmes are not very old as an idea and certainly not in Bhutan, but the picture today is different, where national and international volunteer organizations are being formed year after year which are contributing to the development of the country. Some international associations operating in Bhutan are: The Japanese Overseas Cooperation Volunteers (JOCV), Volunteer Service Overseas (VSO), Volunteer Service Associations (VSA), Save the Children Federation (SCF), German Technical Cooperation (GTZ) and Netherlands Development Cooperation (SNV), and the World Wildlife Fund (WWF).[22]

Table 1: Modern Voluntary Organisations in Bhutan[23]

Voluntary Organizations	*Estd Year*	*Purpose*
United Nations Volunteers (UNV)	1980	Facilitate the placement of international volunteers to Bhutan from many countries to work in wide range of specialist fields; also assist in placement of Bhutanese volunteers overseas.
Social Service Unit (SSU) Sherubtse College	1984	House construction (repair for the poor people); provision of clean drinking water to the nearby villages; provision of food and clothing to old and destitute; medical facilities to sick and non-formal education to villagers.
Royal Society for Protection Nature (RSPN)	1987	To inspire personal responsibility and actively involve the people of Bhutan in the conservation of the kingdom's environment through education, applied research and information dissemination.
Volunteer Service Abroad (VSA)	1987	Program development in coordination with the Royal Civil Service Commission (until now in the field of engineering and finance).
JICA/JOCV	1988	To assist and encourage the activities of young Japanese wishing to cooperate in the economic and social development of Bhutan.
Youth Development Fund	1998	To establish sustainable youth fund for activities related to development of young people as productive citizens of the country.
RSPCA (Royal Society for Protection and Care of Animals)	1999	To inculcate Bhutanese citizens with a sense of moral responsibility for proper care and humane treatment of all animals; Sterilization and anti-rabies campaign, treatment of various diseases and feeding of dogs and other animals.
Singapore Volunteers Overseas	2000	To assist Department of Education in Bhutan in meeting its objectives of promoting IT in schools.
Vertical Bhutan Climbing Club	2000	Train Bhutanese youth, organize rock-climbing events and to promote this sport in Bhutan.
Bhutan Cricket Federation (BCA)	2001	Improve the standard of cricket and attract young players to the game.
Tarayana Foundation	2003	Help vulnerable individuals achieve greater economic security by providing maintenance allowances for people living in difficult circumstances to tide them

		over crisis, help poor students, promote folk craft, medical care for poor and encourage education excellence.
Respect, Educate, Nurture and Empower Women (RENEW)	2004	To provide protection to women against domestic violence. To provide relief and empowerment to disadvantaged women and girls.

All the associations have a written charter except those based in villages. In villages, it is the unwritten rules that are generally accepted. Committees are formed to manage the activities of the association. The two committees are the executive committee which consists of a chairman or a President, a Secretary, Public Relations or a Welfare officer and an Accountant or a Treasurer. The General Committee consists of three or four members. They support the executive committee. The members of both the committees are elected. Their tenures and responsibilities are specified in the charter. The funds to these associations come on contributory basis such as fees or donations. The government has authorised the Bhutan Chamber of Commerce and Industry to collect 40 per cent of the license renewal fees and 0.25 per cent of total value of letters of credit from Bhutanese exporters. Other sources of funds include membership fees and the sale of business license forms. It gets occasional donor assistance for performing services such as the training of entrepreneurs. The National Women's Association used to receive certain grants from the government, but this was discontinued in 1995. Today, its activities are funded by UNICEF. It has also received some assistance from Denmark and the International Fund for Agriculture Development. The main source of funding for the Royal Society for the Protection of Nature is the assistance that it receives from the Bhutan Trust Fund for the Environment. It also collects nominal fee of Nu. 100 from each of its members.

All these Associations require their books of accounts to be audited at regular intervals. While most of the formal associations follow the government's rules and audit their accounts of income and expenditure twice a year, the informal associations audit their books at the end of each year.[24]

Conclusion

Civil society forms an integral part of traditional as well as modern Bhutanese society. People get an opportunity to participate in decision making activities, which affect their day to day life. The mushrooming of the new associations is only an extension to the traditional roots. Most of the contemporary associations are relief based and aim at the uplift of the weaker sections of the society and some even link between the government and the people. They play an important role in economic development, environmental preservation and cultural enrichment. Their efforts have seen that the length and breadth of the country has access to market, health facilities, efficient use of water and proper resource utilisation. Most of the traditional associations in villages are still part of everyday life. Society in Bhutan believes in inter-dependence sharing hardships and joys of life together through cooperation. The scene may be different in urban centres but every home in urban area has its roots in villages and the people migrated to the cities educate their relatives, send money and support them to conduct annual religious ceremonies in family home. State today is seen as a facilitator for providing better life to its citizens. One of the principles followed today by government is of decentralization and devolution of community empowerment 'stimulating local institutions and decision making'. Karma Ura in 2003 wrote in his article *Bhutanese development Philosophy*, "In villages where social and economic institutions are deeply rooted, there are unwritten and internalised rules governing the uses of natural resources and social relations. These institutions bind people together as a community". "Such institutions lying between the state and the family are true indicators of the self-organisational capacity of a community. They are self-regulated through competition, cooperation and control within the community." On cultural preservation, he says further, "As a set of values underlying the harmonious relation between man and nature and between present and future generations, the aim of cultural preservation is to maintain the indigenous basic values in the face of challenges from competing ideologies in world view.

With the demand, new welfare associations commonly called *tshogpas* have emerged especially in urban areas, which cater to the people's need in times of sickness and death. Many new religious and spiritual associations receive full support from Bhutanese people and state as can be seen in case of *Choethun Tshogpa*. The various trust funds such as

Bhutan Trust Fund, Youth Development Fund and Health Trust Fund are examples of full support to state within the civil society.[25]

The government's response can be best summed up in the official document '*Bhutan 2017: A Vision for Kingdom's Future*', Royal Government of Bhutan, Ministry of Planning, 76 –

> First, we can no longer assume that the Royal government should be held solely responsible for the nation's future development. These responsibilities should be shared and new partnerships should be formed with agents of change and development. These partnerships can and should take numerous forms in recognition of the growing complexity and the challenges faced. They should include the private sector as a means for generating self-sustaining growth; they should include the Monk Body as a means for maintaining our commitment to the spiritual and cultural dimensions of development; they should include the growing number of national NGOs that are committed to the principles of justice, equity, social harmony and cultural and environmental conservation.

The most unique feature in Bhutan has been the nature of the monarchy, which has been instrumental in initiating the policy of decentralisation, introduced in early 1980s. Most of the initiatives have been taken by them especially the fourth king His Majesty Jigme Singye Wangchuck. He not only put the country on the path of democracy but also gave the people their first constitution and step by step devaluated the power of monarchy. His philosophy of Gross National Happiness is based on the positive values empowering every citizen with a right to develop as an individual, who contributes fully towards the development of society and the nation. It is an effort to ensure that the Bhutanese progress politically, socially and economically. Civil society in Bhutan has been promoted and nourished so that it can contribute fully towards the development and to fully promote the growth of civil society, changes are being proposed in various Acts so that the proper framework for Bhutanese civil society is envisaged in view of more constructive role.

References

1. Carothers, Thomas and Ottaway, Marina. *Defining Civil Society: The Exclusive Term* in Development Outreach Winter 2002, World Bank Institute.

2. Adapted from *Vaclav Havel's idea and his Civil Society Conception*, Macalester College, Minneapolis/St. Paul, USA, 26 April 1999.

3. CIVICUS is an international alliance establish in 1993 to nurture the foundation, growth and protection of citizen's action throughout the world, especially in the areas where participatory democracy and citizen's freedom of association are threatened.

4. Planning Commission (1999), Vision 2020, RGOB, Thimphu.

5. Dasho Rigzin Dorji, Secretary, Special Commission for Cultural Affairs, Royal Government of Bhutan in A Brief Religious, Cultural and Secular History of Bhutan published on the occasion.

6. Yinhong. S., *The Issue of Civil Society in the Present China and its Complexity*, Beijing: School of International Studies, Renmin University of China.

7. Karma Galay, *Civil Society*, p. 206.

8. CBS (1999), "Final Programmes for the Coronation, June 1974 and the Silver Jubilee Celebrations, June 1999 of His Majesty the King Jigme Singye Wangchuck" Thimphu: The Centre for Bhutan Studies.

9. Lyonpo Jigme Thinley, Values and Development: Gross National Happiness, in *Gross National Happiness*, (Thimphu: Centre for Bhutan Studies, 1999) p. 21. This was prepared as the text of the keynote speech delivered at the Millennium Meeting for Asia and the Pacific, 30th October-1 November 1998, Seoul, Republic of Korea.

10. Lham Dorji, *Understanding Civil Society in Bhutan*, Lham Dorji and Tashi Choden, The Centre for Bhutan Studies, 2005, p. 23.

11. K. Lella, (2002), *Modernisation and Buddhism: Contributions of Ambedkar and Dalai Lama-xiv*, New Delhi: Gyan Publishing House, p. 118.

12. W, Wolters, *The Making of Civil Society in Historical Perspective*, Wolters is the Professor of Economic Anthropology at the Catholic University of Nijmegen.

13. Lham Dorji, *Understanding Civil Society in Bhutan*, Lham Dorji and Tashi Choden, The Centre for Bhutan Studies, 2005, p. 57.

14. Dasho Kunzang Wangdi, Auditor General, Personal Communications, November 2000.

15. Mr. Zangla Namgyal, National Assembly, Personal Communications, November 2000.

16. Brochure, National Commission for Women and Children, Royal Government of Bhutan.

17. Lham Dorji, *Understanding Civil Society in Bhutan*, Lham Dorji and Tashi Choden, The Centre for Bhutan Studies, 2005, pp. 82-83.

18. *Ibid.*, p. 85.

19. http://www.youthdevfund.gov.bt/projects/vast

20. Tashi Dorji, *Understanding Civil Society in Bhutan*, Lham Dorji and Tashi Choden, The Centre for Bhutan Studies, 2005, pp. 67-68.

21. *Ibid*,. pp. 58-59.

22. Karma Galay, *Civil Society*, p. 211.

23. Information is extracted from the website http://www.undp.org.bt/unv/vols.html for tabulation; the 'Volunteers in Bhutan' website was launched in the International Year of Volunteers 2001, and is hosted by UNV/UNDP Bhutan.

24. *Opit Ref* 20, p. 214.

25. Tashi Dorji, *Understanding Civil Society in Bhutan*, Lham Dorji and Tashi Choden, The Centre for Bhutan Studies, 2005, pp. 104-106.

PART-II

Laws of Bhutan

During the period starting from 1950s an effort has been made to pass various laws for a clear preception of how things work in Bhutan. National Assembly has been instrumental in passing laws. Till 1907, Bhutan could not boast of codification of laws, nor were they applicable through the length and breadth of the country. Although, great care has been taken that the laws do take into consideration the local traditions, customs and usages of time, with changing scenario they demand a revision or formulation of the new ones, so that the developments could be catered for.

The Bhutanese legal system is primarily based on Buddhist natural law. It is a response to the evolving culture and the ways of life of the people. The first set of laws was promulgated by Zhabdrung Ngawang Namgyal. The secular laws resemble a silken knot and the temporal laws that of a golden yoke. Codification of law was completed in 1652, during the time of *Deb* Umzed Tenzin Grugyel. These laws include the ten pious acts known as *Lhachoe Gyewa Chu* and the sixteen virtuous acts of social piety referred to as *Michoe Tsangma Chudrung*. The 10th Desi, Mipham Wangpo consolidated and amended certain parts of the Code of Zhabdrung. In the mid 18th century the 13th Desi, Chogyal Sherub Wangchuk, made certain amendments in the code. The first and the second *Druk Gyalpo* made further amendments. During the reign of the third Druk Gyalpo, the National Assembly enacted the first comprehensive codified law known as the Thrimzhung Chhenmo. His Majesty the fourth Druk Gyalpo initiated amendments and legislations to respond fully and effectively to the changing needs of the nation.

The laws of Bhutan seek to do the following:

- Maintain peace and tranquillity in the Kingdom by rendering effective justice;
- Facilitate accessibility to justice by making courts user friendly;

- Uphold and protect due process of law, fair trial, rule of law and review system;
- Make judicial process more responsive, effective, faster, better and easier;
- Build public confidence and respect through continuing professionalism and judicial transparency;
- Harness technology for efficiency and cost effectiveness; and
- Strengthen infrastructure and capacity building.[1]

Broadly law as a system of rules can be categorized into substantive law and procedural law. Substantive law primarily defines rights, duties, obligations and liabilities. For instance, the Bhutan Penal Code, Marriage Act, Land Act, Inheritance Act, Taxation Laws, Movable and Immovable Property Act, Bankruptcy Act, Negotiable Instrument Act, etc., are all substantive laws. The expression "procedural law" denotes legal provisions dealing with various procedures to be complied with for the purpose of proceedings. The Civil and Criminal Procedure Code and the Evidence Act are examples of procedural laws. The Civil and Criminal Procedure Code provides pertinent rules relating to courts, jurisdiction, procedure to be followed for the purpose of initiating legal process and the like. Every aspect of procedural law is significant in the sense that it gives meaning to the substantive rights, liabilities and obligations. Unless procedures for attaining and materialising these rights are detailed and complied with, the envisaged rights, liabilities and obligations merely exist on paper. Towards this end, the procedural law enables the courts to administer these processes to ensure redressal and rendering of justice.

Drawn from the rich historical and religious embodiment of judicial processes as well as the modern procedural practices and laws, the Civil and Criminal Procedure Code of Bhutan contains modern procedural provisions empowering litigants as well as to guide the courts in the administration of justice. Like other standard criminal procedure, the Civil and Criminal Procedure Code of Bhutan outlines comprehensive criminal procedures where the process commences with the arrest of, suspected or accused criminal, and ends with sentencing or acquittal depending on whether the person is found guilty or innocent. The criminal procedure law safeguards against any possible human rights violation of the accused by enshrining principles and procedural rights such as due process, rule of law, right of *Habeas Corpus* (have the body or appearance before a judge), proof beyond reasonable doubt, etc. Besides, the basic premise and purpose of the Civil and Criminal Procedure Code is to *maintain the quality of an unimpaired flowing of heavenly stream of justice* based on the principle that no innocent person should suffer and that no guilty should go unpunished.

Under the Bhutanese criminal jurisprudence, the commission of crime has never been considered out of social context or religious norms. The commission of crime has strong religious and negative significance. Anything that harms living beings, causes injuries, deprives another person wrongfully of possession, takes away any form of life, cruelty in conduct, harshness in speech, and evil in thoughts etc., is considered sinful and non-virtuous. In Buddhism, whosoever commits a crime or engages in sinful acts has to undergo comprehensive and compulsory trial proceedings and an unavoidable "Judgement of the Dead". The basic criminal procedure outlines some of the most fundamental narratives of criminal procedure.

Applicability of Criminal Procedure

The criminal procedure is the main procedural law applicable to all persons throughout the territory or within the judicial reach of the Royal Courts of Justice of Bhutan.

The provisions of the Civil and Criminal Procedural Code are applicable to judicial proceedings. The Civil and Criminal Procedure Code provides that all persons are subject to equality before the law and for the entitlement without any discrimination on the grounds of race, colour, sex, language, religion, political or other opinion, national or social origin, property, birth or other status.

While the general purpose provides a mechanism for the initiation of criminal process and the administration of criminal law, its basic objective is to ensure that the trial is conducted fairly in accordance with the principle of "natural justice". The principle of natural justice demands that no man or woman shall be a judge to hear his or her own cause or sit in the judicial proceeding if any one has personal interest and that no one is condemned unheard or the necessity of hearing either sides. The trial must be conducted by following the principle of fairness and impartiality and a person is convicted only on the basis of facts, evidences and proof beyond doubt.

Court Venue and Sub-Judice

The courts in Bhutan are basically of three-tier hierarchical system. The Sub-Division or the *Dungkhag* Court, the District or the *Dzongkhag* Court and the High Court or *Chethoed Thrimgi Duensa*. However, the Civil and Criminal Procedure Code mandates the establishment of the Supreme Court or the *Ngoenthoed Thrimgi Duensa* as the highest appellate court and forms the four-tiers of courts in the post-Constitution era in Bhutan. The Supreme Court shall be the highest appellate court in Bhutan to be presided over by the Chief Justice of Bhutan and four other *Drongpons* or Justices of the Supreme Court.

The only High Court of Bhutan shall be presided by the Chief Justice of the High Court with other *Drangpons* or Justices of the High Court. The District Court shall be presided over by the *Drangpon* or the Judge of the *Dzongkhags* Courts or by the Chief Judge and such numbers of other *Drangpons* that may preside in a division established from time to time. The Sub-Division Court shall be presided over by the *Dungkhag Drangpon* and may have other numbers of *Dungkhag Drangpons* presiding in a division bench or benches.

THE ROYAL COURT OF JUSTICE

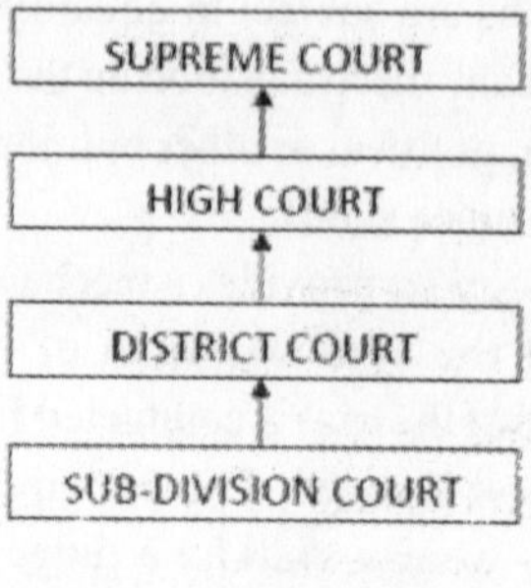

The courts in Bhutan have general jurisdiction and hear both civil and criminal matters. The provisions of the Civil and Criminal Procedure Code specify that the jurisdiction to conduct trial in a criminal matter will lie with the court in whose territorial jurisdiction the crime has been committed. The Civil and Criminal Procedure Code lays down the principle of *Sub Judice* (case in pending), wherein other courts are barred from proceeding with a criminal trial if any defendant or accused for criminal charge is currently being prosecuted in any competent court in Bhutan. The accused may be tried in different courts for a separate offence but not for similar offence. All persons accused of committing crime will have the right to be tried by ordinary courts of law except any ad-hoc tribunals. This means the persons accused of committing any criminal offence must be brought for trial only in a formal court of law.[2]

Some judicial reforms have been initiated in Bhutan which are as follows:

Institutional Reforms

- Introduction of the Annual National Judicial Conference in 1976;
- Appointment of efficient *Drangpons*;
- Abolition of the post of *Thrim-tsap* (acting *Drongpon*);
- Decentralisation of financial and administrative powers from the High Court to the lower court;
- Establishment of *Dungkhag* Courts;
- Introduction of series of workshops, seminars and ongoing training;
- Establishment of a separate judicial cadre in 1990; and
- Establishment of the National Judicial Commission in 2003 under a Royal Decree.

Procedural Reforms

- Strengthened the miscellaneous hearing calendar;
- Streamlined the registration procedure and hearing process;
- Expedited the adjudication process through the introduction of various management principles;
- Strengthened the legal language and Bhutanese terminology
- Enhanced the professionalism and reduced time consumption with the introduction of 75 judicial reforms; and
- Provided inexpensive litigation with nominal court fees.

Penal Reforms

- Under the Royal Command of His Majesty in 1995, the High Court started drafting the Penal Code of Bhutan, which was enacted by the National Assembly in the year 2004. The Penal Code is a consolidation of sections for the existing Acts dealing with criminal offences. It is intended to reinstate dignity to victims of crime and increase possibilities for rehabilitation of offenders. The contents of the Code reflect descriptive and normative functions.
- His Majesty the *Druk Gyalpo* commanded the establishment of Youth Development and Rehabilitation Centre for Juveniles on March 26, 1997. The Centre situated at Tshimalakha provides assistance and support programmes, particularly with regard to nutrition, clothing and housing. It aims at reinstating juvenile back into the society as a reformed and responsible citizen.

Abolition of Capital Punishment

His Majesty the Druk Gyalpo, abolished capital punishment by His Royal Decree on March 20, 2004.[3]

The Citizenship Act 1985

One of the laws which have made a difference in the country's functioning has been the Citizenship Act 1985 which superseded the Citizenship Act of 1958 and 1977. These two Acts were first to define the Bhutanese concept of nationalism. 1985 Act provided for three categories of Bhutan Citizenship- by birth, by registration and by naturalisation. A person whose parents are both citizens of Bhutan is deemed a citizen by birth. A person permanently domiciled in Bhutan on or before December 31, 1985, and whose name is registered in the census register maintained by the Ministry of Home Affairs, is deemed to be a citizen of Bhutan by registration.

Certain categories of residents can apply for Bhutanese citizenship if they fulfil clearly stated conditions to be eligible for naturalisation. The age of 21 years:

(a) The person must have attained the age of 21 years, or 15 years in the case of a person either of whose parents is a citizen of Bhutan;
(b) The person must be mentally sound;
(c) The person must have resided in Bhutan for 15 years in case of government employees and also, in the case of applicants either of

whose parents is a citizen of Bhutan, an 20 years of all other cases; and this period of residence must be registered in the records of the department of immigration and census;

(d) The person must be able to speak, read and write Dzongkha proficiently;

(e) The person must have a good knowledge of the culture, customs, traditions and history of Bhutan;

(f) The person must have a good moral character and should not have any record of imprisonment for criminal offences in Bhutan or elsewhere;

(g) The person must have no record of having spoken against the king, country and people of Bhutan in any manner whatsoever;

(h) The person must be prepared to take a solemn oath of allegiance to the king, country and people of Bhutan.[4]

On receipt of the official Application Form 2 for naturalisation, the Ministry of Home Affairs takes necessary steps to check the particulars contained in the application. The Ministry also conducts written and oral tests to access proficiency in Dzongkha and knowledge of the culture, customs, traditions and history of Bhutan. The decision of the Ministry on the question of eligibility for naturalisation is final and binding. The Royal Government reserves the right to reject any application for naturalisation without assigning any reason what so ever.

A person whose application for naturalisation has been favourably considered by the Ministry of Home Affairs takes the oath of allegiance. He or she is then deemed to be a citizen upon receiving a *Kasho* from the king. The Act of 1985 also provides for termination of citizenship under certain stringent circumstances. For instance, any citizen of Bhutan who acquires citizenship of another country ceases to be a citizen of Bhutan. However, the wife or husband and children of that person, if they are Bhutanese citizens, have the right to remain citizens of Bhutan, provided they are permanently domiciled and are registered annually in the citizenship register maintained by the Ministry of Home Affairs.

Any person who acquires citizenship by naturalisation may be deprived of citizenship at any time if found that naturalisation had been obtained by means of fraud, false representation or concealment of any material fact, or if the person shows by act or speech to be disloyal to the king, country or people of Bhutan.

To the Citizenship Act of 1985, a new provision was added later by a resolution of the National Assembly. It cancels the citizenship of those whose parents are Bhutanese, who have left Bhutan of their own accord, without the knowledge of the Royal Government, and whose names are also not recorded in the citizenship register.

A second National Assembly resolution requires any citizen of Bhutan who has been deprived of citizenship to dispose of all immovable property in the country within one year. Failing this, the citizen's immovable property is confiscated by the Ministry of Home Ministry on payment of "fair and reasonable compensation".

At the 67th session of the National Assembly in 1988, there was a debate on the Citizenship Act of three years before. Some of its rigours were pointed by members, particularly those regarding the claims to citizenship of Bhutanese men or women married to foreign nationals. The king, who was interested in the debate, said that in course of his expansive tours of southern Bhutan, he had noticed the citizen's concern about Bhutanese married to non-nationals. The king ruled that the three Citizenship Acts placed on the statute book in a span of 27 years would each apply to determine the citizenship status of Bhutanese married to other nationals. Marriage between Bhutanese and foreign nationals was not prohibited, declared the king, as long as the marriage took place in accordance with the Citizenship Acts and the marriage laws of Bhutan.

The king declared that the Citizenship Act of 1985 had been formulated and passed by the National Assembly, taking into account the present circumstances. In accordance with the Citizenship Acts 1958, 1977 and 1985, the children of Bhutanese men married to non-nationals prior to 1985 would be automatically eligible for citizenship. In the case of a Bhutanese woman married to a non-national, her husband and children would, according to the law, not be considered citizens. It was not the intention of the Royal Government to separate parents and children, or husbands and wives from living together. In consideration of their welfare, His Majesty suggested that non-nationals married to Bhutanese, who are not eligible to citizenship according to the provisions of existing laws, could be granted special residence permit. They would also be entitled to health, education and other social benefits extended to the citizens of the country.[5]

The *Vision of* His Majesty the king is an inspiration for the young people of Bhutan to grow up as responsible, productive and happy citizens of the country. For this to happen, the Royal Court of Justice recognises the need for Bhutanese children and youth to grow up as informed citizens, prepared to live a full and harmonious life in society. Children and youth must, therefore, be made aware of the laws of the land and of their rights as citizens of Bhutan.

An important legislation is the Penal Code. The Penal Code encapsulates the spirit of rightful living and reflects a broad range of the offences and behaviour that youth should refrain from for the well-being of themselves, their families and the country.

The Penal Code and the Child

According to the Code, the minimum age of criminality of a child is ten years. The child, who is ten years and below shall not be held liable for any offences committed by him/her and hence cannot be convicted. If the child is of above ten years, the court may sentence the child to a minimum of half of the sentence prescribed for the offence, and can only be convicted if s(he) has attained sufficient maturity of understanding to judge the nature and consequences of his/her conduct on that occasion.

(A) Offences in the Code that every child should know

Sl.	*Offences*	*Sections*
1.	Illegal abortion	146/147
2.	Complicity in suicide	150/151
3.	Assault	156/157
4.	Battery	158/159
5.	Criminal elopement	169/170
6.	Escape from Lawful custody	171/172
7.	Incest	207/208
8.	Indecent exposure	209/210
9.	Bestiality	211/212
10.	Unnatural sex	213/214
11.	Arson	231/232
12.	Trespass	237 to 239
13.	Larceny	240 to 244
14.	Larceny of property lost, mislaid or delivered by mistake	253/254

15.	Possession of stolen property	255/256
16.	Theft of services	257 to 261
17.	Unauthorised use of property	262 to 264
18.	Reckless endangerment of property	269/270
19.	Auto stripping	273/274
20.	Pick pocketing	275/276
21.	Lewd and lascivious conduct	381/382
22.	Public intoxication	383/384
23.	Use of tobacco or other health hazard substances	385/386
24.	Malicious mischief	396/397
25.	Black-marketing	402/403
26.	Environmental pollution	408/409
27.	Criminal nuisance	410/411
28.	Disorderly conduct	460/461
29.	Prowling	464/465
30.	Unauthorised opening of mail and parcel	470/471
31.	Tampering with computer materials	472/473
32.	Unlawful possession of computer materials	474/475
33.	Computer pornography	476/477
34.	Illegal possession of firearm, ammunition, explosive or other lethal weapon	480/481
35.	Illegal pointing of a firearm	484/485
36.	Brandish/display of weapon	486/487
37.	False alarm	488/489
38.	Illegal transaction of controlled substances	498/499
39.	Possession of a controlled substance	500/501

(B) Offences in the Code against the child

Sl.	*Offences*	*Sections*
1.	Statutory rape	181/182
2.	Rape of a child above twelve years of age	183/184
3.	Gang rape of a child below twelve years of age	191/192
4.	Gang rape of a child above twelve years of age	193/194
5.	Custodial rape	197/198
6.	Child molestation	203/204
7.	Child abuse	221/221
8.	Endangerment of a child	223/224
9.	Pedophilia	225/226
10.	Trafficking of a child	227/228
11.	Prostitution	373 to 380
12.	Illegal sale of tobacco or other health hazard substances	387 to 389
13.	Illegal sale of alcohol	390 to 392

The concern for the children is evident from the emphasis, which has been made to protect them legally and to respect the cultural values of the society. The child has the right to be protected from the work that threatens his/her health, education or development. The state shall set minimum ages for employment and regulate working conditions. The child also has right to protection from the use of narcotic psychotropic drugs and from being involved in their production or distribution. As His Majesty the fourth king said, "As the future of Bhutan lies in the hands of our people, it is our responsibility to make sure that the future well-being of our country is secure in the hands of the Bhutanese people and that our younger generations can successfully shoulder the sacred responsibility with complete loyalty and dedication."[6]

One of the important legislations passed by the National Assembly after a vigorous discussion was an amendment to the Marriage Act submitted by the *lhengyal shungtshog* or cabinet. While the amendments covered six sections of the Act, namely marriage certificate, adultery, marriage after adultery, divorce, custody and child support, the *chimis* got intensely involved in child support. The Chief Justice of Bhutan who was present in the house, because it was debating a legal issue (a unique feature of Bhutanese democracy, which is nowhere else to be found), explained the amendments and answered legal points raised by the *chimis*, who warmed up particularly to the substantial increase in allowance for the support of both legal and illegitimate children. The king reminded the *chimis* that while the custody of a child in Bhutan was given to mother till the child was nine years old, thereafter, the child had the right to choose the parent s(he) preferred to live with. This was the practice in Bhutan for many years, an old socio-cultural custom legalised in the marriage laws. The king rightly claimed that this was a special feature of Bhutan's legally streamlined social fabric. Even the very advanced countries continue to deny this freedom to the children of divorced parents; some have lately started making laws in this regard.[7]

According to *Bhutan 2020*- A Vision for Peace, Prosperity and Happiness:

The further development of our institutions must be accompanied and supported by the further development of national law and our judicial system. The main priority is to ensure that the independence of judiciary is maintained and that the systems of law and jurisprudence continue to evolve in response to the needs of a society in development. The further evolution must be guided by four main principles:

· All Bhutanese have equal and unimpeded access to the law and legal process;
· The legal system is able to dispense justice swiftly and efficiently;
· The judiciary is able to perform its tasks and execute its responsibilities with the highest degree of professionalism;
· Law must be accepted by all Bhutanese as being fair, responsive and relevant.
· In order to deliver justice, the mechanism to implement the law must be strengthened.

Our system of law has traditionally been retroactive, responding to changes within society and to emerging needs. Given the nation's rapid pace of development, we must seek to ensure that law is, wherever possible and appropriate, proactive in terms of its capacity to anticipate change and the legal instruments required to deal with it. This implies that the further evolution of our traditional system of law must be supported by measures to enlarge our capacity to undertake action-oriented research on law and jurisprudence, with the aim of identifying ways in which systems that remain anchored in Buddhist principles, beliefs and values can maintain their relevance as a positive force for change in the next millennium.[8]

Reference

1. Pamphlet, The Judiciary of The Kingdom of Bhutan, Royal Court of Justice, High Court, Thimphu: Bhutan.

2. Judge Dubgyur Lungten, 'Criminal Justice in Bhutan; A Handbook on Criminal Procedure', 2006, Royal Court of Justice, Research Division, High Court, pp.1-6.

3. Opcit. reference 1.

4. Gupta Bhabani Sen, Bhutan: Towards a Grass-root Participatory Polity, p.35.

5. Ibid, pp.36-37.

6. Pamphlet, Know the Law- To Protect Your Rights, Royal Court of Justice, High Court, Thimphu: Bhutan.

7. Gupta Bhabani Sen, Bhutan: Towards a Grass-root Participatory Polity, p. 112.

8. Bhutan 2020: A Vision for Peace, Prosperity and Happiness, Planning Commission, Royal Government of Bhutan, Part-I, pp. 55-56.

8

Progress and Analysis

Bhutan is one of those nations in the world, where the strength and weaknesses of geographical location, resources and population have been carefully studied and guarded policies which have desired results. The effort has always been to convert its negative points in positive. The role of the Wangchuck dynasty has been one of a guardian, giving the right direction to the Bhutanese people and making them aware of how they could use the limited resources and formulate their own policies. This process began with the laying of infrastructure during the time of the third king Jigme Dorji Wangchuck, a man who understood the importance of development and knowledge. He firmly believed that isolation or backwardness ought to be fought with the tools which may usher a new beginning for the Bhutanese people. Small population made it easy for implementation of the policies, but the remoteness was a big challenge. How to reach the far flung areas in the high mountainous region was a major question.

The third king asserted that the country cannot live only in one time frame. He, with the help of India, embarked on development and implemented the First Five Year Plan. He also realised the importance of education and started English as a medium of education. Alongside an effort was made to open government schools and health units. His efforts ushered advent of change for a country with no roads, telephones, mail service, airports and non-existent international relations. In 1958, the visit of Indian Prime Minister Jawaharlal Nehru and his daughter Indira Gandhi was the beginning of good neighbourly relations between the two countries.

Bhutan became the largest aided country and the First Five-Year Plan was entirely funded by the Government of India. India still remains the largest contributor, though, many new countries and agencies are funding today. Bhutan receives a significant proportion of its investment needs as bilateral aid primarily from Denmark, Switzerland, The Netherlands, Austria and Japan. Multi-lateral aid continues to be extended by the United Nations Development Programme, the World Bank, the European Community, the International Monetary Fund, and the Asian Development Bank. ADB has supported capital projects relating to communications infrastructure, particularly road construction.[1]

The third king's efforts bore fruits during the fourth king Jigme Singye Wangchuck's reign, when Bhutan opened itself to development and modernisation keeping abreast with globalisation, liberalisation and privatisation in the world. Bhutan concentrated on material and economic aspects of development, but did not want to leave the quality of life and its rich culture unattended. The result was the origin of the idea of Gross National Happiness. It was famously said by the fourth king in 1984, when he attended a summit meeting of non-aligned countries, "We are more interested in Gross National Happiness than Gross National Product". The GNH meant careful balancing of material, technological and economic development with a concern for good quality of life, natural environment, good governance and sustainable development.

The theory caught the imagination of other countries initiating a debate whether only economic development can be the parameter for judging progress. The consolidation of policies and implementation of the new ones made Bhutan emerge from medieval existence to modern as the expansion of education percolated at all levels, beginning from primary education to secondary and even higher and vocational education. Efforts were made to give free education to both the genders and to bring scientific knowledge to the entire population. Those who could not pursue education earlier or had to drop out for various reasons could pursue through distance education.

In Bhutan, free health and education services given by the government to its people are praiseworthy. Most of the institutions are government run and a close monitoring of the working of these educational institutions is done. Children who can not afford to come every day due to long distance of walking are given free residential facilities. The poor families as well as the people living in distant areas have largely benefitted from it.

The government of Bhutan shares the concern and goal of women associations of Bhutan and actively works for the education of girls and women. It is also recognised that women with at least basic literacy could function better in traditional roles as mothers, agriculturist and home makers and can also contribute in the development of Bhutan. As a result of lack of females in higher education, their presence at decision making positions is dismal. Promoting greater female enrolment into professional, technical and vocational institutions can change this scenario. Easing of transition of females from secondary to tertiary level and reducing female drop out rates after completion of secondary education is also a must. Focus should be on raising literacy rate among girls and women particularly in rural areas.

The goal that the Education Department had established in 1976 was: 'In the process of educational development, the primary need is to prepare the type of educated manpower required for all round development of our country'. During my visits to Bhutan in 2008, 2010 and 2011, I found that Bhutanese education system is catering to the basic need of preparing citizens aware of their ground realities and know their traditions and culture along with modernisation which is part of Bhutan today. The scene is set for a change, as more women are realising the importance of professional studies and aspiring for higher positions.

Bhutan has rigorously followed past systems and traditions, which were very carefully and painstakingly nurtured by their forefathers. Even when the modern development started, it was kept in mind to tackle problems which have caught up with other societies, therefore strict vigil has been kept on the social environment. There is a lot of appreciation for modern changes and technology with a commtitment to preserve Bhutan's social values and identity. The lower enrolment rates and high drop outs of girls has been taken very seriously. Among the many solutions underrtaken are expanding of boarding facilities for girls, curriculum and faculty development and distance education. The Gross National Happiness is inseparable part of the curriculum. The peace and happiness of Bhutanese people should be achieved through social and economic transformation of the country.

The economy of Bhutan has undergone several structural changes and has concentrated along with traditional sectors like farming and weaving to new areas mostly in public sector–such as hydro-power projects for which financial support comes through donors. India is the largest consumer of electricity produced by these hydro-electric plants.

There has been free trade and commerce between India and Bhutan since the signing of the India Bhutan Friendship Treaty in 1947. However, a formal Agreement on Trade, Commerce and Transit was signed between Bhutan and India in 1972, reviewed and renewed over the years. The agreement was last renewed in July 2006 for a period of 10 years.

The first step to promote trade between Bhutan and Bangladesh was taken in 1978. Subsequently, Bhutan entered into a preferential trading arrangement with Bangladesh in September 1980. A protocol to the trade agreement was signed in February 1984. During the visit of the Prime Minister of Bangladesh H. E. Sheikh Hasina in November, 2009, the bilateral trade agreement was renewed and signed.[2]

Various macroeconomic and human development indicators have improved significantly since 1980. In the first six years of the present century, the country has experienced a sharp acceleration in average annual growth rate of real GDP to 7.9 per cent from 5.9 per cent in the 1990s. In 2007, the country's per capita income was USD 1,810. Privatisation began in the late 1980s with corporatisation and divestment of government shares in state owned enterprises to the private sector.[3]

To develop the economy, the Royal Government approved the nation's first Economic Development Policy, 2009. The policy is the apex by virtue and serves as a guiding document for all ministries and agencies to stimulate economic development. It identifies key areas of economic opportunity and provides incentives to stimulate investments in these sectors. Building Brand Bhutan has been prioritised and national regulatory reforms are to be carried out.

To take into account the changes and development that have taken place since the first FDI policy in 2002, the Royal Government is reviewing the earlier policy to make it more liberal and open more sectors for FDI. It has been recognised that FDI will be an important component of economic development.

For the next five years, growth rate of economy is projected around eight per cent with a focus to stimulate faster growth in productive sectors, particularly agriculture and industry, to a higher rate than achieved in conjunction with continued investments in further development of hydro-power sector.

As in past plans, the major stimulus for growth owes to the energy and construction sectors with the peaks in GDP growth coinciding with the start of construction of planned hydropower projects and their commissioning.

The future of the Bhutanese economy will mainly be guided by the Economic Development Policy (EDP) that has a time frame until 2024. In its pursuit, the Royal Government will provide an environment for private sector and in particular, the promotion and development of high quality green services, agro and forest based products, energy, information and cultural industry, transport and related services, construction, natural resources, etc. that have competitive advantages.[4]

Bhutanese economy appeared to be staggering through a crisis for a short while in June 2013 as the end of the 10th Five Year Plan on June 30, 2013 was marked with controversy due to subsidies on LPG and Kerosene oil being stopped by India, exactly in midst of the second general elections. The decision bred discontent and anxiety among the Bhutanese public about the efficiency of the ruling PDP in of maintaining cordial relations with India. However, the crisis was sorted out as Indian government described the matter as just a coincidence of lapsing of the Tenth Five-Year-Plan and the timing of general elections. The agreement on subsidies had to be renewed in June 2013, while coincidentally there was no government in Bhutan due to elections. The subsidies were restored shortly thereafter in July 2013.

The Eleventh Five-Year Plan (2013-18) lays emphasis on planned development and welfare of the people. Chapter One presents the development planning framework, efforts towards operationalizing Gross National Happiness (GNH) and key milestones to be achieved by 2020. A notable paradigm shift of the Eleventh plan is the adoption of Results-Based Planning (RBP) framework that articulates clear outcome and outputs to realize the Eleventh plan objective of "Self-reliance and Inclusive Green Socio-Economic Development".

The underlying objective of the Eleventh plan is to achieve "Self-reliance and Inclusive Green Socio-Economic Development". Self-Reliance meets our national development needs as articulated through our Five-Year plans by 2020. Inclusive Social Development requires reducing poverty and inequality by enhancing the standard of living and the quality of life of the most vulnerable sections of our society. Green Development means ensuring carbon neutral development at all times.[5]

To realize the Eleventh plan objective of "Self-reliance and Inclusive Green Socio-Economic Development" 16 National Key Result Areas (NKRAs), key national outcome and outputs, need to be achieved over the next five years, categorized under each of the four pillars are defined as:

- Under the pillar of Sustainable and Equitable Socio-economic Development, there are four NKRAs namely Sustained Economic Growth; Reduced Poverty and MDG Plus achieved; Sustained Food Secure; and Full Employment. The achievement of these four NKRAs will be measured by corresponding Key Performance Indicators (KPIs) such as the annual GDP growth rate, inflation, poverty, enrollment, mortality, employment, cereal sufficiency target etc.
- Under the pillar of Preservation and Promotion of Culture, there are two NKRAs defined as Strengthened Bhutanese Identity, Social Cohesion and Harmony; and Indigenous Wisdom, Arts and Crafts Promoted for Sustainable Livelihood. The corresponding KPIs to measure progress include GNH Index, rural households engaged in cultural industries and jobs created.

- Under the pillar of Conservation and Sustainable Utilization and Management of the Environment, there are four NKRAs namely Carbon Neutral/Green and Climate Resilient Development; Sustainable Utilization and Management of Natural Resources; Water Security; and Improved Disaster Resilience and Management Mainstreamed. The NKRAs have corresponding KPIs to measure performance. Water is given special focus in the Eleventh plan in view of its importance for the basic survival of living beings and for hydroelectric projects and agriculture. It has been one of the major difficulties faced by the Dzongkhags and communities and therefore an ambitious target of ensuring 24 hours water supply has been set.
- Under the pillar Promotion of Good Governance, there are six NKRAs covering Improved Public Service Delivery; Democracy and Governance Strengthened; Gender Friendly Environment for Women's Participation; Corruption Reduced; Safe Society; and Needs of Vulnerable Group Addressed. The KPIs such as reducing turnaround time for Government to citizen, government to business and government to government services; monitoring government performance; drafting legislation to ensure quota for women in elected offices; reducing female unemployment; implementation of national anti-corruption strategy; and reducing crime per 1,000 population will be the basis for tracking progress towards these NKRAs.

The main strategic thrust to achieve the national outcome and outputs will be on

i) inclusive social development, ii) accelerated green economic development and iii) strategic infrastructure development.

- Inclusive social development will focus on reducing income and multidimensional poverty, address social issues and improve social outcome in health and education sectors. The targeted key interventions include the Rural Economy Advancement Programme (REAP) to address extreme rural poverty at village and community levels; the National Rehabilitation Programme (NRP) to enhance the productive asset base of marginalized households; the Local Government Empowerment Programme (LGEP) to enhance decision making capacity and improve service delivery through essential equipment, machinery and Nu. 2 million per year per Gewog; special programme for vulnerable groups such as senior citizens, differently-abled persons, and youth; and targeted health and education interventions to reach the unreached for Dzongkhags with poor health and education outcome.

- Green Accelerated Economic Development will focus on economic diversification through non-hydropower sectors and by fostering dynamic private sector that catalyzes green economy. Key interventions include the Economic Stimulus Programm to address the credit crunch and make finances available for productive sectors; Rapid Investment in Selected Enterprises (RISE) Programme, the flagship programme to accelerate growth, self reliance, end-to-end development of non-hydro sectors such as tourism, agro-processing, construction, small and cottage industries including cultural industries and manufacturing and mining; optimizing opportunities of accelerated hydropower development local trade and commerce, participation of local private sector and workforce and aligning corporate social responsibilities of hydropower projects with local needs and plans; enabling environment through simplification of policy and regulatory framework and facilitating vital infrastructure development such as surface and air transport, dry ports and industrial estates.
- Strategic Infrastructure Development will focus on development of critical infrastructure complementing efforts under the thrust areas of the Eleventh plan objectives. The investments will primarily be in urban, transport, ICT, energy, economic, social and cultural infrastructure. These include the development of two regional hubs and infrastructure facilities and services in Dzongkhag headquarters and towns; expansion and improvement of road and air connectivity; expansion of ICT infrastructure including national data centre, government intranet system, national broadband master-plan and facilities for G2C, G2G and G2B services; expansion of energy infrastructure through accelerated development of 10,000 mw of hydropower, construction of transmission lines and substations and expansion of rural electrification; the development of dry ports in Phuentsholing and Jigmeling or Nanglam and industrial parks in Mongar, Samtse, Samdrup Jongkhar and Sarpang; and construction of educational and health infrastructure and renovation/construction of Dzongs.[6]

India and Bhutan held the second round of talks in New Delhi on November 26, 2013 for Bhutan's 11th Five-Year plan. The Bhutanese delegation to the second Bhutan-India development cooperation talks for the 11th Five-Year plan, was led by foreign secretary Yeshey Dorji while the Indian delegation by additional secretary of development partnership administration in the Ministry of External Affairs, Sujatha Mehta. The Indian government committed a total of Rs. 4,500 crore for the 11th Five-Year plan and a separate package of Rs. 500 crore for the economic stimulus plan.[7]

The talks centered on the 'project tied assistance' under which India has committed Rs. 28 Billion. The talks approved 39 projects under PTA, with 42 projects after submitting more information. It was agreed that projects above Rs. 500 million shall require detailed reports.[8]

Monarchies in the world have faced the question for change and even struggle to materialise it. Bhutan is an example, where there was no demand from elite as well as the common people for change. Even today, if one talks to an ordinary Bhutanese they are not ready to accept that Bhutan can exist without monarchy. For them, the kings are synonymous with the nation. But, the changing times, the conditions especially in neighbouring Nepal may have been influencing the fourth king to lend democracy as a gift to his people, which can be termed 'revolution from above'.

In the words of the Chief Justice of Bhutan Sonam Tobgye, "As a witness of the past, we must address the future". We felt this was the time to do the political engineering. So what we did is, and again, this is His Majesty's vision, he felt, there should be a multi-party system at the primary level, and thereafter, the two parties getting the maximum votes will contest the general elections to the National Assembly. So, will have a stable government in parliament, and also have a multi-party system at the primary level. The tyranny of two-party system will be avoided, and the perpetuation of certain rules will not continue. This is perhaps unique in our constitution. Political party structure is probably not mentioned in any other Constitution.[9]

Along with accelerating the pace of development which took the country to progress, the fourth king hastened the political process. He is credited to give Bhutan democracy and a system of good governance when he said, "I have always made it clear that the people are more important than the king. We can not leave the future of the country in the hands of one person who is chosen by birth and not by merit". The process of constitution making was complete on August 18th 2008, when the fifth king Jigme Khesar Namgyal Wangchuck signed the first written constitution It was a historic moment witnessed live on television by the Bhutanese people when the king said that the power that the Bhutanese people had reposed in him and his forefathers was now bestowed on them.

The focus which the fourth king shifted in the past has culminated in making the present monarchy the 'democratic constitutional monarchy'. It paves way for restructuring new generation of political leaders, emerging with media. Some new constitutional agencies have come up like the Election Commission and the Anti-Corruption which made a difference to the working and the administration.

The elections of 2008 saw the hard work put in by the Election Commission to educate the people, the need to vote and how to vote. It was a success as nearly 80 per cent of the people voted and became partners in the change. The local elections in 2011 added to the constitutional glory. The second general election in 2013 was a challenge for the election commission to conduct in fair manner and seek the participation of every adult Bhutanese in the process. It was interesting to see the Bhutanese society which considers monarchy as pivot around their lives take decisions signifing new trends. The erstwhile reigning party–The People's Democratic Party (PDP) was shown the door by dissenting voters while the opposition party Druk Phuensum Tshogpa (DPT) came in power on the promise of strengthening relations with India, winning 37 out of 42 seats.

Elections have added to the new phenomena in the united society of winners and losers. The Bhutanese have learnt to disagree and question even the authorities, a shift in the public and social life.

Bhutanese politics with the introduction of democracy has brought about a new way of thinking. There is a need to understand the role of the king, the concept of state and government, the concerns of the common

Bhutanese people and a need for greater transparency in every aspect of life. The question is where will the economy, society, politics and the changing culture head to? Will the goal of Gross National Happiness be accomplished? Certainly, the answers to these questions will testify the position and intention with which the betterment of the society was carried forward.

On December 9th 2006, the fourth king abdicated his throne, made way for the crown prince and introduced, parliamentary democracy. Although, he had announced to retire before 2008, it happened sooner than expected, when he was only 51. It was a voluntary move with no pressure from any quarter. He was bestowing on his inheritors a nation which he nurtured carefully for 34 years of his reign to support ordinary people by channelizing resources. The relations with India remained progressive and massive external aid was mobilised. Efforts were made to generate domestic revenue. The people were not taxed. In fact, government extended help and support for development of one and all.

Bhutanese monarchs have a good record of mobilising resources from alternative sources rather than taxation but investing for the ordinary people and the monastic community. The spirit is reflected in the fifth king's speech on his coronation:

"Throughout my reign I will never rule you as a king. I will protect you as a parent, care for you as a brother and serve you as a son. I shall give you everything and keep nothing. I shall live such a life as a good human being that you may find it worthy to serve as an example of your children; I have no personal goals than to fulfil your hopes and aspirations. I shall always serve you, day and night, in the spirit of kindness, justice and equality. As the king of Buddhist nation, my duty is not only to ensure your happiness today but to create the fertile ground from which you may gain the fruits of spiritual pursuit and attain good karma. This is how I shall serve you as King."[10]

The transition period in Bhutan may throw up many challenges for its people. Socially, a close knit society may have to grapple with disintegration of the joint family system. The movement from rural to urban areas is contributing to nuclear families. The rising cost of living and smaller spaces in bigger towns do not permit for extended families. The problem of child care with working parents has started rearing head. There is an urgent need for crèches and day-care centres. The situation is similar for the elderly people. With better health facilities, their population is rising and in the projected 2030 Census by the National Statistical Bureau, Bhutan, their number stood at 58,110. Only recently the, first old age home has been opened in Radhi gewog in Trashigang Dzongkhag. We may see the pressure in future on government to open more such homes.

The youth of Bhutan face the problem of unemployment as large number of them is getting primary and secondary education. This can not be ignored for long and the government has to find new avenues to harness their potential. Alcoholism and drug abuse are grave areas. Youth has outlet to the world and no longer can they be convinced without reasoning. So, there is a need to develop private sector as well to tap this energy in various fields.

Women have left their traditional secure arena and entered new areas. There is a need to review their maternity leave period, help at home and infantcare. Bhutan till today is primarily a Buddhist country with emphasis on festivals, mask dances, food and national sport archery. To retain the essence of culture, utility ought to be explained and ingrained in the youth.

The cultural diversity which Bhutan enjoys can only be preserved by respecting heterogeneity.

Bhutan is a land–locked nation and 68 per cent of its people are still engaged in agriculture. Hydroelectric generation and tourism being the major economic activities, they will have to make an effort to see that some more industrialisation be carried out. Most of the poor people live in rural areas. The benefits of development should reach them.

The challenges may be enormous but as the fifth king His Majesty said in the Madhavrao Scindia Memorial Lecture on December 23, 2009:

"After many years of observing my father, working with the government, touring the country, living in the villages and meeting the people, I learned that you don't just become a leader for a prescribed and planned situation, you have to offer leadership whatever the circumstances. Now, having assumed the duties of kingship of this small Himalayan nation in the midst of a globalising world that changes in an instant, it is even more clear that there is no way to foresee the circumstances and plan for leadership in such a world."

"So my guiding principle has been born and nurtured on the simple instinct that in order to do the job I have been given as best as I can, first and foremost, I must strive to be a good human being. So while the wider vision is crucial to me, it is more important for me as a king whose aspirations are lodged within those of my country and people, to be able to crystallise that vision, to fulfil the ultimate aspirations of the people, in the form of simple daily acts carried out from moment- to-moment."

"I take each day as it comes. If someone in a village has something to tell me, I stop and listen. If an old man's house must be rebuilt after a natural disaster, I try and stay there to see it through. It may take an extra few minutes or months but it must be done. Not only is it the duty of a good human being, but each moment, each action is to me, a building block that will one day take shape in the wider vision. Besides, it's all very well to have a vision that stretches to the top of the peak, but unless you are walking a little up the hill every day, you will never get there."[11]

The above words reflect the deep commitment of the monarchy for the welfare of its people and a desire to see the smooth functioning of the government, where the people will derive benefits with development. For India, a strong and stable Bhutan is welcome in troubled South-Asia.

References

1. Michael Rutland, Bhutan: From the Medieval to the Millennium, p. 288.
2. Window on Bhutan, Exploring New Avenues, Issue VII, 2009, "The Bhutanese Economy on the Rise", p. 30.
3. *Ibid.*, p. 29.
4. *Ibid.*, pp. 30-31.
5. Eleventh Five Year Plan, Volume 1, Main Document, 2013-2018, Gross National Happiness Commission, Royal Government of Bhutan p.23.
6. *Ibid*, pp. 33-35.

7. India, Bhutan held second round of development talks" 2 Dec, 2013 http://economictimes.indiatimes.com/articleshow

8. *Ibid.*

9. Interview with Sonam Tobgye, Chief Justice of Bhutan by Suhrid Sankar Chattopadhyay in Thimphu, Frontline, May 9, 2008, p. 47.

10. Kinga Sonam, Polity, Kingship and Democracy, 2009, Bhutan Times Ltd., Ministry of Education, Royal Government of Bhutan, p. 340.

11. Window on Bhutan, Exploring New Avenues, Issue VII, 2009, The Madhavrao Scindia Memorial Lecture, delivered by His Majesty Jigme Khesar Namgyal Wangchuck, King of Bhutan, December 23, 2009, New Delhi, p. 13.

Appendix-I

His Majesty's Address to the Joint Sitting of the First Parliament on May 8, 2008

"It is with deep personal satisfaction and happiness that I address this inaugural session of Parliament. After all, it is in a time of unprecedented peace and prosperity that we are gathered today to celebrate our nation's historic achievement of a unique democratic transition.

Therefore, I commend the sense of duty and service that motivated the members of our first Parliament under Democratic Constitutional Monarchy. You have been a part of a transition that shall enter the history of our nation as one of our greatest endeavour.

Our nation has always provided security, tranquillity and happiness for our people irrespective of the dramatic changes that have taken place in the world and the region around us. The primary reason for our achievements has been the hard work and sacrifices of our forefathers and the selfless leadership of successive kings since Gongsa Ugyen Wangchuck, the first king of Bhutan. Shining even amidst our proud history of service, loyalty and affection for our nation, is the legacy of His Majesty Jigme Singye Wangchuck, the fourth Druk Gyalpo. In the 34 years of his reign, we have grown far beyond our own expectations and created history today as a nation that has not only given birth to the unique philosophy of Gross National Happiness, but also achieved an unprecedented transition to democracy. His Majesty has shown that there is no other duty for a king than to serve the people.

Therefore, I take this opportunity to offer on behalf of all Bhutanese, our gratitude to our forefathers, our kings and to the fourth Druk Gyalpo. Let us abide by their great example and pledge our unwavering loyalty and service to the Tsawasum.

The highest achievement of one hundred years of Monarchy has been the constant nurturing of Democracy. This has culminated today with the first sitting of Parliament and the start of democracy, whereby my father the fourth Druk Gyalpo and I, hereby return to our people the power that had been vested in our kings by our forefathers one hundred years ago. We do so with absolute faith and confidence, offer our complete support and our prayers for the success of democracy.

As *king*, henceforth, it is my sacred duty to ensure the success of our new democracy so that it will serve to fulfil the aspirations of our people always.

As you, the members of Parliament, begin to shoulder the immense powers and responsibilities as representatives of the people, I wish to share own hope for Bhutan. It has always been my prayer that we will all be united in our efforts to build a stronger nation, so that at the end of our lives, when we hand over our country, our children will inherit a stronger nation, where all obstacles to their happiness and prosperity will have been overcome and we have created the conditions for the fulfilment of their aspirations. And above all, that they will be better than us, more qualified and capable. We should not have insecurities in this regard. If Bhutan is to excel, our future generations must always be better than those before them.

To realize this prayer, we must first build a strong democracy. In doing so, our new politicians must be mindful of the experiences of nations where democracy failed and hardship, disunity, internal strife and violence have plagued their people. We must never allow, at any time, the conditions to develop for such occurrences in Bhutan. Our effort to build a democracy is another important step towards strengthening our country. It continues the work of nation-building started by our forefathers and our kings. We must remember that our greatest strength throughout history has always been the unity of our spirit and purpose of our people. One nation, one vision.

Members of the first Parliament of Bhutan; Speaker; chairperson of the National Council; Leader of the Opposition; ministers of Lhengye Zhungtshog, Lyonpo Yeshey Zimba, Lyonpo Khandu Wangchuck, Lyonpo Wangdi Norbu, Lyonpo Ugyen Tshering, Lyonpo Zangley Dukpa, Lyonpo Minjur Dorji, Lyonpo Pem Gyamtsho, Lyonpo Nandalal Rai, Lyonpo Thakur Singh Powdyel, Lyonpo Dorji Wangdi; and the first Prime Minister under democracy, Lyonpo Jigmi Yoezer Thinley- from this day forth, we place in your hands our unique nation, our greatest treasure in this world.

As democracy's first government, you have the responsibility of setting the right example, laying strong foundation and promoting the best practice of democracy. We, the people and *king*, have complete faith in the new government. As long as you work to serve the country and people, you will have our full support. If you should falter in your service to the nation, then the duty to counsel you also rests with the people and the *king*.

However, with your experience and qualification, and your loyalty and commitment to the *Tsawasum*, I am confident that you will work hard to bring greater progress and growth for our people.

May the unity of our people and the fruits of democracy ensure that the sun of peace and prosperity continues to shine on our nation, the Land of Buddha's Teachings; blessed by *Guru Padmasambhava* and our Guardian Deities; and founded on the vision and legacy of Zhabdrung Ngawang Namgyal and Jigme Singye Wangchuck."

Appendix-II

His Majesty's Address at the Signing of the Constitution on 18 July, 2008

"On this day of destiny, in the blessed land of Pelden Drukpa, we, a fortunate people and king, hereby resolve to bring into effect the root and foundation-the very source- of all law in our nation.

On such an auspicious occasion, on behalf of the people, I offer gratitude to His Majesty the fourth Druk Gyalpo. During his reign, His Majesty built a strong nation and secured the hopes and aspirations of the people through the process of democratisation and the enlightened vision of Gross National Happiness. His Majesty has also laid a clear path for our future through this Constitution.

The significance of His Majesty's unique achievements as leader has transcended the experiences of our country and been acknowledged by the world. In our own country, many generations into the future, the Constitution will continue to inspire our people as it stands testimony to a selfless and extraordinary leadership.

This Constitution is the most profound achievement of generations of endeavour and service. As it is granted to us, we must remember that even more important than the wise and judicious use of powers it confers, is the unconditional fulfilment of the responsibilities we must shoulder. Only in understanding our duties will the exercise of our powers be fruitful. If we can serve our nation with this knowledge and in this spirit, then an even brighter future waits our country.

It is my fervent prayer that through this Constitution we will, with our body, speech and mind work with complete commitment and conviction as we strengthen the sovereignty and security of Bhutan; secure the blessings of liberty; ensure justice and peace and enhance the unity and happiness of all Bhutanese, now and always.

Lastly, this Constitution was placed before the people of the twenty *dzongkhags* by the *king*. Each word has earned its place with the blessings of every citizen in our nation. This is the People's Constitution.

And today, through this, my Hand and Seal, I affix on to the Constitution of the Kingdom of Bhutan, the hopes and prayers of my people."

Appendix-III

Coronation Address of His Majesty the Fifth King

It is with immense joy that we are gathered together on this most auspicious day. In these last 100 years, the dreams and aspirations of our forefathers and the vision of our kings have been fulfilled beyond all expectations. The wise and selfless leadership of our kings, the sacrifice and hard work of generations of Bhutanese and the special bond between the people and king have given us this unique and special nation- a jewel of the earth.

Two years ago, at a time of profound change I came onto the Throne as a young King. You, my people, in the spirit of generations past, worked with me with complete faith and gave me your wholehearted cooperation and goodwill. Thus, in these two short years while we have taken gigantic steps towards strengthening our nation, we have done so in calm, deliberate manner in complete harmony. It is with great pride that we stand as new democracy, having successfully completed an unprecedented and historic transition.

Yet, we must always remember that as our country, in these changing times finds immense new challenges and opportunities, whatever work we do, whatever goals we have-and no matter how these may change in this changing world-ultimately without peace, security and happiness we have nothing. That is the essence of the philosophy of Gross National Happiness. Our most important goal is the peace and happiness of our people and the security and sovereignty of the nation.

Our generation of Bhutanese have been gifted a strong, dynamic nation by our forefathers. I am confident that as long as we are willing to work with commitment and dedication and follow their example we can bring greater peace, happiness and prosperity to our country.

I am confident because I know the worth and character of our people. You are the true jewel of this nation. As citizens of a spiritual land, you treasure the qualities of a good human being -- honesty, kindness, charity, integrity, unity, respect for our culture and traditions, love for our country and for God. Throughout our history, our parents have upheld these values and placed the common good above the self.

My deepest concern is that as the world changes, we may lose these fundamental values on which rest our character as a nation and people. It is critical that we are able to recognise Bhutanese character irrespective of how far we look back into the past or into the future. The Bhutan we see is vastly different, even unrecognizable, when compared to the Bhutan in the time of our first king. Yet, the character of our people and the nature of our fundamental values have remained unchanged. Henceforth, as even more dramatic changes transform the world and our nation, as long as we continue to pursue the simple and timeless goal of being good human being, and as long as we strive to build a nation that stands for everything that is good, we can ensure that our future generations for hundreds of years will live in happiness and peace.

It is not because I am *king* that I ask these of you. Destiny has put me here. It is with immense gratitude and humility that at this young age, I assume the sacred duty to serve a special people and country. Throughout my reign, I will never rule you as a *king*. I will protect you as a parent, care for you as a brother and serve you as a son. I shall give you everything and keep nothing. I shall live such a life as a good human being that you may find it worthy to serve as an example for your children; I have no personal goals other than to fulfil your hopes and aspirations. I shall always serve you, day and night, in the spirit of kindness, justice and equality.

As the king of a Buddhist nation, my duty is not only to ensure your happiness today, but to create the fertile ground from which you may gain the fruits of spiritual pursuit and attain good *karma*.

This is how I shall serve you as *king*.

I cannot end without addressing our most important citizens-our youth. The future of our nation depends on the worth, capabilities and motivation of today's youth. Therefore, I will not rest until I have given you the inspiration, knowledge and skills so that you not only fulfil your own aspirations but be of immense worth to the nation. This is my sacred duty. A strong motivated young Bhutan guarantees a strong bright future.

The future is neither unseen nor unknown it is what we make of it. What work we do with our two hands today will shape the future of our nation. Our children's tomorrow has to be created by us today.

I end with a prayer for Bhutan- that the sun of peace and happiness may forever shine on our people. I also pray that while I am but *king* of a small Himalayan nation, I may in my time be able to do much to promote the greater well being and happiness of all people in this world, of all sentient being.

Tashi Delek.

Appendix-IV

Interview with Lyonpo Thakur Singh Powdyel, Honourable Minister of Education and Chairman Commission of Women and Children

(Taken by Dr. Madhu Rajput on October 20, 2011, at his office in the Ministry of Education, Thimphu, Bhutan)

Q. What are your views about education in Bhutan? It is said that every child has right to education, but sometimes poverty makes it difficult to access education.

Ans: No scheme is complete without including education. Education for me is the bottom line. Any nation aspires to do anything good and succeed, has to make education its foundation especially for small systems like Bhutan- a small country with a small population, we have to do the best that we can in those areas where we feel we have some advantage and the advantage here is smallness, its size; but this is also a disadvantage, so thereby that means, we have to make up in term of quality what we do not have in terms of quantity. For a small country, its people are very important, that is the only wealth that we have. We have to invest in people. We have to make every Bhutanese man, woman and child a productive contributing member of the society. The best way to invest in people and the building of people is through education. So, even though this modern education began only in early 1960's, we feel that we have come a long way in the past six decades or so. We had a very long system of education dating back to several centuries. I look at education in Bhutan in terms of waves. The first wave we call-the Monastic Education Wave that would have started somewhere in eighth century, that wave still continues. Somewhere in the early 1960's, we started the big Modern Education Wave. Today's professionals, bureaucrats, administrators, managers, diplomats, members of parliament, civil servants, all these people, belong to the second wave. The third wave we call the Non-Formal Education Wave. Because in the early 1960's, when the modern education began, there weren't many schools. Lot of our people could not go to school, either because there were no schools or because there were too many compulsions that kept them at home. So a large number of our people lost that opportunity. They became farmers, business people but we felt that especially now, with modernization, democratic processes having been in place, we feel that every citizen must be able to make sense of the political process, democracy, they must be able to participate meaningfully in the process. So, we had to introduce a third wave called the Non-Formal Education Wave. This programme was meant for people who missed their opportunity when young. We feel they must be given a second chance in life. So, we started the Non-Formal Education Program for housewives, the villagers, our farmers who could not go to school early on, and this caught on very well. Today, a lot of our local leaders are graduates of the Non-Formal Educational Wave. Our housewives have been able to learn how to read and write, read the newspapers, use their mobiles, communicate to each other, learn and listen to the news and also make informed decisions. Quality of home life has improved. Health and hygiene has improved. Our mothers are able to manage home affairs much better and the general standard of living has improved. So, this has been a very important third wave of education. Since, we have been doing fairly well, in 2009 the UNESCO awarded the Confucius Literacy prize to Bhutan, for success in the Non-Formal Education Program.

In the recent past, we have also realized that there are lot of people in the civil service who started working after finishing Grade VIII, Grade X, because, there was a need for people, educated people in system. So, they got into jobs even before they were able to complete their education that they would have wished to, there was a need now for us to upgrade their qualification and knowledge. We started the fourth education wave which is called the Continuing Education Wave. Lot of people have benefitted from this wave.

The fifth wave we feel will be the Digital Education Wave. These are the waves through which I look at the progress of education. In the early 1960's, we had a difficulty in getting people to school—because that is the main thing. The government literally had to do some conscripting of young men and women from villages to come to school. Now at the moment, we are very glad that people have understood the value of education. Parents want to send their children to school. There are economic challenges for people to send their children to school in remote areas. However, our parents believe that education is the way to better life, a better future.

Our enrolment especially at the primary level is close to 98 per cent. In the next couple of years, we want to make sure that every single child is in school, who should be in school, is in school. The constitution of kingdom of Bhutan provides for eleven years of schooling. Class X is supposed to be the basic education level. The government is required to provide basic education to all the children of Bhutan. So, standard X is the basic education level. It is based on eleven years of schooling with one year of primary education. After the basic education level, graduation to the pre-university level is merit-based. We send about 40-45 per cent of class X graduates to do pre-university. From pre-university to go to undergraduate programmes, the selection process becomes still much more merit-based, progressive. We take in between 20 to 30 per cent of class XII graduates in the first year degree programme. The process is fairly steep as we go up. So, we see education both as a means to an end as well as an end in itself. Means to an end because we are still building our infrastructure. We are still building our society, still building many institutions and education has to be used as a means to an end. We also feel that education is good in itself. It is good to have educated people in the society. If there are learned, educated and wise people in the society, that's a good society. We see education both as a means as well as an end.

We launched a massive nationwide education reform program in 2010. The new academic year began in February 2010; that we call 'Education for Gross National Happiness'. Every nation has to have a dream just as every individual has. If a nation has a dream which is a big, worthwhile and good dream, the sub sectors, the sub systems of the nation will have to support the dream. They have to advance the dream. Gross National Happiness being the developing goal of this country, the long term vision of this country, the education system has to take ownership of the dream and cater to advance the dream. We began a programme called 'Educating for Gross National Happiness'. It not only allows us to advance our national development goal, but we feel that educating for Gross National Happiness allows us to return to the essential goal of education. What is the purpose of education? What's the goal of education? What is the core function of education? This programme of Educating for GNH actually allows us to return to the basic goal of education. Around the world if you look, whether it is at the school, college or the university level, there is so much happening in the name of education, which is not education. Education is meant only as an entry into the job market, prepare people for employability. People are not talking even about employment. They are talking about employability which means the system makes big schools, colleges and universities only to prepare people for job market, to be employed and to serve a certain end. We feel that is not the only purpose of education. Education has a bigger role. It has a bigger responsibility. That's why education is called the 'Noble Sector'. No other sector is called the 'Noble Sector'. Some great minds in the past thought education must be called the 'Noble Sector', but in more systems around the world, education system has lost that nobility. Nobility has gone out of the noble sector. If education is not noble, some sector in the society doesn't make people aspire for noble things, for the sublime things of life, which sector will they look up to? Something has to shine as the North Star. Something has to aspire people; it has to be education.

Agriculture is very practical. Industry is very practical. Business is the market based and very practical. Health has got to be very practical. Education has to be pragmatic as well as idealistic, positive as well as normative. It has to inspire people. That's why educating for Gross national Happiness is for us a very powerful instrument. It needs to make us return and to rediscover the essential goal of education and at the same time helping advance the developmental goal of this country. Educating for gross national happiness is a very important and powerful goal. We are looking at education not only as an instrument to prepare people for the job market, but would like to use education as an instrument to build people and engage young men and women—not only to aspire for careers, but to look at what is going to be important for this country. It is a tremendously important service that we provide through education. Education has to build the society. That's how we look at education.

Q. Education should be for developing their inner talent. You were precisely talking of developing them uttermost and making them a responsible citizen of this country.

Ans: If education doesn't do that, we are failing in our responsibility. It's unfair to young people. We owe it to young people, not only to provide and prepare them for the job market but to prepare them for life.

Q. What would you like to tell us about the higher education, do you intend to expand it more?

Ans: We have to, because we have a university. It's a federative system. The colleges spread across the country are supposed to be centres of excellence in their own rights. We do not have enough of them. A large number of young men and women have still to go outside to India and beyond. We have to build higher education centers, but even in higher education, we have to see whether it is education that is limited to preparing people for career or employment or whether higher education should enable societies to discover their intellectual potentials. Higher education should act as the same means as a great conserving space in the sense that Bhutan should be able to look at higher education as a means of tapping into innovation, development, progress achieved by cultures and civilisations around. We look at higher education both as a symbol of our society and nation coming of age. We should be able to participate in the intellectual awakening of the 21st century. At the same time, we should be able to treasure and promote what we have inherited from our own heritage, culture and wisdom of the past. We look at higher education as a means of reconciling, harmonizing the best of the old and the new. Higher education in Bhutan is in the process of growing, developing. We have to do more.

Higher education basically has three functions. One is 'knowledge function', because higher education has people who are the most educated lot in the society. They have to discover new frontiers. They have to expand the frontiers of human mind, frontiers of the society. The knowledge function of higher education is very important. We look upon our higher education system basically as building those intellectual frontiers. The second important function of higher education is 'training function'. We need to prepare people for the different sectors of the economy, to serve in different sectors of the society. By providing higher knowledge, higher expertise, higher training, we have to prepare people to shoulder responsibility in the different sectors of the economy for which training function is very important. Finally of course, higher education should serve 'Public Service Function'. By virtue of the fact that our colleges, universities are supposed to have the most educated and learned people, higher education system owes it to society—to provide 'Consultancy Services', to provide new knowledge, new directions, new pathways. What should be the direction of the economy. What should be the direction of our diplomacy? What should be the direction of our development? It should be the responsibility of higher education to provide those pathways. Higher education should be seen as something that will enable public discourse, provide new pathways for thought building.

We see higher education as a symbol of growth of our education. It will make us reach a level of maturity and confidence that will provide Bhutan the necessary tools to engage our minds. At the same time, it should also enable us participate in the promise, innovations, development that is happening around the world in different cultures and civilisations.

Q. Education has to be internationally linked. It has to have its roots in the local. All the policies have to come up keeping our local demands and traditions in mind. We can be influenced by anybody but our policies should always reflect our own growth.

Ans: Absolutely. Mahatma Gandhi said that India is like a big house with many windows through which lot of fresh air should come in. The house should be so strong that the blast doesn't topple it. In same way, education system should be able to honour what we have and at the same time allow us to receive the goodness and virtues of systems around the world. University by definition is precisely that. Allow young people, men and women to celebrate what they have received through their heritage and culture, keeping their minds open to receive good ideas, knowledge and wisdom from around the world. Otherwise we could be very insular and to that end very limited.

Q. What do you think has changed the role of teachers in present context? The earlier role teachers had really has changed. How do you feel a teacher should be a role model for the students?

Ans: In any education system, the teacher is the kingpin. The teacher is the central pillar. Otherwise, we may have fabulous facilities, great policies, wonderful programmes, great resources, very motivated children. If the teacher is not motivated, engaged and initiated, we can go only so far and no further. The teacher is so important that s (he) can actually compensate for the deficiencies in other areas. We may not have very good resources or facilities. We may not have the most highly motivated children. If we have a highly creative, imaginative, engaged and motivated teacher, this person can compensate for deficiencies in other areas. The teacher is the upholder of the profession, of culture, and of disciplines. He is the medium through which the knowledge of different disciplines passes to succeeding generations.

What has changed in the status of teachers? I think all around the world, there is a sea change in the way the role of teacher is perceived. I am sure especially in our part of the world, in the earlier years, the teacher was the only source of knowledge in the community. The teacher was the most qualified, knowledgeable and respected person. If a letter came to the local headman from the government, the local headman would run to that teacher to read it out. If a response is required to be written, it was again the teacher who had to write that response. Nobody else was educated like the teacher. So, the teacher occupied that exclusive space as the most powerful and knowledgeable person. Everybody respected him or her. The teacher was seen as the exclusive source of knowledge. Today, there are many sources of knowledge. Knowledge comes to children from the internet, advertising, the television, the mass media, from educated parents and, from neighbourhood which is much more literate. There are so many source of knowledge today. The teacher is not the only source of knowledge. His exclusive space is today shared by many other players.

The teacher has to work very hard to keep ahead. Otherwise his or her space is going to be taken away by others.

Why there is a change in the attitude towards teachers is that the exclusiveness that the teacher enjoyed in the past is no longer the case. There are so many other players. There may be far more knowledgeable people in the society than him. The children could easily get information from many other sources but I still feel that despite the smart technology we have, the state-of-the-art equipment we have, the human teacher is still important. A machine cannot speak the language of the teacher. The machine doesn't feel, so the human teacher with flesh and blood is still a very important part of the whole scheme. We have teachers even to this day, who are highly revered. We would like to reclaim the noble profession by situating the teacher in a respectable position. If you cannot respect your teachers, you cannot expect to learn. Respect for teachers is the fundamental condition for learning. You can't treat your teacher as a machine. The teacher is a very precious part of the scheme of teaching and learning. Of course, today there has been such a change, transformation that when we look at the status of teachers, it is no longer as glamorous and respectable as it was in the past.

Teaching is a very difficult job. Perhaps, it is the most difficult job in the world. They are dealing with young children, young minds. You do not know how young minds operate, as complex as the human mind is. Especially, if it is young mind, that is more difficult. Teacher's job is not even a job, it's a mission. One has to be cut out to be a teacher. It is not anybody and everybody becoming teachers. Only some people can become teachers. It's difficult, risky and dangerous. You can be miseducating a lot of people if you do not know who you are as a teacher. Education or teaching is the only profession in the world, dedicated to making people better, i.e., making the world a better place. Every time, a teacher does something good to the class, he has already made the world a better place. Anytime you teach a child a new sound, a new concept, a new meaning, a new idea, you have already made the world a better place. That's why, it is a great civilising force. We need a new civilization. I feel it is going to be called a new educational civilization.

Other civilisations have been very weak. So to save it, to retain the society what we need is the nobility of the noble sector. What education can change people, transform society, transform the world.

Q. What are your views on present Bhutanese women? How have they evolved over the years? They were always powerful in a family but now, they are visible everywhere. How things have changed over the years for them?

Ans: I think Bhutanese society is evolving, Bhutan as a nation is dynamic, is forward looking, futuristic and with the evolution of the society there has also been a remarkable evolution on the status of women. Bhutanese women have always been very strong. They have been the bulwark of our families, homes and society. More and more women have entered the modern sector, thanks to education. Education is a great leveller, thanks to democracy. It's a great leveller and thanks to the vision of our kings and our leaders. They have always believed that men and women have to move together.

We have achieved a lot over the years. We have several members in the parliament. The number should even be greater than what we have now. Lot of our local leaders are now women. That number has to increase. Our enrolment at the primary school level is very balanced. As a matter of fact, we have more girls than boys. We have achieved gender parity at the middle, secondary level, and are close to achieving gender parity at the higher secondary level. We have to do some work at the tertiary education level to achieve gender parity. We believe that we will be able to create more space for women. We have actually equal number of men and women in the country. As a matter of fact, there could be a few more women than men. We have to engage the genius the creativity and the talent that is hidden away in our women. Otherwise, our society cannot move forward. It will move forward, but it will be so much stronger if both women and men move together. They have made rapid progress, women who have been in power, in positions of importance, have done an incredible job, they have given a wonderful account of themselves—very strong, very capable, resourceful, imaginative, creative and bold. I am very glad about the way our women have been involved and played the role in building of this nation. We have close to 90,000 girl students in our education system. They are doing wonderfully well. Many of the top positions at public examinations are taken by girls. They are a great inspiration.

Q. It is true that education has played a revolutionary role in changing their lives and has empowered them to progress furher.

Ans: In many ways, one of the indices of the society is the way you treat your women.

Q. Right from my childhood I always thought of one thing, all of us who are born, have a right to be humans.

Ans: Definitely, if anybody thinks otherwise is absolutely blighted.

Q. We should have the opportunity of development, rest is up to us.

Ans: The former French finance minister, now the current IMF chief Christien Laggart, said that if the laymen brothers had been laymen sisters, perhaps we would have been spared the financial crisis the world went through. The great resources in the men and women must be channelled to serve life, society the nation and the world.

Q. Many of my friends disagree with me I always say that men and women were created with equal kind of mind but their work was different. So a woman cannot ignore her home, but she has to develop in other areas. I never believe in those theories where you neglect one thing and you want to do something else. You have to know the art of balancing.

Ans: The virtues of being a man, the virtues of being a woman, those virtues we cannot spurn. Man should make the most of being men. Women should make the most of being women. We should try to be the most we are. Do the best of who we are, be the best of who we are.

Appendix- V

Interview with Deki Pema, Election Commissioner of Bhutan

(Taken by Dr. Madhu Rajput in June 2010, at her office in Election Commission of Bhutan, Thimphu, Bhutan)

Q. How have been the two years after election? What has been your work during this time?

Ans: It's been good because we have had an opportunity for introspection. We looked at our organisational structure. We did learn from experience. We went over rules and regulations and tried to find out what needed to be changed, given our experience. It was like housekeeping in many ways. Earlier, we were quite loosely organised, whoever was around did whatever was necessary. Now, we have to be much more systematic. There has to be professional development. At that time, we didn't have that option. We just learnt on the job and did the best we knew. A great enthusiasm was there. People were willing to put in 15-16 hours without a grudge. It's not fair to ask in every election. The time between the elections was the most important. We were kind of regrouped and better prepared for the next elections. We had the time to reflect and did a major organisational review on our understanding. We have looked at the way we are organised, our staffing pattern. What would be the ideal state so that we try and go there. We also identified the gaps in professional development. We have come up with a plan which we hope we will be able to implement over the years. We are looking forward not only for the next elections but at 2020. That's a long term plan. We also have been preparing ourselves for the local government elections. Having said that, not all the pieces are together yet.

Q. Last time you had to teach the people each and every thing regarding elections. Do you think this time they are more aware of the procedure?

Ans: Definitely, even the roles that the different houses have to play, it's one thing to talk about and another thing for people to actually see it happening—to see the houses in section; to see how decisions are made; how issues are being discussed and how the decision making process is coming in. When you talk, it becomes very abstract. When you see it happening, you realise. Oh! Opposition means this.

Q. Do you think you need to upgrade the electoral list that you had at the last census?

Ans: In the last elections, we used the Civil Registry. It was more or less correct, but over the years more people would have turned 18, or have died. We have to continually upgrade to maintain the electoral roll to ensure that it is up-to-date. Some people are to be transferred on to the electoral roll of the other place, as they change their citizenship, like from one district to the other, in which case their constituency and polling station will change. We have to keep updating the list.

Q. Do you face any problems in such a huge exercise?

Ans: Actually, it's not such a huge problem. We have a Civil Registry which is an ongoing process with the Ministry of Home and Cultural Affairs. We derive our electoral roll. It is really helpful but few things are to be taken care of, the age limit of 18, and the religious figures are not voters. The Civil registry has the total registration of all citizens. These are the elements we have to separate while preparing the electoral roll.

Q. I think the Election Commission has done a good job. Though, it is still being debated in the outside world as to how democracy will fare in your country, it is too early to say anything at present. How do you feel being a woman Election Commissioner, it is something very closely followed by everyone? How has been your experience at this position?

Ans: I think it's not because I am a woman in this position. Anybody in this position will firstly feel very grateful for the privileges that come with the role entrusted to him or her. It's an honour to have an opportunity to be in an organisation, which is quite crucial for the whole process of transition from monarchy to democratic constitution. It's historic and very important to the national goal. It is something which will really define my life. Even if I work here only for five or eight years, it will still be the highlight of my life. It doesn't mean I didn't believe what I was doing earlier or what I will do later, but because this, in the life of the nation was such a crucial point. That I have an opportunity to be involved at such close range and in such an intimate manner was an honour. I didn't really have a problem as a woman. There was no problem even earlier as it is my 19th or 20th year of working. Earlier, I worked in the Ministry of Agriculture. I used to work in the Policy and Planning Division. I never felt there that because of my gender I got either opportunities or I was denied one. I had the opportunity to do my best and interact with my colleagues as well as my seniors in a comfortable way. I can't say that this is the case with everybody. Personally, I never had a grudge.

Q. How do you feel being here in the Election Commission?

Ans: It was a privilege and an honour. I can say it was not only for me, but all of us who worked for the first elections. We did it with such a sense of occasion. We were so aware what the occasion was and of the opportunity that we had in helping the transition and increasing procedures for those who will come later. They worked on the rules, regulations, procedures, and the organisational structure. We are setting precedence. We were very conscious of the fact that we were creating precedence. It is because that we did it with a lot of joy. We had to work very long hours, which we did without grudge. We realised that we were very fortunate to be here. Now, we have the local elections. The dates are not confirmed yet. That will complete the whole cycle. We are all geared up for work as well as mentally prepare.

Q. It will give you more insight into how your electorates react to it?

Ans: Definitely.

Appendix-VI

Interview with Sonam Tobgye, Chief Justice of Bhutan and Chairman of the Constitution Committee

(Taken by Dr. Madhu Rajput on 19 October 2011, at the Supreme Court, Thimphu, Bhutan)

Q.Sir, in one of your articles you have used the word constitutional monarchy for your present political system, which was given by His Majesty the fourth king. Could you put some light on that?

Ans: This is the constitution timeline. On September 9, His Majesty the fourth king had summoned chief justice, prime minister, all the cabinet ministers that we will have the constitution. After that the whole process took place. There were three processes. The first process is the election of the members of drafting committee, nomination from the government, from the clergy and the judiciary. On November 30, His Majesty signed and then in November 2001, drafting of the constitution began. First draft of the constitution was submitted on December 9th, then the present draft. The first draft was presented, then Mr. K. K. Venugopal was consulted. It was presented to His Majesty again. On 22 November 2004 his Majesty the fourth Druk Gyalpo presented it to the cabinet. The draft constitution was distributed among people. His Majesty began public consultation, which was like the Constituent Assembly. Constitutional monarchy came from the third meeting of the drafting committee.

Q. As far as your Supreme Court is concerned, will it be something like we have in India?

Ans: Yes, it is something like India. We have the general jurisdiction. It is almost like India, British and American model. We have general jurisdiction of the cases. We do not have a separate court for the constitutional cases. Unlike your system, the whole administration of the judges and the whole country comes under Supreme Court. In your case, it is taken over by law department and is on the State list. Unlike that, there is a total separation of powers from Supreme Court to the lowest court in Bhutan. From Apex court to the lowest court, it is totally separated from the executive and legislature.

Q. Does it have the power to give decisions on other administration?

Ans: Yes, it is clearly mentioned in the judicial review in Article 1 Section 10, that we have full judicial review. In India, America and elsewhere, it is through implied interpretation. In our case, it is the explicit provision.

Q. Before the establishment of the Supreme Court, you had the High Courts. Now that the Supreme Court is there will it be easy for people from far flung areas to approach? As some cases are directly administered, while in other cases first you have to go to the lower court, then High Court and then the Supreme Court, so even in Bhutan is it going to be the same?

Ans: Yes, it's similar. We have no limitation unlike your country where there are some limitations, such as pecuniary cases; but here it can come generally till Supreme Court in the process of appeal. One process is by 'Appeal' and the other is by 'Special Leave of Appeal'.

Q. What is the 'Special Leave of Appeal'?

Ans: 'Special Leave of Appeal' is when the Superior Court grants the appeal. The other one is general 'Right to Appeal'.

Q. As the Chief Justice of Bhutan, what do you feel about the present judicial system?

Ans: Obviously, I have been in this system for so long and to say wrong will be self-inflicting.

Q. Still the system today is a little different from the system we have been seeing in Bhutan. So, what is the difference?

Ans: The only difference is that earlier there was appeal from the High Court to His Majesty. Now, it is the Supreme Court and Supreme Court is final. There are more responsibilities. We are the final appellate court. We have greater responsibilities to dispense justice.

Q. Do you have a system like India that even after the Supreme Court's decision, there is a provision for the petition to the President?

Ans: That's different. That comes under 'Review Petition', Pardon, Reprieve; it is there under the Constitution.

Q. In your case, will it be to the King?

Ans: Yes, to the king.

Q. How lengthy a process it was for you to draft the constitution?

Ans: The first draft was 10 months. It took thereafter three to four years, between 2002-05. Three years was time for our discussion, like consulting K. K. Venugopal in India and within our system. Corrections took about three years. Drafting took another ten months.

Q. You must have kept the entire Bhutan in mind while drafting?

Ans: There were 39 members in the Drafting Committee. 20 people were elected for drafting the constitution, and six members were elected by the people for the National Advisory Council. We had the National Advisory Council , who were also elected, then the Speaker. There were 27 members from the public. We had clergy two, the government had 13, and judiciary had three. Everybody was represented. We had to think of the whole country.

Q. Though, it happens everywhere, I think in Bhutan it is even more prominent that there are not many women lawyers. Is there a woman judge?

Ans: Yes, we have a woman judge. Women judges are few, but women lawyers are many. Many are studying law in India. At the lower rung, there are many, but at the senior level, at Supreme Court, we were going to have one woman judge. Unfortunately, we couldn't have her. At that time, she was not in the country. At the High Court we have one woman judge. At the district court we have, and not as many as men but at the lower rung, there are many.

Q. Is there any proposal of opening Law School?

Ans: There is a proposal; We are considering to do so.

Q. The more the expansion, the more people will be required to settle the disputes.

Ans: I think within 2-3 years, we will have an oversupply, In India alone, there are around 250 law students. In Bhutan, there are more than 100 scattered around. So, in human resource we do not have a problem.

Q: You have been in the legal system for so long, what are the kinds of cases which come in the largest number?

Ans: The number differs between three types. Number one – is land because it still is an agrarian society. Number two is loan, and the number three is matrimonial.

Q: We understand that divorce is not a complex affair here.

Ans: It is quite a simple system here.

Q: But if one party wants a divorce, is it possible?

Ans: Unless it is under the principle of incompatibility. If somebody wants a divorce, s(he) can but that will become a defaulting party. Therefore, there will be more concern, because the defaulting party looses certain rights. Those who want a divorce without reason unless on cruelty or incompatibility, then what the law says is that half of the property goes to the person who is right, another quarter goes to the children, the defaulter gets only one quarter.

Q: What is the definition of incompatibility?

Ans: The law has mentioned it as a long separation. Incompatibility generally has to be mutual. Judges will accordingly interpret the definition.

Q: In India, it takes a long time to get a divorce; in fact it takes more than one's lifetime.

Ans: In Bhutan, the cases are decided within twelve months. If there are some complex cases like currently we have 80-90 cases which are beyond 12 months, otherwise all the cases are decided within one year.

Q: Have you started getting any corruption cases?

Ans: Yes, we have corruption cases. Now quite a bit is coming. Corruption was always there. The law took very serious note of it. We have heard the closing statement of another big corruption case. Our judgement will be out in November. It will be on our website.

Q: This case is from which department?

Ans: It is an individual vs. Anti-Corruption Bureau case. Anti-Corruption Bureau had filed the case, represented by the Attorney General.

Q: May I ask you what drives man to corruption, to become a criminal because we established these laws to make a better life for ourselves?

Ans: I think there are about three to four factors. First factor is the lack of moral authority. In short, there is no self-restraint. One should be able to realize that it is wrong. Number two is lack of timely or appropriate action. The law must be punitive and deterrent and must say that you must not enjoy the fruits of that labour called a poisonous tree. I think the third aspect is some systemic problem. We have to bring up the system.

Q: In India, we keep on saying that the system is faulty but don't you feel that the society is made of individuals and we contribute in a bigger way as individuals, families, a community, town, state and a country? This is the way a country is made.

Ans: Blaming on society is negation of one's duty. It means you don't want to do anything. You have to do a positive action. The positive action is–if there is something wrong, improve the education, in the society, improve morality through education, sensitize people through dissemination of thoughts. Knowledge is power and knowledge is a deterrent measure. If you talk about society, I think we have to inform them,we have to make them realize. How much society can do? To a great extent, government has to play the preventive role. The moment you say society, then the law becomes weak for you can't punish the society. You can punish the institution. When I talk about systemic problem, it's our laws. Basically, our laws are made up of suspicion. I think laws should be positive. It should not only to punish the corrupt, but also to encourage non-corrupt person. If we do not encourage the virtues, we can never discourage the vices. Our laws are mostly there to control. The very fact control means approval.Approval means that there is a favour to be asked and in return of some favour. Hundred per cent it can't work but deregulation is necessary. Number one is deregulation. Number two is simplification. Number three is transparency. As Lord Denning says, "Under the veil of secrecy, the world thrives". This is the way we are asking for murky situations. We cannot hide the scintillating stars under that murky veil.

Q: Do you think people in remote areas know their rights as citizens, the rights that are given to them by laws?

Ans: It is knowing and not knowing. I think it is very condescending. which is right? Is this a God given right ? Is it because the court gives that right or that the constitution gives that right? I feel it very insulting. Constitution and law are basically the recognition of inalienable, inherent, inviolable values. Each individual holds them and that our past sages have reminded us. In India and South East Asia we have more gods and goddesses, not because these areas were overpopulated but because they symbolised virtues. Something to look forward as an example is to do right and detering us from doing wrong. God means doing all that and that exists in the heart of every individual. Be it in the village, or in the remote corner or in the ivory tower of Thimphu. I do not believe that people in Delhi are more aware than in Gujarat or U. P. or in far flung places. Why? They are made up of flesh and blood. They are attacked by same hunger. They also feel pain. They react to happiness like all of us. Basically–laws are a recognition of inherent virtues of human being and the values. So, to say that they do not know is wrong. Yes, somebody may say on internet or something like that they you have no right of hacking or something like that. Is hacking known only in Thimphu or in Delhi? I don't think the word hacking will be known only among in the computer literates. I think it's very subjective views. Any subjective views will have a negative impact losing objectivity, I think they know but yes, nevertheless, we cannot take a passive role by saying they ought to know. It is in our values, that is also not true. If there is dissemination or empowerment, it is then to complement and supplement and to reinforce the very values that we owned. Hindus and Buddhist in particular, I am not talking about other countries. The values are inherent and even among Christians and Muslims, it doesn't say theft is right, I never heard murder is right in any religion,Law says only that much. In Mahabharata the very fact between Arjuna and Lord Krishna upholds the duty from where, the right comes. So to say that people in remote corner of Bhutan don't know, I think this is somewhat wrong.

Q: Many times hiring an advocate and coming to the court may not be possible.

Ans: That is access to justice. That is not ignorance, but that is access to justice. When they know about it, there should be a path. Destination and journey are very important, and interrelated. Access to that justice is the journey. It is the responsibility of the state. We had three types of access to justice. Access to justice is–when one is aggrieved, there should be one place or one window, one stop. O.k. you report, you go and file the FIR, that is the first access. The second access is that filing alone is not enough. There must be some rights for that person. s(he) cannot stay indefinitely, because it is done. No duty terminates but a simple act. We must give a limitation to that. In Bhutan, we have given limitation of ten days to act. In civil cases, it is 100 days to act. If you have a headache today, I can't ask for *crosine* tomorrow or paracetamol day after tomorrow. Timely medication relieves pain and deters complication. So, that is the second access to justice. Third thing is that when they know these things are accessible, people then get deterred not 100 per cent, but they will be deterred. Oh! If I do like this, tomorrow I will be in the police station or in a court. So, the access to justice is there in our court procedure and more so under Article 21 Section 1 of the constitution the judiciary shall dispense justice timely, without undue delay in accordance to the rule of law for the delay or expeditiousness must be accompanied by the rule of law as it comes under that.

The concept of rule of law is not an invention of the West enunciated and started by the Magnacarta in 1258 A. D., it is there in Hindu and Buddhist values and even among Christians. What it says that the values of the Dharm Raja in Hindu concept is different from the Buddhist concept but in Hindu concept he is a leader. Rajan actually came with that concept, and what kind of Raja is he? He is a Dharam raja. What is a Dharma? It is combined by rule. So, the rule of law for the Hindus and Buddhist came with Dharma Raja not Adharma Raja.

Q: How would you like to describe the position of women in your society today?

Ans: Position of women today is mentioned in Mahabharata. It is something like "salvation of man lies in the strength of a woman". I think that is the basis of a woman. Number two is *Tantric*. In India, the word *Tantra* is misunderstood. What does *tantric* mean? It's the union of male and female and that is represented in Buddhism also. Women are wisdom, male are method. It is a combination which is inseparable. Any person, who does not honour women, dishonours himself. In some of the context, you talk about *Manusmriti*. There is only one section in *Manusmriti* which talks against women but don't throw away the whole document. If my little finger is problematic, I don't commit suicide, I may amputate that. So, woman is a very important part. If a nation is to progress, society is to be strong, morality is to be enhanced, it's the woman because the first influences starts in one's life with the mother.

Q: Do you feel that for working women in modern context, it is little problematic to manage the work and the home because the children have to suffer a little bit in that?

Ans: Yes, this is not woman working. It is because of the nuclear family. True when a mother and father both go to work, most probably children suffer. Because, they are under the nannies or whoever they are, but what had happened was our women were never back to kitchen in the past, at least in Bhutan it was not that way. Jhansi ki Rani was not only in the kitchen, she saddled in the work, Queen of England Elizabeth the First said, "My body may be weak but my heart is not." We have voluminous and innumerous examples to strengthen our conviction and not to enfeeble us. I think the problem is the nuclear family. As we are getting more and more conscious of ourselves, the value for our grandparents is decreasing. I feel grandparents are perhaps more loving to the children than to their parents. So, it is not an abdication of responsibility by women working in offices. They are going to supplement the economy. It is laudable that we are empowering them to be independent. Shortage or denial of extra income is deterrent to the growth of children to whom we owe our responsibility. They are not there by their own choice but are the creation of mother and father. Having created them, we must provide best of the facilities so that they grow to their fullest and that is provided by some supplementary income. The basic problem is that we are not looking after the old parents. In fact about two or three years ago the Supreme Court of India had given a very landmark judgement on the responsibility of children to look after them. My daughters can go for work because my wife is there at home. To grandparents, it's a delight to see the young children growing and they can tell Ramayana to them, sing lullabies to them, it will transmit the values and ethic ensuring the survival of our values and culture.

Q: Our Supreme Court has given some landmark judgements. In India, especially the social norms are very hard to touch but they are touching them such as the live-in relationships are being recognised. The laws also have to match with the times.

Ans: You have rightly mentioned, it's the right word, I do not know whether you made it intentionally. Supreme Court is rendering judgement in recognition. Law is not a static stream. As Lord Denning said, "Real laws must not enslave but liberate us". As the very liberating laws if they can restrict us, then our growth is stultified. It's nothing new, it was always there but somehow over the years, there was a taboo on that, so that you must recognise but you can't do it immediately.

Q: Who inspired you to get into law?

Ans: Many things are imposed on you. The fourth king exiled me into this.

Q: People always say that what was begun by your third king was taken ahead by the fourth king. It was a lot of hard work, digging into the right thing. He made a road which was slow, steady and when he understood that now that things can go, he opened things. So how would you describe the fourth king as a man?

Ans: Obviously, he is a great king who has been absolutely compassionate, He has looked after his people well. In short in speech he always served the people, in action he fought and served the people and in deeds he made the people progress. We can say, in the years to come, one may scarcely believe that such man has walked in flesh and blood.

Q: And I think Bhutan will owe a lot to him.

Ans: Obviously. With all our kings we have been very fortunate.

Q: They understood the depth of the need of your people and they were able to protect you and give you the right things. I think they were the right kind of parents you needed.

Ans: All our five kings have been very wonderful. As I said earlier everything must spring from the inner self. It must be truthfully reflected. Satyamev Jayate! truth alone shall prevail.

Appendix-VII

Interview with Aum Neten Zhangmo, Chief of Anti-Corruption Commission of Bhutan

(Taken by Dr. Madhu Rajput in June 2010, at her office in the Anti-Corruption Commission, Thimphu, Bhutan)

Q: Since I have been in Bhutan, I have been hearing a lot about you.

Ans: You will definitely hear, because I work in Anti-Corruption Commission. (laughs)

Q: What do you think are the essential qualities in a human being that make him a confident person, who has the inner strength to work and accomplish successfully?

Ans: Be yourself! Don't try to be something else that you are not. Have conviction in yourself. Of course the values of honesty, self-esteem, honour are very important in life. These are the qualities which brought me so far. And you are at peace with yourself, but if you try to be someone else then you have problems.

Q: When did you begin your career? Before coming to this prestigious post, you must have been working somewhere?

Ans: I have been a rolling stone moving from one place to another. I worked at the polytechnic as a lecturer for six years. I was transferred to a vocational school, where you train plumbers and electricians.

Education Ministry under the section called the Technical Vocational Education Division looks after vocational training institutions. I moved to the Planning Ministry-Planning Commission then to the cabinet from where to Foreign Ministry and now I am here. So, I have worked in many agencies, but by profession I am an engineer. I studied in Birla Institute of Technology, Ranchi in India. This working in many agencies and with different groups of people gave me an exposure to lot of situations and learning opportunities. It's also useful that you don't become rigid. If you are working in one position and one organization then you have fixed ideas and fixed mindset, which is very difficult. Working in various organizations has been a learning process for me.

Q: I would like to know what makes a man corrupt?

Ans: Greed, I guess. In our context, it could also be social pressures. In a small society, you have a closely knit family. You have to look after your nieces, nephews, uncles and aunties. There are lot of expectations and that places lot of social compulsions. We did a survey because people say that it's not because of greed. It's because of need. We did a survey to know whether it is need or greed,but people agreed that it is not because of greed. Often the popular argument is that people are not paid well. They stoop to all sort of means to augment their income. I keep saying that if that is the problem then solution is also simple. Next day you enhance their salary by 100 per cent or 200 per cent then see if corruption stops. It will not. At the end of the day, it is to do with your inner self as to what values you espouse. Saying that salary is not being sufficient, is the easy part. But, the more difficult part is what is in you as a character.

Q: In my country, I think there is lot of corruption.

Ans: It's everywhere. Bhutanese are no saints. (Laughs)

Q: What measures are you trying to take at your level to check this corruption, because I think wherever we go there are so many posters? I feel you cannot instil anything by just displaying something. You have to lead by example. If there is this fear that if you are caught you will not be let go. It has to be there as by nature man needs that pressure to make things go right. What are the measures that you are taking at your level?

Ans: In fact I will go one step further. I will say that the Anti-Corruption Commission is established, so you are fearful. I will say that people should be responsible. Perhaps, the starting point could be fear. Some time after it should graduate to be responsible. We have a three-fold strategy, public education advocacy, sensitizing people on the forms of corruption that prevails in the society basides the cost. At the end of the day, it is the ordinary people who face the brunt of corruption. They are the victims of corruption. So, public education advocacy is one part, raising the responsibility that you have the ultimate responsibility to fight corruption. It is very difficult, because unlike other crimes, corruption is something that you can't see and find victims. If it is a robbery or murder you can identify the victim. In the case of corruption, somebody has embezzled few hundred thousand in an organization, but you don't see the victim. At the end of the day, we all become victims.

The other thing is the preventive aspect. Looking at the systems that allow corruption to perpetrate, rules, regulations, laws. Look at these and even in terms of administration, as you said we must lead by example. We have this slogan 'Lead by example', 'If you care, you will dare' and that ACC is the nation's conscience. It's also plugging the loopholes in the system.

Third part is the punitive- the investigation. When cases of corruption are reported, we investigate like the CBI. We are a combination of CBC and CBI in India. These three strategies we adopt in fighting corruption. We have always been saying that ACC can only do so much, on our own we cannot do anything. We need to fight together. It's a collective battle, unless there is support from all agencies, we just can't manage. If we talk about the systems, we don't have the expertise. They have the expertise, perhaps we would have the tools to identify the loopholes in the systems. They have the expertise in how the systems are operated. It's all about partnership, working together. The other strategy is learning from each other. We have partnership with our counterpart agencies in other countries.

Q: How do you feel being looked upon?

Ans: This is not a matter of consideration for me. Whether they look up to me, I don't care. Most important for me is that I do what I am to do, because if I start thinking that people are looking up to me, I better be careful then you don't become yourself. As I said you have to be yourself and have conviction in yourself. At the end of the day, my conscience has to be clear. I keep telling people that you don't have to be accountable to your superior-the king or the ACC. You have to be accountable to yourself, because you cannot lie to yourself. When you look into the mirror, don't look at your beautiful eyes and nose, look at what is inside you.

Q: Working here over the years, you must have faced many challenges.

Ans: Obviously, many challenges. In fact this is the best job I have got. People laugh at me. They think that I am stupid. Here, we have to investigate people.

Q: It blends very naturally with your personality, I suppose.

Ans: I love this job, though it is a bit difficult in a small society. Everybody is connected to everybody, whether through blood or matrimonially. You could be hurt also, even if you are not hurt your friends/relatives could be hurt but at the same time you know that you can make a difference. You can bring about changes in people's perceptions and behaviour. You can empower the citizens. This is what is most satisfying and rewarding for me.

Q: It's like putting your hands in dirty things. As you said you may be hurt, because corruption involves both the persons who does corruption and who is making it possible. You can't leave any of the parties by saying who did what and you have to be very careful dealing with cases. Because, your basic idea should be to investigate honestly. I am talking about big scandals in India, I have seen people who try to be very honest, it comes out one day in the newspaper that they are the most corrupt. You must have had chances of talking to these people. They are people in very responsible position, trying access to huge money for nation building. Why do they try to hoard so much wealth for themselves? What do they do when they take it home? What is their idea behind?

Ans: Leaders lead a different life altogether. We have big scam in mining sector. I guess it's more of an ego thing that they want to have more and more money.

Q: Don't have they the notion that they are betraying the nation?

Ans: Corrupt people are the last, who would care about it. They don't even worry that they will be caught. What we are trying to do is that corruption has to be made very costly and risky which is not the case right now. That's why the cost that I pay as a corrupt officer is very minimal. So might as well get corrupt. Get as much money as you want and be convicted for one or two years. You don't even have to go to the prison, you just pay in lieu of that and then carry business as usual.

Q: We are living in a society where people don't look down on people who are corrupt. It's OK that they have done something. Something has been done against them. They have huge money, that is more influential than anything else. The same happens with salaried people, who are bringing more money to their families. Suddenly, one day they are caught then people say that we didn't know. How didn't you know. When people were bringing more money and you are spending more than your salary, then how are you supposed not to be corrupt? During the French revolution, when corruption issues were being debated in National Assembly, Mirabeau said, "If you elect people and give them charge of positions, they are bound to be corrupt because they are going to come from all sectors where they have not seen money." So, he said that you should never have such people in charge of the treasury, because what will happen is that every time a new person will be there and when they see so much wealth, it is difficult for them to resist. That is why we have seen more scandals in democratic countries, where we elect representatives. In India, we have felt it. The heat is so much that we have stopped talking about it.

Ans: That's why the electorate has to be blamed, why are you electing such people?

Q: Many people outside say that Bhutan does not have a democracy. They say it's an eyewash and the power lies with one particular person. In India, we have never met our MPs and MLAs. The system of giving ticket is such that when you are spending crore in getting elected, how can we expect you not to extract back that money? The corruption is starting at the highest level. It has gone so deep that it has got roots. What do you feel on this acceptance of corruption in society?

Ans: This is the biggest problem. One of the sustainable ways of curbing corruption is intolerance. Right now in fact, we are also very accommodative. Even if a person is corrupt and has got convicted, as long as he has money and influence, he is very well regarded. We are saying this should not be tolerated. Within the government system, strict accountability has to be fixed. If somebody has embezzled funds, such and such an MP has siphoned government fund. We have this constitution development fund, if s/he has misused, s/he should be thrown out. Citizens should compel this person to leave. If acceptability is there, it is a serious problem.

Q: Corruption cannot be related to money only. It is related to the corruptions of the society, though they may not come under this purview. If such corruptions exist and there is acceptability, the idea of making a society in which you have equality for everybody does not exist. Corruption itself makes one person in a higher position; you are able to put other person down when you are able to squeeze something out of him.

Ans: We have this corruption tree. There are roots of corruption, in it you will find sleeping government, indifferent citizen. In the causes of corruption, you can see the tension in the society. You can see poverty being entrenched. You can see the divide between the rich and the poor. The rule of law been undermined. You can see at the end of the day, the *Gross National Happiness* becoming absolutely irrelevant. As you mentioned that people say that Bhutan is not a democracy, I believe that Bhutan is more democratically inclined than most of other democracies. Whatever the form of the government, what matters is how well the government is serving the people, what sort of opportunities people have. If the system provides it, it's not necessary to have party politics. I am quite fearful of this party politics. I am very much worried. India is not doing bad. I admire India and what your Prime Minister is doing. What the citizens are doing citizen-driven programmes, wonderful in terms of accountability, transparency, service delivery. Look at Nepal, Bangladesh. Look at these countries! These are democracies but serving whose purpose? If you are happy with such democracies, so be it.

Q: What do you plan to do after your retirement?

Ans: Retiring to the mountains. I have opened up a CSO (Civil Society Organisation). I want to work for the people, especially the ordinary people and be their voice. Let's see. This is what I really want to do. You are then your own master. You do what you want. I can hardly travel to the villages, my colleagues do. I want to go to the villages, work with the people, understand them, empower and in fact make them understand what democracy is.

Q: Not to get into politics?

Ans:Politics, I do not know. In fact I was just joking with my colleagues that I will join politics, not to win but to set ethical standards. The money that you get from the government, one lakh or so for your campaigning, how to use that. I will also make people understand that it's not for throwing parties or bribing. It's basically for our mobility. I don't care if I don't get a single vote or I get 90 per cent of votes. So, when you have such agenda, you are very clear. You can offer it honestly. When you have other agenda of winning, stoop to all sorts of things, and you become compelled, I want to see clean politics, just for that reason; otherwise I can work through the people via CSOs or NGOs.

Q: I always say no child is born-corrupt. It's the society which makes him corrupt.

Ans: Absolutely.

Q: We were never born corrupt. Many times we try to go for short cuts in life and that makes it difficult to leave. The first time in life when you make a compromise, that is the beginning of you making endless compromises. One day you may find yourself not in a position to say anything.

Ans: When we talk about corruption, it's all about values. How a young girl is growing up in family, environment community and school. How she develops, she is bribed by her grandfather to get cigarettes. In that environment how she grows up. When she becomes a mother, she bribes the teacher to get her daughter admitted in a school. That shows how the environment affects the character of a person.

Q: I think this is to do with our society. Most of us have this feeling that somebody is with us till you do something right. It has to be the opposite. We have to have this confidence that somebody should be there with us even if we go wrong. If we have done something wrong and somebody can tell us, we can correct ourselves and go the right way. We unknowingly commit a mistake so many times. I always say that if you do something for the first time, I don't blame because either you were so captivated by your environment, by the person who was with you that you couldn't see right or wrong. It should not be repeated for the second time. If it comes, then it is that you believe in something. I think the same is with corruption. If somebody is caught the first time and with a small thing, we have to understand that if somebody is very hungry and he has stolen something to eat, we have to tell him that you have to work hard and earn this. It's not easy in this society. If I go asking for something, I don't think anybody will give me even a pen. If I have one rupee less for my tickets, I think nobody will lend me. People will only lend me money when they know I have a good salary and I will repay that debt. This human aspect was one part of your 'Good Governance'. It is said that rigid things always break, no matter how strict you are. You have to make that consideration all the time in your life. With whom you are dealing, and what you are dealing. But as you rightly said that tolerance part should go away. The dealing tactics should be increased gradually with time. I think you must have taken these things in consideration.

Ans: Absolutely, especially people who have done it out of innocence, we try to accommodate those people, guide and counsel them so that they don't repeat. But repeated offenders have to be dealt with stringently.

Q: Do you take any pressures from anywhere?

Ans: No, if they try to pressurize me, they will be pressurized. It will be the rich and influential who will try to pressure you. Who will take care of the ordinary citizens?

Q: Who can pressurize are already in positions where they can take care of themselves. So, don't you take any pressure?

Ans: No, they should not. Ask them to try! If the government is sincere about fighting corruption, it must prove it in action.

Q: Before I came to Bhutan, I was very naïve. I thought there was no corruption here.

Ans: Somebody else was shocked. There was a conference in which somebody was surprised that there was corruption in Bhutan, for they think of it as a Shangrila and a happy nation with *Gross National Happiness*. I said first of all Bhutanese are also human beings. Corruption is a human weakness. We are no saints. May be the only difference is in the degree. we are not as corrupt as other countries. Corruption is there as long as there is civilization. It was there even in Buddha's time and Christ's time. The developed countries come here and tell us 'do this, do that', we tell them first you take care of your own countries where the nature of corruption is sophisticated and in crossed boundaries. At least here the corruption is in the bureaucracy, we can handle it. Yesterday, we were discussing a case where you can see huge flow of government funds into the personal account. Anybody will be tempted unless we have very high moral principles. All of us will be tempted. First may be 1,000 here, then 10,000 there, then may be hundred thousands, especially if you are able to take your kids to Bangkok for holidays or send them to Canada for studies. You have big fleet of cars, a big building until you are caught. That's why I feel corruption has to be made highly costly.

Q: In India, some of the officials were found keeping money in their floors. I wonder that they did corruption of all sorts, gave money to relatives, who took that money because that was black money. At the end, I don't know what they get because they have to clear their names from so many people. And even there, they are cleared because they are able to bribe. What is the use of such money, you can't use it.

Ans: There is always this fear of being caught. At the end of the day, you also drag your family. Your wife and children may not have known about it and the shame. Especially, if you have young kids going to school, it is flashed in the media that your father had so many millions inside the walls or sofa. It's very traumatizing for kids. Parents must realize the impact it will have on the kids.

Q: I think it is a fight within more.

Ans: It is. We keep saying that fight against corruption is the fight against self. It begins from within. That's why, we stress a lot on personnel, the people who you appoint as Heads of agencies–one person can make a difference.

Q: New things have started in your country. If a close watch be kept now, I think things may not go beyond control.

Ans: We can do a lot. There is a table on corruption perception index. The best countries in the index are Finland, Denmark etc. In Bhutan, we have the opportunity to be the best. You look at the king. He is the anti-corruption champion. We are a very small country. Here, we are talking about 10 ministers and a population over 600,000 we can manage. We have this statement of *Gross National Happiness*, We have very good leaders. We can do very well. Unless you set that culture now what we have, in future it will be worse. We are very fortunate; right now, in future we may have corrupt politicians.

Q: You are one of those people who lead by example. As far as work is concerned, even I get much inspiration from you, sometimes I do lose my temper but don't think you might be losing your temper.

Ans: I lose temper but remind myself that you should not be doing it sitting in this office. At the end, it only harms you. Now, I have improved a bit. In school days, just at the drop of the hat, I would lose my temper. Now, I can't afford. It's very unhealthy. It gives you heart attacks but our office is very well located. We have the hospital next door, we also have the chorten, If you need some spiritual refuge, you go there. Go to the hospital, if you have heart attack.

Q: Do you have lady doctors working in this hospital?

Ans: Ya, we have two.

Q: Are they specialists?

Ans: Yes, they are, gynaecologist and paediatrics. Others, I do not know.

Q: How many working hours do you have?

Ans: 32! (laughs), ordinarily it is 9 to 5, but during investigation, you can't wait for 9 to 5, so it depends. Normally I go till 7 o'clock or so.

Q: You must be investigating people?

Ans: Yes, in fact right now, interrogation is going on. It's an everyday affair. I don't do, my colleagues do.

Q: You are so calm about everything. How come?

Ans: Spirituality. I was asking my master how to apply compassion in my work. People say Buddhism and your work do not go together. I say no, in fact what I am doing is very much religious and spiritual. He was telling me that you are paid to do your job. You must do it. You must think the person you are investigating is your only child and shall have compassion. Whatever s/he is going through will change her/him. People say that as a Buddhist you should not be investigating people and putting them behind bars. This person is making life miserable for others. It's better to kill him and save thousands like Buddha did. In a ship, there was a pirate. He killed that pirate to save 500 other sailors.

Q: It's true. It's like a disease. You have to act like a surgeon. If some part is giving you trouble, either you cure or remove it. How would you like to put that in the end?

Ans: Be yourself, Be honest, Serve the people because you are being paid and be satisfied. Do your best. I keep telling my colleagues–don't be sad. If something has not worked be happy that you have done your best.

You have not left anything unturned to get something done. If the result is not the way that you anticipated, doesn't matter.

Q: There must be days when things have not gone your way. You must have gone home with a very heavy heart. Sometimes, you must have done something which otherwise you wouldn't like but had to do as your duty.

Ans: Absolutely, because I am also human being. For example, I had to investigate my friend. It's a very difficult task. Somebody who is very close to you but he has done something wrong. You have to do your job. It saddens you, but what to do? It's unfortunate. Recently, we had planned an investigation, but things just fell out. My colleagues were so disappointed. I can't be disappointed like them. Yes, you feel annoyed that morning till evening you had planned it, then late in the night and then early morning, when this has failed you have to anticipate about that.

Q: What do you do with the people who don't approve of your ways? Just ignore them?

Ans: What can I do? It's their problem, not mine. I do reflect, if there is a lot of criticism and such perception is almost general then you begin to look into yourself and the organization. Could we have done it better? Normally people don't like me because I just spit it out. People have advised me not to be too hard as you want their cooperation. I say that I am not working for my father's organisation. Politicians say that we support you. I say you are supporting yourself.

Q: Do you take your work home?

Ans: I used to when I was at the polytechnic and was just beginning my career but now I have stopped. Teaching was the most difficult profession. My mother used to stay awake till midnight as I prepared for lessons. I used to work on weekends also, even in HQs but now no because it doesn't help anybody and least of all yourself.

Appendix-VIII

Interview with Dorji Wangchuck, Director, College of Natural Resources, Lobesa

(Taken by Dr. Madhu Rajput on 11 June 2010 at the residence near the premises of College of Natural Resources (CNR), Lobesa)

Q:What are the professional courses in this very prestigious college of which you are the Director?

Ans:We offer programs at two different levels- Diploma and Degree. We offer Diploma in Agriculture, Animal Husbandry, and Forestry. Basically it's about training extension agents, who after graduating from this college, will work in different parts of the country, mainly with the farmers. Sometimes being paid and working as experts, most of the times facilitating as a friend or co-workers. Basically to enhance farm production, animal production, sustainable use and management of natural resources.

Degree programs are for the Diploma graduates we have already trained here. The degree students are in-service people who are already working for the Ministry of Agriculture. Now we are upgrading their qualification from Diploma to Degree. That is mainly to cater to the requirement in the fields. With the changing times, even the level of services required at the farms is going up. In degree programs, we have

B.Sc. Agriculture, Forestry, and Animal Science. These are the six programs we offer.

Q: Are your programs directly connected with employment?

Ans: Yes, the degree people, after graduation go back to work places. They are already working, so there is no problem about employment. For diploma students, it will be different. This year all the diploma people we have produced are being employed by the Ministry of Agriculture. The University was established in 2003. We were inducted in 2004 as one of the member college. We had to enrol students up to the optimum level. The Ministry of Agriculture guided us as to how many students are to be taken for the diploma. Once they graduated, all of them, (100 per cent) were employed. Now, Ministry of Agriculture may not take in all the diploma graduates we produce. They will take only as many they require in different sectors. There is no guarantee of 100 per cent employment to them. Some may have to look for employment outside the ministry. It has not happened yet, but it can.

Q: The knowledge you impart here may be very beneficial for rural areas. That needs to be taken care of. It's an infrastructural requirement to have good and innovative crops. The knowledge how to recycle them and how to have the best seeds is very important.

Ans: I would fully agree with you. In fact, if some of our diploma graduates, not employed by the Ministry of Agriculture, go back to rural areas and work as farmers, let's say, progressive farmers because they are trained and educated, I will be very happy. The problem is our young people don't want to go back to rural areas. They always look for a job other than working at the farm where there are opportunities. If not employed by the ministry, they might find a job elsewhere. As long as they have this choice, they will not go back but if they do, they could actually do very good job on the rural areas, especially Agriculture and Animal Husbandry diploma graduates. If you look at the contents of these programs, they can very well start farm business on their own.

Q: They can have good farms of their own, which can be very contributive to the economy, like education, agriculture is very important to be looked after.

Ans: It's a very important sector for us.

Q: How many girl students opt for these courses, keeping with the tradition that most of the Bhutanese women were peasants?

Ans: Not only women, even men.

Q: Yes, both. Even men contributed a lot. How many girl students are now opting for these agriculture courses?

Ans: We have been asked this question by many visitors. In fact, we did a calculation on this among several batches. We found that starting from the first to the fifteenth batch, about 20 per cent of our diploma students are girls. We have just started the degree program this year only. We have about 7 or 8 girls, out of 72.

Q: I think even among teachers, you don't have many women?

Ans: Even lecturers we have more of men than women. Only four of them out of 31. In the support sections like library, I have women.

Q: What has been your experience on having women employees and colleagues?

Ans: I never felt any difference between a male and a female colleague from the point of view of how they work, how they contribute. No bad experience.

Q: What I have gathered is that teaching is a profession women have opted for in large numbers, in schools and colleges. Most of them have very specifically pointed out the demand to have an extended maternity leave. Do you agree?

Ans: Right now they get three months. Of course, if I look at myself as a mother, I will be happy if I am given six months.

Q: They say doctors advise that you should feed your baby for at least four months. It is very difficult coming to the office. Even when they come to their work place, go back in lunch hours to feed their baby; their mind is not free from the baby. They are still worried about their health.

Ans: Extending the maternity leave, I would support if I had the power. I have one of my colleagues with baby. It is quite fortunate that her house is nearby. So, in between the office hours she has to go and breastfeed the baby and come back to work. She has taken three months, but even after three months, breastfeeding is required. It should be four months, I believe.

Q: How long have you been in service?

Ans: Nearly thirty years.

Q: How have you seen Bhutan change in these years in terms of education and development?

Ans: If I just use one word- very fast, very rapid, only in few places. A very rapid change in Thimphu. I was born there. In 1967, I was just a school kid. I know how Thimphu used to look those days and it has changed now: Paro, Punakha, Wangdue and even Mongar have changed but the rural areas, even in Punakha, things are still same, except a firm road has gone in those places. Change is concentrated in the cities, towns, places near the roads and people are making a little more income and improving the houses.

In the field of education, we have changed a lot. If you look at the number of schools, the number of people graduating from High School, education has made a very huge success. There was a time when for any development activity, we used to depend on consultants but now there are many qualified Bhutanese people. We know enough what we want. If at all, we hire consultants, it's because of the attitude of policy makers, who attach importance to consultants. Bhutanese people may have ideas, but it's not easy to get them implemented. It is easier for somebody coming from outside to suggest or recommend. I think Bhutanese people can do it now.

Q: There is a very cautious approach. From higher levels in Thimphu, they say that we want to change keeping everything intact. We want to move ahead in the field of development, but don't want to destroy any of the things we have inherited. Do you think it is possible to maintain such balance, which has not been possible in any country in the world?

Ans: I think we should try our best to the extent possible. Changes are very powerful. We have to realise why we have to accept change. Actually, we have no choice, the changes are coming. We can't totally avoid changes; it is natural but at the same time make conscious effort to preserve what we have. We can slow down the change that way a bit but we cannot stop change itself.

Q: As of now you don't have the problem which countries face of their best brains going to other countries.

Ans: Not yet we can say, at a large scale, but few people are now going out. It's not at the scale as happening in India or elsewhere.

Q: How things have developed in the field of agriculture?

Ans: I think agriculture has contributed a lot. It has improved the life of the farmers. I will give you one example. We know a farmer on the way to Thimphu. In fact through a religious ceremony, he is connected to my wife. We used to visit the farm very often, because it was nearby. There was a time when that farmer used to find it difficult to have even good cups to serve tea. Over the past few years, they have really progressed. They have improved the quality of their lives. Inside the house, there are rice cookers, television sets. They have even bought a power trailer. They were mainly dependent on agriculture.

Q: You are in such responsible position. You must be seeing the change in your college among young people. What challenges do you feel Bhutan face in future?

Ans: The biggest challenge would be not to lose the young people to western culture. It is so powerful that they just want to look, behave like what they see on t.v. Another is the use of drugs. These are the emerging problems for the young people.

Q: As far as development is concerned, Bhutan is a very different country. Development ought to be watched with close-guarded eyes rather than destroy the natural beauty of the country. Do you think monetary gains will be forsaken for preservation of natural heritage? I came to this place two years back and it is very different today.

Ans: If you look at the policy of the government and the constitution, I think we have a very strong policy for the conservation of the environment.

Q: Do you think it possible to retain 60 per cent forest cover as directed in the constitution?

Ans: Already people question whether we could maintain 60 per cent of our land area under forest cover. It is going to be quite a challenge. But the important part is to be cautious how important environment is for us, for everything. If we make a conscious effort, even if the percentage goes lower, we might keep, it close to 60. Otherwise, we might lose our forest altogether.

Q: Do you think GNH is the right political philosophy for the country and people agree to come along?

Ans: Not only for Bhutan, GNH as a philosophy would be applicable to any country in any part of the world. Growth and development are driven by money. GNH talks quite differently. We need money to have decent life but not to the extent of modern economical model. GNH talks about happiness as the ultimate purpose. Why do you want to have buildings, cars, so much of land? Is there a limit? If we are not able to set limit, we will never have enough. If we do not have enough, we will never be happy. GNH from that point of view is a very profound philosophy. We can look at GNH from two different levels- at national level, it means the society being happy, not 100 per cent, that will never be possible but society at large being happy. To achieve that, we will have to extend important services such as roads, telecom communication, education, medical facilities. Various Acts, laws, orders ought to be there to ensure smooth functioning. If I want to send my children to school, there is a school. If I am sick, there is a hospital where I can go and take medical services. If I have some problem related to law, the court is there and justice is delivered. If I want to travel from one place to another, the road is there where the private or public transport will ply that I can go. These services have to be there for nation as a whole, for the society at large.

It has to come down to the level of the individual. At this level, most important would be knowing how to set limit to your wants. If my wife is sick, I have a car so that I can move to hospital, this has become a necesity. At one time, a watch used to be a luxury; slowly it has become a necessity. What is necessary has to be there. If necessary things are there for me, I think I should be happy. I have enough income to pay school fees, to pay electricity and telephone bills, then I should tell myself, "OK, enough for you, what you need, you have. So, be happy". GNH is not something the whole country is going to draw from the sky, from the mountains, we had to cut into pieces and share. It lies in our own heart.

Q: How do you see education changing the girls' position in the society?

Ans: For us, it is quite open. There is no discrimination between boys and girls. Of course, some people say there is gender bias in Bhutan. I am not saying this because I am a man, but we are not a biased society. Opportunities are equally given to both the girls and the boys. Today, if we have more men holding higher positions, it is because in earlier days, when you had to make a choice who will go to school and who will stay at home, that choice is quite natural. It's safer for the boys to go out, travel more while girls will do a better job at home. We have lesser women holding important positions at the moment but now the time has changed. If I have four children two girls and two boys, I can afford to send them to school and whoever does well in studies, will progress. That decides who will hold important positions. Even here in this college, once we were discussing if we should give special concession for girls for admission, but if we do it, we would actually be gender-biased, so we decided that let's not do it. Just keep it open as it is, let's not change anything.

Q: Working women are an accepted fact now.

Ans: Yes, they are everywhere. They can contribute as equally as men.

Q: Yours is one of the countries where crime is not much. You have not got a big graft. In other countries, crime has risen with modernisation very drastically, especially against women. In Bhutan, it is not such a big rise.

Ans: Now it is rising, especially in urban centres like Thimphu. If we compare to the earlier days, it is becoming less and less safer but specifically targeted at women.

Appendix-IX

Interview with Sonam Namgyel, Director, Sherubtse College, Kanglung, Trashigang

(Taken by Dr. Madhu Rajput on 04 June 2010 at the Director's office in Sherubtse College, Kanglung, Trashigang)

Q: When did you join this college?

Ans: Almost three years ago.

Q: Where were you earlier?

Ans: I was in College of Education in Paro, where we train teachers.

Q: How many women you had in faculty and how many do you have today?

Ans:The number has increased, especially in the past two years. When I joined in 2007, the number was slightly less than what we have now. We have few Assistant Lecturers. In 2007, we didn't have many Assistant Lecturers. A good number of them are female.

Q: As a Director, do you find them fully competent and doing work well?

Ans: They are doing well. They are young, new. They take lot of initiatives. Very co-operative. They want to learn and contribute in their own ways to the college.

Q: Are they available even at emergency times, when you want to call at odd hours?

Ans: Yes. as far as possible, we do not like to call at odd hours. Sometimes, our meetings go beyond office hours, as late as 8.00 p.m. Then, they are there.

Q: Let me talk about the days when you were in College of Education. It is felt that the field of education was the safest for women. Do you agree?

Ans: I have not thought about it from professional angle. If you look at the number, we had good number of teacher trainees who were girls. Many girls tend to join teaching. If you look at the statistics in the primary section, you will find more female teachers.

Q: It is a general opinion I am talking about. The working hours are fixed. It is said that education is the best field for girls. The girls are opting for other careers, irrespective of working conditions. Do you feel in Bhutan girls would like to join the fields considered 'High Risk Areas' such as Armed Forces or becoming a pilot?

Ans: In the recent past, I have been observing this change. Some years ago, which the ladies thought was not their job, now increasingly they are taking part in them, including the Armed Forces. We have a lot of police women. Even if you look at this college's statistics, the number of girls is increasing year by year.

Q: During my interviews, most of the women wished the maternity leave be extended from three to six months. Do you agree with it? In India it has already been extended, because they feel they need this much time to bring the child up.

Ans: We have to look at it from two sides. On one hand, we have to think of women and children. If the mother is with the child for six long months, it is better for the health of mother and the child. On the other hand, we have to consider the economic situation of the country whether we could pay someone without working for months. Once our country is rich, probably we can consider this option, but it is not about somebody being paid or not paid, whether the country is rich or not. We have lot of other administrative issues. For that duration, to find somebody to take her place, be it teaching or other office work, we have to get additional employees.

Q: Do you have a working wife?

Ans: No.

Q: And your daughter?

Ans: She is working.

Q: Do you feel women have to try harder to prove themselves at their work place?

Ans: As far as my daughter is concerned, no. Sometimes, she tells me that there is lot to be done, and she is tired. Sometimes, things cannot be done on time. She has to sometimes stay late in office, not always. I personally observe she is young and has the necessary qualification. This should be alright she can do it. She should be able to manage. She is working in a bank. Sometimes, she seems to be struggling to do well, sometime, I think she can, but doesn't have to struggle so much.

Q: As a Director, while giving an assignment you must be thinking of the competence of the person.

Ans: As I mentioned earlier, if somebody has something to be considered in a family, yet that person is paid as a colleague as others. As a Director, how long can I continue to consider domestic affairs? It is not fair to discriminate the responsibilities on domestic grounds. Although, at the back of my mind, I would like to consider, we do consider but how long and how much, that I have to weigh. Men and women are working. When women have babies, they keep going home to feed the baby, sometimes missing the official responsibilities. Other colleagues understand but after a while they complain. I have to balance and support both.

Q: Have you any complaints from girls' hostel about mismanagement?

Ans: When you talk about management, lot of factors come into play. I may have two females looking after hostels, both have young child. It may so happen that one is doing perfectly OK, other may not be doing well. If you look at these individuals, they have the same problem, similar capability but one may outdo the other. Sometimes, we have to see beyond what we consider capable and not capable. Regarding management, I have not received any formal complaint but observe myself that if somebody is weak in the management of hostel, I have to tell. More problems are with the girls. They are not following the rules. I often see more girls wandering in a particular hostel where they are not supposed to. I tend to question the women who are looking after the hostel.

Q: What change do you perceive in the women's attitude today? Are these changes positive? Are they more assertive about their position or go by others' decision?

Ans: There is a change. I think women are trying their best to make a difference, to become prominent and claim as equal to men. What men can do they can also do. I see that concerted effort made by women. These have been facilitated by our environment. There are lot of agencies, laws, and this democratic form of government is giving them opportunities to come out. That's why we see some changes. I may be biased. I personally tend to see some artificiality. 'I can do' they say but when it comes to certain things, they cannot. Biological make up is such that few things cannot be done by them. Although, there is change, but there are certain limitations. If you make a particular reference to the Bhutanese society, in certain things, I think, women overshadow men, especially in terms of trying to make themselves look attractive. This change is more obvious in the girls.

Q: May be they are being more confident. That may be the right word.

Ans: Yes, they have become more confident.

Q: People say women are not in higher position as of now because they didn't have access to education, but they are getting education and exposure, they can make use of the opportunity and shoulder responsibility of nation building in the coming years.

Ans: It will happen.

Q: You see young girls in your own college. Are they taking responsibility seriously?

Ans: Yes. When girls are given responsibilities, they take it seriously as much as boys. I think it will improve further. In certain professions, there are more men as of now like doctors, engineers, executives, in next 15 to 20 years we would like to see 50-50 per cent of men and women.

Q: Would you like to encourage them as a person in a very responsible position in your country?

Ans: I would encourage. I think they can do that. In certain positions, more women are at present as in primary level teaching. They will have to prove themselves in new fields. We say that we should make a woman come to a position but not on charity basis, or humanitarian grounds but due to her capability.

Q: The situation will then change that they come for work only to shoulder the burden of family rather than doing something for pleasure, choosing the career which they want. It is said that if you love your work, you will do it in the best possible way, if not, you will just finish it off and go.

Ans: That is true.

Appendix- X

THE BHUTAN CITIZEN ACT, 1977

Conditions required for the grant of Citizenship:

KA 1. In the case of government servants, an applicant should have completed 15 years of service without any adverse record.

2. In the case of those not employed in the Royal Government, an applicant should have resided in Bhutan for a minimum period of 20 years.

3. In addition, an applicant should have some knowledge of the Bhutanese language both spoken and written and the history of Bhutan . Only those applicants who fulfil the above requirements may apply for grant of Citizenship to the Ministry of Home Affairs, which will ascertain the relevant facts and submit the application to the Royal Government for further action.

Eligibility and Power to Grant Citizenship:

KHA 1. The power to grant or reject an application for Citizenship rests solely with the Royal Government. Hence, all applicants who fulfill the above conditions are not necessarily eligible for grant of Citizenship.

2. Any applicant holding the Citizenship of another country or with criminal records in other countries or those who are related to any person involved in activities against the people, the Country and the King shall not be granted Citizenship even if all the other required conditions are fulfilled.

3. A person granted Citizenship by the Royal Government is right to register his/her name in the record of the Royal Government from the date of the grant of Citizenship.

4. All those granted Citizenship are required to take the following oath to be administered by the Home Minister;

i) Henceforth, I owe elegance only to His Majesty the Druk Gyalpo of Bhutan.

ii) I shall abide by and observe the Laws and Rules and Regulations of the Royal Government with unswerving reverence.

iii) I shall observe all the customs and traditions of the people of Bhutan.

iv) I shall not commit any act against the TSAWASUM OF BHUTAN (the country, the people and the King).

v) As a citizen of Bhutan, I hereby take this oath in the name of Yeshey Goempo and undertake to serve the country to the best of my ability.

Special Grant of Citizenship:

GA 1. A foreigner in possession of special or extraordinary qualifications who specially require for the country will be granted citizenship without consideration of the required conditions, except for the administration of the oath of allegiance.

Renouncement and Re-application of Citizenship:

NGA 1. In case of a Bhutanese citizen, who having left the country returns and applies for citizenship, the Royal Government shall keep the applicant on probation for a period of at least two years. On successful completion of the probation period, the applicant will be granted citizenship provided the person in question is not responsible for any activities against the Royal Government.

2. A foreigner who has been granted Bhutanese Citizenship may apply to the Royal Government for permission to emigrate with his/her family. Permission will be granted after an investigation of the circumstances relating to such request. After grant of permission to emigrate, the same person may not reapply for

Bhutanese citizenship. Any family member amongst those who seek permission to leave the kingdom, who do not wish to leave and makes an application to that effect, the Home Minister will investigate the matter and will permit such persons to remain in the country after ascertaining that the country's interest is not harmed.

3. If anyone, whether a bonafide Bhutanese citizen or a foreigner granted citizenship applies for permission to emigrate during times of crises such as war, the application shall be kept pending until normalcy returns.

Procedure for Acquisition of Citizenship:

CHA 1. When a Bhutanese woman is married to a foreigner, only she is a citizen, her husband and their children will not be considered as Bhutanese citizens. If they desire Bhutanese citizenship, such cases will be considered in conformity with the procedure laid down in this Act applicable to foreigners applying for citizenship.

2. When a Bhutanese man is married to a foreign woman their children will be considered Bhutanese. The wife will have to fulfil the requirements of this Citizenship Act as applicable to foreigners applying for Citizenship.

3. In the case of Bhutanese citizens residing in other countries, the citizenship Law sub-head KA-12 No: 2 which is reproduced below, shall be applicable.

Reproduction of Thrimyic KA 12- 2:

KA-12-2 with the exception of a genuine Bhutanese, whose family is domiciled in Bhutan but s(he) her(him) self has to stay away in another country in connection with the service of the Royal Government, private business or religious practices, all others who live in foreign countries and serve the government and people of such countries or have settled in a foreign country or are holding official posts in a foreign government are considered non-nationals.

Registration Procedure:

CHHA 1. All children born of a father, who is a Bhutanese citizen should be registered in the official record within one year of their birth-whether the children are born inside or outside the country.

2. All children born within the country are required to be listed with the Dzongkha or the Dungkhag of their birth. Children of Bhutanese parentage born in other countries should be recorded with the Royal Bhutanese Embassies. Where there are no embassies nearby, the information should be conveyed to the Home Ministry through correspondence.

3. If a child is more than one year and is not still registered in the official record, registration is not permitted but may be applied for to the Home Ministry by the concerned local authority. The Home Ministry will then investigate the matter before granting permission for the registration.

Validity of Census Record:

JA 1. All census records must bear the seal of the Royal Government and the signature of an officer not lower in rank than a Dzongdag. Other records will not be acceptable.

Enquiry of Kashos:

NYA 1. All Kashos with the people which were not granted by His Majesty will be investigated by the Home Minister and reported to the Royal Government.

Penalty for Violation of Rules:

TA 1. Anyone having acquired Bhutanese citizenship if involved in acts against the King or speaks against the Royal government or associates with people involved in activities against the Royal government shall be deprived of his/her Bhutanese Citizenship.

2. In the case of any person knowingly presenting false information at the time of applying for citizenship, the Kasho granting him/her citizenship will be withdrawn after due verification of the false information presented.

THA Status of the provision:

1. In case of conflict between the provisions of this Act and the provisions of any previous laws, rules and regulations, the provisions of this Act shall prevail.

Appendix- XI

The Bhutan Citizenship Act, 1985

1. This Act may be called the Bhutan Citizenship Act, 1985. It shall come into force from twenty third day of the fourth month of Wood Bull year of the Bhutanese calendar corresponding to 10th June, 1985. In case of conflict between the provisions of this Act and the provisions of any previous laws, rules and regulations relating to citizenship, the provisions of this Act shall prevail.

2. CITIZENSHIP BY BIRTH

A person whose parents are both citizens of Bhutan shall be deemed to be a citizen of Bhutan by birth.

3. CITIZENSHIP BY REGISTRATION.

A person permanently domiciled in Bhutan on or before 31st December,1958, and, whose name is registered in the census register maintained by the Ministry of Home Affairs shall be deemed to be a citizen of Bhutan by registration.

4. CITIZENSHIP BY NATURALIZATION.

A person desiring to apply for Bhutanese citizenship to the Ministry of Home Affairs in Forms KA-1 and KA-2 must fulfill the following conditions to be eligible for naturalisation:

(a) The person must have attained the age of 21 years, and 15 years in the case of a person either of whose parents is a citizen of Bhutan;
(b) The person must be mentally sound;
(c) The person must have resided in Bhutan for 15 years in the case of Government employees and also in the case of applicants, either of whose parents is a citizen of Bhutan, and 20 years in other case, and this period of residence must be registered in the records of the Department of Immigration and Census.
(d) The person must be able to speak, read and write Dzongkha proficiently;
(e) The person must have good knowledge of the culture, customs, traditions, and history of Bhutan;
(f) The person must have good moral character and should not have any record of imprisonment for criminal offences in Bhutan or elsewhere;
(g) The person must have no record of having spoken or acted against the King, Country and People of Bhutan in any manner whatsoever, and
(h) The person must be prepared to take a solemn Oath of Allegiance to the King, Country and People of Bhutan according to the prescribed From KHA.

On receipt of the application Form KA-1 for naturalization, the Ministry of Home Affairs will take necessary steps to check the particulars contained in the application. The Ministry of Home Affairs will also conduct written and oral tests to assess proficiency in Dzongkha and knowledge of the culture, customs, traditions and history of Bhutan. The decision of the Ministry of Home Affairs on the question of eligibility for naturalization shall be final and binding. The Royal Government of Bhutan also reserves the right to reject any application for naturalisation without assigning any reason.

5. GRANT OF CITIZENSHIP:

(a) A person, whose application for naturalization has been favourably considered by the ministry of Home Affairs, shall take the Oath of

Allegiance according to Form KHA of this Act and then His Majesty the King may grant citizenship Kasho.

(b) A person shall then be deemed to be a citizen of Bhutan upon receiving a Kashog from His Majesty the King of Bhutan according to Form GA of this Act.

6. TERMINATION OF CITIZENSHIP

(a) Any citizen of Bhutan who acquires the citizenship of another country shall cease to be a citizen of Bhutan. The wife/husband and children of that person if they were Bhutanese citizens, shall have the right to remain as citizens of Bhutan provided they are permanently domiciled in Bhutan and are registered annually in the citizenship Register maintained by the Ministry of Home Affairs.

(b) Any citizen of Bhutan who has acquired citizenship by naturalisation may be deprived of citizenship at any time, if it is found that naturalisation had been obtained by means of fraud, false representation or the concealment of any materials fact.

(c) Any citizen of Bhutan who has acquired citizenship by naturalisation may be deprived of citizenship at any time if that person has shown by act or speech to be disloyal in any manner whatsoever to the King, Country and People of Bhutan.

(d) If both the parents are Bhutanese and in case of the children leaving the Country of their own accord, without the knowledge of the Royal Government of Bhutan and their names are also not recorded in the citizenship register maintained in the Ministry of Home Affairs, then they will not be considered as citizens of Bhutan. (Resolution No.16 (2) adopted by the National Assembly of Bhutan in its 62nd Session).

(e) Any citizen of Bhutan who has been deprived of Bhutanese citizenship must dispose of all immovable property in Bhutan within one year, failing which, the immovable property shall be confiscated by the Ministry of Home Affairs on payment of fair and reasonable compensation.

Bibliography

A History of Bhutan 19th to 20th Century, Department of Educational Ministry of Social Services, Royal Government of Bhutan, Thimphu 1991.

Adrol Mridula, British Relations with Frontier States, New Delhi, 1974.

Aris Michael, Bhutan: The Early History of Himalayan Kingdom.

Aris Michael, Views on Medieval Bhutan, the Diary and Drawing of Samuel Davis 1783, London, Washington, 1982.

Arora Prem Chandra Prakash, International Relations, New Delhi, 1991.

Asirvathan Eddy, Political Theory, Tenth edition, 1974.

Baker David P., Wiseman Alexander A., Education for All: Global Promises, National Challenges, Emerald Group Publishing, 2007.

Bell Sir Charles, Tibet Past and Present, 1924.

Benegal Sir Rau, Indian Constitution in Making, 1960.

Bhutan and Sikkim, Published by Information Service of India, Political Offices, Gangtok Sikkim, 1969.

Bonn: Gisela and Wirsing, Giselher, India and the Sub Continent: An Introduction to India, Pakistan, Bangladesh, Nepal, Sikkim, Bhutan, Oxford and I.B.H., Publishing Co., New Delhi, 1974.

Carothers, Thomas and Ottaway, Marina, Defining Civil Society: The Exclusive Term in Development, Outreach Winter 2002, World Bank Institute.

Coelho V.H., Sikkim and Bhutan, Indian Council for Cultural Relations, Delhi, 1970.

Collister Peter, Bhutan and the British, London Serindia, 1987.

Das Nirmala, The Dragon Country, Orient Longman, New Delhi, 1973.

Dasho Kunzang Wangdi, Auditor General, Personal Communications, November 2000.

Dasho Rigzin Dorji, A brief Religious, Cultural and Secular History of Bhutan, The Asia Society Galleries, New York, 1989.

Deb Arbind, Bhutan and India: A Study in Frontier Political Relations (1772-1865), Calcutta, 1976.

Dogu Tshering (ed), Bhutan: Himalayan Kingdom, Royal Government of the Kingdom of Bhutan, Thimphu, 1979.

Dorji, C.T., *A Brief History of Dogar Dobji Dzong*, Fortress of the Dragon, National Museum of Bhutan, Paro, Second Edition, 2009.

Dorji, C.T., Proceedings of the 5th Colloquium on "Tangible and Intangible Culture of Bhutan", National Museum of Bhutan, Paro, Bhutan.

Dorji, Dasho, Rigzin, A Brief Religious Cultural and Secular History of Bhutan, The Asia Society Galleries, New york, 1989.

Dorji Lham, The Wangchuck Dynasty, 100 Years of Enlightened Monarchy, The Centre of Bhutan Studies, 2008.

Dorji Lham, Tashi Choden, Understanding Civil Society in Bhutan, The Centre for Bhutan Studies, 2005.

Dorji Tandi and Sithey Gyambo, Drukyul Decides, The story of Bhutan's first democratic elections, Thimphu, Bhutan, 2009.

Eden Ashley, Political Missions to Bhutan Comprising the reports of Hon'ble Ashley Eden 1864, Captain R.B. Pemberton, 1837, 1838, with Dr. W. Griffith's journal and the account by Baboo Kishan Kant Bose (Calcutta, 1865 Reprint, New Delhi, 1972. with the addition of the Truth about Bhutan by one who knows it, originally published in Calcutta, 1965.)

Edmunds, Tomowen, Bhutan: Land of the Thunder Dragon, London, 1988.

Francoise Pommeret, Introduction to Bhutan, Hongkong: The Guidebook Company Limited, 1990.

General Eavas, The Dragon Kingdom, 1970.

Griffith William, Journal of travels in Assam, Burma, Bhutan, Afghanistan and the neighbouring countries (Calcutta, 1847)

Gupta B.S., Bhutan, 1999.

Gupta Bhabani Sen, Bhutan: Towards a Grass-root Participatory Polity.

Gupta Shantiswarup, British Relations with Bhutan, Panchsheel Prakashan, Jaipur, 1974.

Harrat Bikamajit, History of Bhutan: Land of the Peaceful Dragon, Educational Department, Royal Government of Bhutan, Thimphu, 1980.

Hhickman Katie, Dreams of the peaceful Dragon: journey into Bhutan, London, 1987.

Jenkins Jr. William, The Himalayan Kingdom: Bhutan, Sikkim and Nepal Princeton, 1963.

Judge Dubgyur Lungten, 'Criminal Justice in Bhutan; A Handbook on Criminal Procedure', 2006, Royal Court of Justice, Research Division, High Court.

Karan Pradjumma P., Bhutan: A Physical and Cultural Geography, Washington, 1967.

Kharat S. Rajesh, Foreign Policy of Bhutan, New Delhi, 2005.

Kinga Sonam, Polity, Kingdom and Democracy, A biography of the Bhutanese State, Ministry of Education, Royal Government of Bhutan, 2009.

Kohli Manorama, India and Bhutan: A Study in Interrelations 1772-1910.

Kohli, M.S, 'A Kingdom in the sky', Vikas Publishing House, 2004.

Lella K., (2002), Modernisation and Buddhism: Contributions of Ambedkar and Dalai Lama-xiv, Gyan Publishing House, New Delhi.

Lyall Sir Alfred, Rise and Expansion of the British Dominance in India, 1964.

Maj. Gen. (Retd.) Sood Shubhi, Bhutan: Hundred Years of Wangchuck Vision, 2008.

Mehra G.N., Bhutan: Land of peaceful Dragon, Vikram Publishing House, Delhi, 1974.

Mele Pietro Francesco, Bhutan: New Delhi, 1982.

Menon K.P.S., China: Past and Present, Asia Publishing House Bombay, 1968.

Michel Peissel, Lords and Lamas, 1970.

Michael Rutland, Bhutan: From Medieval to the Millennium, London, 1999.

Mishra H.N., Problem and Policies of Bhutan, Heritage Publisher, New Delhi, 1988.

Mitra Debamitra, Indo-Bhutan Relations, Political Process, Conflict and Crisis, Delhi, 2010.

Morgenthau J. Hans, The Struggle for Power and Peace.

Nishimizu Mieko, Portrait of a Leader, The Centre for Bhutan Studies, 2008.

Olschack Blanche C., Ancient Bhutan: A Study on Early Buddhism in Himalayas, Zurich Swiss Foundation for Alpine Research, 1979.

Parmanand, Bhutan: Retrospect and Prospect, New Delhi, 1992.

Parmanand, Political Development in South Asia, Sterling Publishers Private Limited, New Delhi, 1988.

Penjore Dorji, Love, Courtship and Marriage in Rural Marriage, A Preliminary Ethnography of Wamling Village in Zhemgang, Galing Printers and Publishers, 2009.

Phadnis Urmila, Muni S.D. and Bhadur, Kalim (Ed), Domestic Conflicts in South Asia, Volume 2.

Pommaret Francoise, An Illustrated Guide to Bhutan: Buddhism Fort of the Himalayas, The Guide Book Company, 1990.

Pommaret Francoise, Introduction to Bhutan, Hong Kong, 1990.

Pommaret Lmaeda, Francoise and Lmaeda Yoshiro, Bhutan: A Kingdom of the Eastern Himalayas, Time Books International, New Delhi, 1989.

Rahman Atiur, The Political Economy of SAARC, New Delhi Sterling Publishers, New Delhi, 1986.

Rahul Ram, Modern Bhutan, Vikas Publications, Delhi, 1971.

Rahul Ram, Rise of Nepal and Bhutan, New Delhi, 1984.

Rahul Ram, Royal Bhutan, Motilal Banarsidas, Delhi, 1983.

Rahul Ram, The Himalayas as Frontier, Vikas Publishing House Private Limited, New Delhi, 1978.

Rajput Madhu, Bhutan: From Theocracy to Democracy, Jaipur, 2010.

Rajput Madhu, Indo-Bhutan Relations through Prism of History, Manak Publications, New Delhi, 2011.

Rasgotra M., Chopra V.D. and Mishra K. P. (eds), India's Foreign Policy in 1990s, Patriot Publishers, New Delhi, 1990.

Rathore L.S., The Changing Bhutan, Jain Brothers, New Delhi, 1971.

Rennie D.F., Bhutan and story of Dooar War, London, 1866.

Ronaldshaj, Earl of Lands of the thunderbolt, 1923.

Rose Leo E., The Politics of Bhutan, Cornell University Press, Ithaca, 1977.

Rustomji Nari, Bhutan: The Dragon Kingdom in Crisis, Oxford University Press, Delhi, 1978.

Rustormji Nari, Enchanted Frontiers Sikkim Bhutan and Indian's North Eastern Borderlands, Oxford University Press Bombay, 1971.

Rustomji Nari, Imperiled Frontiers: India's North Eastern Borderlands, New Delhi, 1983.

Sandhery G.S., Bhutan the Unknown State, 1897.

Sharma Rasmi: Bhutan and SAARC, New Delhi, 2007.

Sherubtse College, Kanglung, Bhutan and its Natural Resources, Vikas Publishing House Private Limited, New Delhi, 1991.

Sinha A.C., Bhutan: Ethnic Identity and National Dilemma, Reliance Publishing House, New Delhi, 1991.

Singh Amar, Kaur Jasbir, Himalayan, Bhutan Triangle: A Historical Survey of British India's Relations with Tibet and Sikkim.

Singh I.J. Bahadur, Indians in South Asia, Sterling Publishers Private Limited, New Delhi, 1984.

Singh Mohanjeet, Himalayan Art, London 1968.

Singh Nagendra, Bhutan: A Kingdom in Himalayas, A Study of the Land, its People and their Government, New Delhi, 1978.

Singh Nagendra: Bhutan: A kingdom in Himalayas, New Delhi, 1988.

Snelling John, The Buddhist Hand Book, London 1987.

Steele Peter, Two and Two halves to Bhutan, Calcutta, Oxford X IBM, 1970.

Trevelyan G.M., British History in 19th Century, 1782-1901.

Turner Captain Samuel, Account of an Embassy to the Court of Teshu Lama in Tibet, 1800.

Uni Wikan, The Situation of girl child in Bhutan, Mimeo, Thimphu, Bhutan 1990.

Upreti B.C., Bhutan: Dilemma of Change in a Himalayan Kingdom.

Ura Karma, Leadership of the Wise: Kings of Bhutan, 2010.

White J. Claude, Sikkim and Bhutan: Twenty One Years of the North East Frontier, 1887-1908, London, 1909, Reprint, Delhi, 1971.

Wolters W., The Making of Civil Society in Historical Perspective.

Yinhong. S., The Issue of Civil Society in the Present China and its Complexity, Beijing: School of International Studies, Renmin University of China.

25 Years of Enthronement, Gross National Happiness, Centre for Bhutan Studies.

ARTICLE

Abdi, S.N.M., Rumbling of Discontent, The Illustrated Weekly of India, Bombay 4-10 November 1990.

Aiyar, Swaminathan S. Anklesaria, Anguished Voices of a Double Tragedy, The Sunday Times of India, New Delhi, October 7, 1990, p. 17.

Anil R.N., Bhutan's Dilemma, Unity International, New Delhi, Vol. 15, No. 6 April, 1991. p.5.

Aris Michael, Bhutan: Internal development and relations with outside power upto 1952, in Robinson, Francised, pp. 161-164.

Bardoli Utpal, Human Rights in Bhutan-I; the issue has been grossly exaggerated, Deccan Herald, Bangalore, June 1 1990.

Basu Taru, Trouble in Himalayan's Kingdom, India Abroad, New York, Vol. 22, No. 23, 6 March 1992, p. 25.

Bhanumathy K.P., Bhutan: Some impressions, Mainstream, New Delhi, August 18, 1990, pp. 25-26.

Bhattacharaji Romesh, Bhutan: The Land of the Dragon, Frontline, Madras, May 14, 1988, pp. 53-57.

Bhutan 2: Monarch stresses dialogue to resolve conflict: the king speaks out, Far Eastern Economic Review, 20 December 1990, p. 26.

Bhutan Today-I: Road to two countries two Peoples, The Statesman, 25 October 1990, pp. 7-8.

Bhutan Today-II: Terrorist disguised as democrats. The Statesman, 26, October 1990, p. 7.

Bloodshed in Bhutan-I: Simmering Ethnic Fury in Shangrila, The Times of India, New Delhi, October 5, 1990, pp. 1-6.

Bloodshed in Bhutan-II: King willing to hold talks with dissidents, The Times of India, October 6, 1990, p. 9.

Bose Shikha, Anti- ULFA Drive: Bhutan wary of Joining in, January 28, 1992, p. 4.

Breeveld Jim, Bhutan: Land of the Peaceful Dragon, The Illustrated Weekly of India, January 30, 1977, pp. 36-39.

Chadha Kumkum, Bhutan: The Tremors within, The Hindustan Times Magazine, New Delhi, November 17, 1991, p. 1.

Chakrabarti Ashie, Bhutan stir, Shadow in Darjeeling, The Hindustan Times, May 5th 1991, p. 19.

Chaudhari Kalyan, A Captive Ruler: Peace Intrigues in Restive Bhutan, Frontline, December 6, 1991. pp. 30-32.

Chaudhary Savitri, Democracy for Dragon Kingdom, The Sunday Times of India, February 16, 1992, p. 14.

Chophel Karma, Democratic Terror in Bhutan, The Statesman, 15th, January, 1991, p. 6.

Clad James, Bhutan –I: Nepali threatens the Hermit kingdom: the Kukris edge, Far Eastern Economic Review, 20 December 1990, pp. 22-25.

Datta Roy, Sunanda K., Diplomatic Realism; New Look at Aims Abroad, The Sunday Statesman, July 21, 1991, p. 6.

Datta Roy, Sunanda K. Druk Past and Present I: Catching up with the 20th Century, The Sunday Statesman, July 10, 1983, p. 6.

Datta Roy, Sunanda K., Druk Past and Present II: Strategies for Survival, The Statesman, July 11, 1983, p. 6.

Datta Roy, Sunanda K., Flight of the Dragon-II: Challenge of Settlement with China, The Statesman, April 28, 1984, p. 6.

Datta Roy, Sunanda K., India's Closest Friend Ancient Oath on Ties with Bhutan, July 20, 1983, p. 6.

Datta Roy, Sunanda K., Influx by Treaty: Pressure of Nepal's Diaspora, The Sunday Statesmen, October 6, 1991, p. 6.

Datta Roy, Sunanda K., Return of the Dragon II: Challenge for Indian Diplomacy, The Sunday Statesmen, July 8, 1981, p. 6.

Datta Roy, Sunanda K., Return of the Dragon- II: Economic Progress without Hussying, The Sunday Statesmen, July 20, 1981, p. 6

Datta Roy, Sunanda K., The Phoney Crisis: Propaganda was against Bhutan, The Sunday Statesmen, September 2, 1990, p. 6.

Desmond, Edward W, Stirrings in the Himalayas: Stony Look Tranquillity is Shattered by Ethnic and Political Unrest, Time, October 29, 1990, p. 13.

Dhar M.K., The Nepalese Sqeeze on Bhutan, The Hindustan Times, July 5, 1993, p. 10.

Dragon Kingdom's urge for an international role, India Quarterly, Vol. 37, No. 2. April-June 1981, pp. 227-249.

Drukpa Banam Nepali: Bhavisya ke Garbha Men Palta Toofan, Saptahik Hindustan, New Delhi, December 1, 1991, p.12.

Dutt, Srikant, Bhutan's International Position, International Studies, New Delhi, Vol. 20, Nos. 3-4 July December 1981, pp. 601-623.

Education and Gender in Bhutan: A Tentative Analysis, Joke Buringa and Lham Tshering, Thimphu, July 1992.

Fear still haunts South Bhutan, The Statesman, October 18, 1990, pp. 1-9.

Ghose Manash, Bhutan's survival at stake: Tsering, An Interview with foreign Minister Lyonpo Dawa Tsering, The Sunday Statesman, June 26, 1992, p. 10.

Gupta Anish, Destination: Unknown Bhutanese refugees Languish Without Hope in Nepal, Sunday Calcutta, pp. 8-14, March 1992, pp. 26-27.

Gupta Anish, Inside Bhutan: An ethnic bomb is ticking away in the Himalayan Kingdom, Sunday Calcutta, pp. 22-27.

Gupta, Rakesh, Small not Smaller is Beautiful, Link, New Delhi, September 29, 1991, pp. 20-23.

Husain Wasbir, Flight from Paradise Insight, Calcutta, Sunday July 5, 1992.

Jagmohan, Terrorism: Causes and Cure, The Hindustan Times, November 25, 1992, p. 11.

Katyal, K.K., Ties with Neighbors: Positive Signs, The Hindu, December 30, 1991, p. 8.

King and Country-I: Why Bhutan needs peace, The Statesman, January 4, 1991, p. 6.

King replies with an edict, Indian Express, May 4, 1990, p. 9.

Kohli, Manorama, Bhutan's Strategic Environment: Changing Perceptions, India Quarterly, New Delhi, Vol. 42, No. 2, April-June 1986, pp. 142-53.

Kottary Salesh, The Last Shangrilla, The Illustrated Weekly of India, October 20, 1985, pp. 44-45.

Kumara, D.P., Appeal to Bhutan Terrorists, The Statesman, October 14, 1990, p. 7.

Kumar Narendra, Uneasy Lies the head........, The Sunday Statesman miscellany, Delhi, July 14, 1991, pp. 4-5.

Kumar Rahul, Enter the Dragon, The Sunday Times, Lucknow, 1993.

Labh Kapileshwar, Bhutan's International Position prior to 1947, International Studies, Vol. 13, No. 1. January- March, 1974.

Lekha J. Shankar, "The Many Hues of SAARC", The Hindustan Times, October 4, 1992.

Lhadon Pema, Women in Development: Bhutan, November 1, 1989 in Labh Kapileshwar, India and Bhutan, Sindhu Publication Ltd., New Delhi.

Lyonpo Jigme Thinley, Values and Development: Gross National Happiness, in *Gross National Happiness*, (Thimphu: Centre for Bhutan Studies, 1999) p. 21.

This was prepared as the text of the keynote speech delivered at the Millennium Meeting for Asia and the Pacific, 30th October-1 November 1998, Seoul, Republic of Korea.

Majumdar Sundip, Bhutan: Once Upon a Time: There was a nice king, News Week, 18 June 1990, p. 21.

Man Singh Surjeet, The King and We, The Hindustan Times, January 19, 1993, p.11.

Martin Brauen, A Village in Central Bhutan, in Christian Schicklgruber and Francoise Pommaret (eds), Bhutan: Mountain Fortress of the Gods (Delhi: Bookwise (India) Pvt. Ltd, 1997), p. 93.

Marwaha Manisha, Consensus at Heart of Indo-Bhutanese Ties, India International, February 15th, 1993.

Mcgrik Tim, A Kingdom in Crisis, The Independent, on Sunday, December 6, 1992.

Menon Ritu, Bhutan: The Dragon Stirs, Indian Express, New Delhi, September 17, 1991, p. 8.

Misra R.C., Bhutan-China Relations, China Report Vol. 17, No. 2 March-April 1981, pp. 43-50.

Misra R.C., Scholarship on Bhutan, China Report, Vol. 18, No. 4 July-August 1982, pp. 25-32.

Misra R.C., Tibetans in Bhutan: Problem of Repatriation, China Report, Vol. 18, No. 5, September-October 1982, pp. 25-32.

Mondal, Sekh Rahim, People of Bhutan: A Study of its Society and Culture in B.C Upreti (ed.), Bhutan: Dilemma of Change in a Himalayan Kingdom', Kalinga Publications, Delhi.

Mountain Shangrila Bhutan: A Voyage of Friendship, Unity International, Vol. 15, No. 4, April 1991, p. 9.

Namgyal Dorji, The History of Paro Ta Dzong, Fortress of the Dragon, Proceedings of the 4th Colloquium, The National Museum of Bhutan, Paro, Second Edition, 2009.

Nanda, Prakash, Foreign Affairs: Is Bhutan likely to do a Nepal on India?, The Times of India, May 11, 1989, Agenda 3.

Narayan Hemendra, Bhutanese Refugees in Nepal: Caught between Frying Pan and Fire, Indian Express, February 19, 1992, p. 12.

Pal Samir, Prime Minister: India will finance part of Bhutan Plan, The Hindustan Times, October 1, 1985.

Pal Samir, Bhutan's Cultural Dilemma, The Hindustan Times, 17, September 1990, p. 13.

Pal Samir, A Significant Upswing, The Hindustan Times, 17 December 1991, p. 18.

Pandey Kedar Nath, Bhutan Today, Anguished Voices of a Double Tragedy Alive, New Delhi, June (second) 1990, p. 20-22.

Parekh, Navnit, A Journey through Bhutan, The Illustrated Weekly of India, April 1, 1979, pp. 29-31.

Parmanand, Bhutan: Misguided discontent, Patriot, November 16, 1990, p. 4.

Parmanand, Bhutan: Monarchy, Modernisation and Internationalisation, Rising Nation, New Delhi, Vol. 2 issue May 5, 1987, 56-59.

Parmanand, Bhutan: Phoney Crisis of Integration, The Times of Nation, 20 November 1991, p. 6.

Parmanand, Bhutan suffers interference, Link, November 10, 1991, pp. 17-18.

Parmanand, India-Bhutan Friendship and Bhutan's Problem of National Integration, Strategic Analysis, New Delhi, Vol. 13, No. 12, March 1991, pp. 11-24.

Parmanand, Indo-Bhutan Relations in the Nineties, in Rasgostra, M. Chopra V.D. and Misra K. P (eds) pp. 325-37.

Phadnis Urmila, Ethnic conflicts in South Asian States, In Phadnis Urmila, Muni S.D. and Bahadur Kalim, pp. 100-120.

Pubby Vipin, Bhutan asks immigrants to leave, Indian Express, January 15, 1991, p. 9.

Pubby Vipin, Is Bhutan Next, Indian Express, May 3, 1990, p. 1.

Rabgye Sonam, Currents Developments in Bhutan and its implication, Unity International, Vol. 15, No. 4, April 1991, pp. 7-8.

Rabgye Sonam, Statement at the Indian International Centre, New Delhi, on October 16, 1990.

Rahul Ram, Making of Modern Bhutan, International Studies, Vol 19, No. 3, July-September, 1980, pp. 515-28.

Ramachandran S., We are restrained in dealing with Nepali subversives: Bhutan King, The Hindu, 25 April 1992, p. 6.

Rattan Kamaljeet, Bhutan; between the two Worlds, India Today September 15, 1989, pp. 134-137.

Rattan Kamaljeet, Jigme Singye Wangchuck: haste to develop erodes our traditions, India Today, 1989.

Sagarika Ghose, Bhutan: the Dilemma of Kingship, The Times of India, New Delhi, Friday, October 9, 1992.

Sagarika Ghose, King of Bhutan to visit India, The Times of India, New Delhi, Tuesday, October 20, 1992.

Sagarika Ghose, All is well in the Tiny Himalayan Kingdom, The Independent, Bombay, November 9, 1992.

Sagarika Ghose, I've come to express solidarity, The Times of India, New Delhi, Thursday, January 7, 1993.

Sagarika Ghose, Refugees and Ngolops, Asian Survey February, 1993.

Sagarika Ghose, Uneasy Heads in Dragon Kingdom, The Times of India, Lucknow, April 12, 1993.

Sanghvi Hemen C., Images Bhutan: A Photo Essay on a never Never-Land, Destination South Asia, New Delhi, Vol. I, No. 1, October-December 1997, pp. 41-43.

Sen Antra Deva, Neighbours: Trouble Hills, Sunday October 28, 1990, pp. 22-26.

Sen Gupta Uttam, Bhutan: Slow, Steady Pace of Change, The Hindustan Times, January 8, 1988.

Sen Gupta Uttam, Bhutan: Cracks in Paradise: Ethnic Strife Threatens Kingdom's Peace, India Today, September 30, 1990. pp. 159-60.

Sharma L.K., No Diplomatic Ties with China and Bhutan, The Times of India, May 16, 1985, p.16.

Shroff Vandana, Indo- Bhutanese Relations: Example of Good Neighbouringliness, 13 February 1993.

Sonwalkar Prasun, Trouble Brewing for Bhutan King, The Times of India, March 21, 1990, p. 4.

Sriram K., India, Bhutan for World Peace, Indian Express, September 30, 1985, p.1.

Thakur Singh Powdyel, Honourable Minister of Education, Bhutan, 'From Innocence to Passion- Bhutan's Tryst with Education' in the book 'Education Reform in Societies in Transition: International Perspectives, Ed. by J. Earnest, D. Treagust, 2006, Chapter 4.

The King may seek India's help, Indian Express, May 5, 1990, p. 9.

The Kings of Bhutan, The Hindustan Times, 21 February 1985, p. 9.

Trumbull Robart, Bhutan Planning Four Roads to India, The New York Times,p.4.

Upreti, Sonia, Status of Women in Bhutan, in Pamakant, Ramesh Chandra Misra, (eds) Bhutan: Society and Polity, Indus Publishing House, 1996, p. 53.

Victors Cecil, Bhutan and Greater Nepal, Patriot, November 8, 1991.

Vinayak M., Unrest in Bhutan: the voice of people uprooted, Frontline, April 17, 1991, pp. 19-11.

Wangchuck Seeks Better ties among South Asian Nations, the Hindustan Times, New Delhi, Thursday January 7, 1993, pp. 1-12.

Warning to Bhutan Terrorists, The Statesman, October 13, 1990, pp. 1-7.

We are not fighting for the throne, (An interview with King Jigme Singye Wangchuck), The Hindustan Times Magazine, November 17, 1991, p. 2.

Primary Sources

Achievements in Planned Development (Review of Sixth Plan) 1987-92, Thimphu, September 1991.

Achievement in Planned Development, Review Sixth Five-Year plan, Planning Commission, Royal Govt. of Bhutan, Thimphu, September 1992.

Adapted from *Vaclav Havel's idea and his Civil Society conception*, Macalester College, Minneapolis/St. Paul, USA, 26 April 1999.

Annual Report, 1995-96, Department of Commerce, Ministry of Commerce, Government of India.

Anti National Activities in Southern Bhutan: A Terrorist Movement, Department of Information, Royal Government of Bhutan, September 1991.

Apa. B. Pant Papers: Notes: File No. 10, Conference of Heads of Indian Mission in Asian and African Countries.

1. "India's Relations with Sikkim and Bhutan".
2. "Problem of Nepalese Population in Bhutan".

Bhutan: A traditional Order and Forces of Change, Ministry of Foreign Affairs, Royal Government of Bhutan, 1993.

Bhutan at a Glance 2009, National Statistical Bureau, Royal Government of Bhutan, Thimphu, Bhutan.

Bhutan: Development in Himalayan Kingdom, World Bank Report, 1984.

Bhutan in Focus, New Delhi, Royal Bhutanese Embassy, December 2003.

Bhutan 2020: A Vision of Peace, Prosperity and Happiness, Planning Commission, Royal Government of Bhutan, 1999.

Brochure, National Commission for Women and Children, Royal Government of Bhutan.

CBS (1999), Final Programmes for the Coronation, June 1974 and the Silver Jubilee Celebrations, June 1999 of His Majesty the King Jigme Singye Wangchuck, Thimphu, The Centre for Bhutan Studies.

Chinese Interest in Bhutan: Evolution of the British Indian perspective, China Report, Vol. 19, No. 4, July-August 1983, pp. 37-45.

Colombo Plan Bureau, Progress of the Colombo Plan, 1963, (Colombo).

Crins, Reiki, Religion and Gender Values in a Changing World, The Spider and Piglet, Proceedings of the First International Seminar on Bhutan Studies, ed. by Karma Ura and Sonam Kinga, Centre for Bhutan Studies, 2004.

Druk Gosel, Quarterly Published by the Department of Bhutan of Information, Royal Government of Bhutan, Thimphu.

Educating for GNH, Nurturing Green Schools for Green Bhutan-A Guide to School Management, Education Monitoring and Support Services Division, Department of School Education, Ministry of Education, Thimphu, Chapter 3.

Eighth Five Year Plan (1997-2002) Main Document, Vol. 1, Ministry of Planning, Royal Government of Bhutan, Thimphu, September 1996.

European Union Election Observation Mission, The Kingdom of Bhutan 2008, Final Report.

Gender Focal Point, Royal Bhutan Police (RBP), Thimphu.

Inaugural speech of Ambassador of Bhutan to India His Excellency Lyonpo Dago Tshering as delivered on 24th Oct. 2008 in Malviya Hall, University of Lucknow on the occasion of National Seminar on Bhutan.

Interview with Sonam Tobgye, Chief Justice of Bhutan by Suhrid Sankar Chattopadhyay in Thimphu, Frontline, May 9, 2008.

Interview with the Honourable Minister of Education and Chairman Commission of Women and Children Thakur Singh Powdyel, taken by the author (Dr. Madhu Rajput) on 20 Oct. 11, in his office at the Ministry of Education, Thimphu, Bhutan.

Labour Force Survey 2006, Ministry of Labour and Human Resource, Royal Government of Bhutan.

Labour Force Survey Report, 2010, Labour Market Information Division, Department of Employment, Ministry of Labour and Human Resources, Royal Government of Bhutan.

Main Plan Document, Seventh Five-Year Plan, 1992-1997, Vol. I, Planning Commission, Royal Government of Bhutan, Thimphu, December 1991.

National Plan of Action for Gender 2008-13, Gross National Happiness Commission, National Commission for Women and Children, Royal Government of Bhutan.

Pamphlet, Know the Law- To Protect Your Rights, Royal Court of Justice, High Court, Thimphu: Bhutan.

Pamphlet, The Judiciary of The Kingdom of Bhutan, Royal Court of Justice, High Court, Thimphu: Bhutan.

Population and Housing Census of Bhutan, Office of Census Commissioner, Royal Govt. of Bhutan.

Speeches by the fourth King compiled by Bhutan Times.

Speech Record of King Jigme Singye Wangchuck when first draft of constitution was drafted in 2002.

Statistical Year Book of Bhutan, Central Statistical Office, Planning Commission, Royal Government of Bhutan, Thimphu, 1989.

Statistical Yearbook of Bhutan 2009, National Statistics Bureau, Royal Government of Bhutan, Thimphu, Bhutan.

Tenth Five Year Plan 2008-2013, Main Document, Vol. I, Gross National Happiness, Royal Government of Bhutan.

The speech of Lyonchhen Jigmi Y Thinley, Prime Minister of Bhutan, at the National Consultative Meeting on National Anti-Corruption Strategic Framework, 26 March 2009.

Towards Gross National Happiness: A Journey with UNDP, Annual Report, 2008-09.

Translated from Dzongkha Source, Source Kuensel, Windows on Bhutan 2007-2008, Welcoming the Winds of Change.

UNHRC General Comment, Number 25, Point 12, Information and Material about Voting should be available in minority languages.

Window on Bhutan: A Moment in History, Vol. VI, Royal Bhutanese Embassy, New Delhi, 2008.

Window on Bhutan, Exploring New Avenues, Issue VII, 2009, The Bhutanese Economy on the Rise.

Window on Bhutan: Welcoming the winds of change, Royal Bhutanese Embassy, New Delhi, 2007.

Years of Service to the Tsa-wa-Sum, Army Welfare Project Establishments, Phuentsholing, Bhutan, 1999.

News Papers (Bhutan)

Bhutan Observer. Various dates.
Bhutan Times. Various dates.
Bhutan Today. Various dates.
Kuensel. Various dates
The Journalist, z2 October 2011, Dorji Tshering, 'The Journey Ahead'

Internet Sources

http://en.wikipedia.org/wiki/Paro_Taktsang

http://www.bhutanmysticbliss.com/bhutan-travel/festivals-of-bhutan.html

http://www.lonelyplanet.com/travelblogs
http://www.tourism.gov.bt/bhutan/about-bhutan/people-and-society
http://www.undp.org.bt/unv/vols.html

http://www.youthdevfund.gov.bt/projects/vast

www.bhutantimes.bt, Tenzen Karma, Article 'Female Voters Dominate LG Elections', 23 January 2011

Index